SUCCESSFUL CLASSROOM MANAGEMENT

Real-World, Time-Tested Techniques for the Most
Important Skill Set Every Teacher Needs

Richard H. Eyster and Christine Martin

sourcebooks

Published by Sourcebooks, Inc.
P.O. Box 4410, Naperville, Illinois 60567-4410
(630) 961-3900
Fax: (630) 961-2168
www.sourcebooks.com

Library of Congress Cataloging-in-Publication Data

Eyster, Richard H.
  Successful classroom management: real-world, time-tested techniques for the most important skill set every teacher needs / by Richard H. Eyster and Christine Martin.
      p. cm.
  Includes bibliographical references and index.
  1. Classroom management. 2. Problem children--Behavior modification. 3. Teachers--Professional relationships. I. Martin, Christine, 1949 Sept. 25- II. Title.
  LB3013.E97 2010
  371.102'4--dc22
                                   2010009842

Printed and bound in the United States of America.
        VP 10 9 8 7 6 5 4 3 2

We dedicate this book to the educators of today and tomorrow—
to those who spend their days among the young, working to forge
connections, inspire success, and foster ongoing growth.

CONTENTS

ACKNOWLEDGMENTS...IX
INTRODUCTION TO THE FIRST EDITION....................XIII
HOW TO APPROACH THIS BOOK...........................XIX

Part 1: Creating a Positive Tone
Chapter 1: The Image of an Effective Teacher.....................3
Chapter 2: "We're All in This Together" 9
Chapter 3: The Power of Praise 15
Chapter 4: Ten Ways to Praise 33
Chapter 5: Setting High Expectations.........................39
Chapter 6: An Unshakable Sense of Trust 45
Chapter 7: Knowing the Whole Child 51
Chapter 8: The Culture of a Class 57
Chapter 9: Final Thoughts on Creating a Positive Tone.............63

Part 2: Establishing Discipline
Chapter 10: Establishing Discipline: Overview.....................67
Chapter 11: How to Be the Marshal of a Wild West Town 73
Chapter 12: The Popularity Temptation.........................81
Chapter 13: The Power of "No"...............................85
Chapter 14: The Power of Silence 91
Chapter 15: Preventative Discipline: Seating Arrangements 93
Chapter 16: Isolate the Individual: The Private Version.............99
Chapter 17: Isolate the Individual: The More Public Version 103
Chapter 18: Sending a Student to the Office 105
Chapter 19: Enlisting Parent Support.........................111
Chapter 20: The Solo Intervention: Enough Is Enough............117

Chapter 21: When It Is Beyond Your Control: The Mediation 123
Chapter 22: The Intervention: Martial Law 131

Part 3: Structuring Your Class

Chapter 23: Planning for the Year. 141
Chapter 24: The Power of the Opening Days 147
Chapter 25: Expectations Sheets. 151
Chapter 26: Daily Planning: Overview 157
Chapter 27: In the Beginning: Before Even Starting a Lesson Plan 161
Chapter 28: Ensuring Variety in a Lesson Plan. 165
Chapter 29: The Successful Beginning of Class: Checklist. 169
Chapter 30: Leading the Centralized Dynamic 175
Chapter 31: Small Group Work 191
Chapter 32: The Final Three Minutes 199

Part 4: Optimizing Assessment and Feedback

Chapter 33: Assessment and Feedback: Overview 207
Chapter 34: Tests. 211
Chapter 35: Grades, Feedback, and Comment Writing 219
Chapter 36: Homework: Overview 227
Chapter 37: Homework: Collecting It. 233
Chapter 38: Homework: Correcting It 237
Chapter 39: Writing Narrative Comments: Six Critical
    Recommendations 241
Chapter 40: Effectively Managing Parent Conference Day 247

Part 5: Beyond the Classroom

Chapter 41: Your Time, Your Life. 255
Chapter 42: How to Establish a Good Relationship with
    Your Supervisor 259
Chapter 43: Key People with Whom to Establish Good Relations. 279
Chapter 44: Making Use of Outside Resources 283

Part 6: Special Circumstances

Chapter 45: Dealing with the Child Who Drives Us Crazy 289
Chapter 46: Supporting Students with Learning Differences 301

Chapter 47: Supporting the Quiet Child. 307

Chapter 48: Thirty-Five Steps for Dealing with a Difficult Class 319

Chapter 49: Twenty-Four Steps for Dealing with Difficult or

Angry Parents. 337

Part 7: Appendices or Worth Noting

Appendix 1: A Whisper about Classroom Etiquette 351

Appendix 2: What Adults Remember: Characteristics of an

Effective Teacher 355

Appendix 3: What Students Want: Advice from the Kids. 359

Appendix 4: A Note on Montessori Education 363

FINAL WISHES 365

THE AUTHORS 367

INDEX. 369

ACKNOWLEDGMENTS

Careers, like lives, span decades and pass through incredibly varied terrain. There are periods spent in relative isolation and there are moments in which a new vista opens up—very often because of the thoughtful guidance of someone met along the way.

In our work together, no one has been more individually supportive than Barbara Swanson, long-time program director at NYSAIS. She encouraged our work from the beginning, recommended us to many others, and opened doors for us along the way. It is no exaggeration to say that this book would not have been written without her visionary support and without the years of evolution and refinement made possible by that support.

When we were looking for a beautiful retreat in which to hold our summer residencies, Arch Smith, head of the Trinity-Pawling School, and Ed Hauser, director of the Physical Plant (and so much more!) responded enthusiastically. Countless schools expressed a willingness to open their doors to us—but of course summer was the time in which renovation and restoration had to be completed. Between Arch and Ed and their remarkable staffs, they have supported our work by timing summer maintenance so that we and the teachers could work in air-conditioned, sleeves-rolled-up comfort.

In Rich's career, as is mentioned in the heart of this book, he owes a permanent debt to his two first supervisors and mentors—Peg Zilboorg and Walter Birge. In his current role, Michele Pierce, Thom Greenlaw, Michelle Marino, and all of his Summit colleagues deserve deep appreciation for the welcome, outreach, and support he has received. Over a longer period of time, three people have played a transformative role in his life—Rosalind Freundlich, Jenny Hankins Barthold, and David Mallery. And to those wise, irrepressible, and utterly faithful sidekicks—Henry, Karen, and Philo—the warmth of a life-long smile, shared late in the afternoon.

For Christine, two people were central to her becoming an educator and a learning specialist—Nancy Henningsen and Debbie Henry. Their enthusiastic support and encouragement continues to guide and inspire her professional life.

During their years working together, Christine and Rich have accumulated considerable professional debt to Geoff Pierson, whose belief, support, and good-humored wisdom helped to shape their professional lives and this program. Bruce Dennis has also offered a generous perspective on behalf of this work.

Cliff, Kevin, and Kristine Ross welcomed Rich into their beautiful world and homes in Santa Fe for the final push to completion of this manuscript.

Sterling Lord believed in this project at once. He knew just where to send it, and where it would be appreciated. A good agent is a good friend.

Peter Lynch, our thoughtful, caring, and incisive editor at Sourcebooks, helped to bring this manuscript to life, to clarify key points, and to push us to offer clear-cut conclusions where we had too readily settled for implication and inference. We couldn't have been in better hands than working alongside Peter.

Finally, our families put up with our hours of preparation and our days of absence, and always welcomed us home with the kind of loving support road travelers come to savor. To Mary (who predicted the existence of this book thirty years ago), deep respect and thanks for the encouragement over the years. To Liza, Becky, and Katherine, a love that knows no limits, a gratitude that knows no bounds. And to Sarah, my generous sister, my Dad, who has always believed in me, and to my wise and literate late mother, all my love and appreciation for your support. To Tony, Anna, Judy, Vicki, and Shirley, my love and appreciation for their unwavering optimism and belief in me. To each of our families, now and always, this book is because of you, and thanks to you.

INTRODUCTION TO THE FIRST EDITION

There are brief encounters, small moments that forever change one's life. I was in San Francisco ages ago, attending just another conference among many. The keynote speaker had just finished his address, and I rose with the rest of the audience to leave. Halfway up the aisle, in the heart of that milling, moving crowd, I stopped abruptly and turned. I had the distinct feeling that someone was watching me.

From far across the ballroom, a young woman was staring intently in my direction. I had no idea who she was. I checked behind me to see if I had mistaken the direction of her gaze, but there was no one behind me. And the mischief in her smile only deepened.

Before I knew it, she was only six feet away. She stopped before me then, her hands folded behind her, waiting for me to give up, but suddenly, I had her. With a suddenness that shocked and delighted me, I caught sight of a nine-year-old child gazing impishly from the eyes of the young woman before me. I burst into a laughing grin and reached out to embrace her.

It was Jennifer Longley.

A dozen years before, I had taught Jennifer as a third grader. I had never seen her again—until now.

She still had a light spray of freckles across her upturned nose and the same devilish glint in her eyes—although obviously much had changed over the years. As we spoke, she began to fill in the blanks of that intervening stretch. Her mother had remarried and had moved to Maine. Her older sister, whom I had also taught, had taken a job with a magazine in New York. And Jennifer had taken a job in California, working through her first year of teaching, serving out an interim year for a teacher on maternity leave.

Our conversation quickly filled the minutes before the next series of workshops. We were headed in different directions, but before we broke away from each other, we agreed to meet for lunch.

I was very excited to have run into Jennifer. Beyond the simple pleasure of such a reunion, I felt a deep, resonant joy that someone as wonderfully bright and good-hearted as Jennifer had looked at the myriad opportunities before her and had chosen to teach. She had been a generous child, with a capacity for reaching out to classmates who struggled. Hundreds of students would come to be touched by her spirit. Many would be forever changed by what she brought to her classroom each day. The teaching profession is enriched every time a Jennifer Longley gives up the chance to achieve fame and fortune to take on the education of the young.

But when we met for lunch, things changed. We seated ourselves at a big, glassy café and began to catch up. She was teaching high school English. It was "fine." It was going "okay." We talked about the books she and her students were reading. I said that it must have been tough taking on a one-year assignment so new to the profession. She nodded, looking down and away. She didn't immediately surface from the nod. Her head remained bowed for too long. When she looked up at last, her eyes were brimming with tears.

She began speaking of the kids, good kids she couldn't really begin to control. She said she even knew how much some of them—all of them maybe—wanted her to be strong enough and sure-handed enough to control them, to keep them on course, but there was this group of boys…her voice trailed away then.

After a moment, she had the courage to meet my eyes and continue talking. Just the week before, she had missed a day because of an illness. The very next day, when she returned, the class was more chaotic than it ever was before. And one of the girls who had really liked her and had been rooting for her all along came up to her at the end of class. With a scalding look, she confronted Jennifer and hissed, "Even the sub could control us better than you can."

And at that confession, right there in the noisy, crowded clatter of the restaurant, Jennifer Longley began to cry.

We spoke for a time. I tried to console her. I wished that there was something I could have said, something I could have done or offered to ease her pain. I wished that I knew what to tell her. I felt helpless in my compassion and care.

After a while, we rose to go our separate ways. I gave her a parting hug. A soft light had begun to return to her eyes, not so much of hope but of the simple relief of having shared such a deep and secret grief.

I never saw Jennifer again, though I thought of her countless times in the days that followed.

Several years later, I went to a reunion at the school where I had taught her and saw a number of her classmates. Several of them had been in touch with Jennifer in the interval. She was now doing "something in marketing."

That had been her one and only year in education. We had lost her. Generations of students who would have had her as a teacher, learning English, decency, an enthusiasm for literature, and their own creative expression, would never know what they had missed.

Jennifer Longley had had a great deal to give, but she wasn't able to last. She hadn't had time to learn the survival skills of classroom management. One quiet June afternoon in a school emptying for the summer, she had packed her books and left, never to return. In so doing, she had left more than just a school behind. She had left education, and perhaps her own self-image, self-esteem, and aspirations were forever diminished.

* * *

This book and the countless workshops and residencies Christine Martin and I have given in the years since have been inspired to some extent by that chance meeting in that San Francisco ballroom. In the same way, they are dedicated to Jennifer Longley and to every teacher in their early years in the profession. These years are a difficult, pivotal rite of passage for most young educators—a time of testing, a time of self-doubt, a time during which our ideals and excitement are often put to the test of simply keeping a class in order.

That challenge is made dramatically more difficult by the ubiquitous and damaging myth that there are those who are born to command respect and those who are not. The myth presupposes that talent for effective classroom management is almost innate—"Some got it, and some don't."

Before the end of her first year of teaching, Jennifer had come to believe that myth. She never lasted long enough to understand education's most important breakthrough lesson. It is the foundation upon which Christine and I have built our work together with more than one thousand young teachers.

Effective classroom management is built upon a foundation of demonstrably learnable skills.

The fact is that educators face a strange, almost singular obstacle in their early growth. Consider the career choices facing the young—and look at how many emerging professionals in other fields have the opportunity to learn right alongside the veterans. Young interns take grand rounds with veteran doctors. Young real estate agents work side-by-side with experienced realtors. Young plumbers apprentice alongside those who have spent their lives amid the pipes. And young attorneys work directly alongside more senior partners.

Those of us who teach, on the other hand, are more or less left to learn on our own. We are given a classroom, a roll book, a teacher's edition, and then we're sent off to learn the craft on our own. Alone. With the door closed.

We don't lack idealism. We don't lack an understanding of our chosen subject. We don't lack a passion to communicate with the young. What we lack is the chance to learn easily from the veterans among us. Teaching has the potential to be one of the most rewarding careers available to any of us. It also has the potential to be one of the most challenging and isolating. Christine and I have taken on the challenge of breaking through that isolation.

Our goal in creating workshops for teachers and our goal in developing this handbook is to make the skill set that underlies successful classroom management explicit, practical, easy to learn, and adaptable to any teacher's style in the classroom. In preparation for this, we have visited hundreds of classrooms, watching teachers young and old with an analytic eye for what works and what doesn't. In the pages that follow, our objective is to distill the inevitable, slow-motion knowledge gained from classroom experience into a high-speed, tightly crafted series of lessons. We want to do nothing less than to jump-start the learning process for those newest to the profession with the best practices of those who have been at it for years.

* * *

Teaching matters. Be under no illusion that it is easy, that the young will flock to us that very first morning and appreciate all that we are giving to them—and giving up for them.

Have no doubt. Every one of us will be tested—on the most professional and on the most personal of levels. Christine and I have created this guide for one reason and one reason above all—to help each and every educator pass that test. We missed the chance with Jennifer. We never want to lose that opportunity again.

Our goal is, in part, to provide every relatively new educator with the tips, tricks, and techniques of the most accomplished veterans by sharing with them those structures and skills that underlie great teaching. Our goal beyond that is to enable as many Jennifer Longleys as possible to fulfill their aspirations and to find the richness of success and satisfaction that can arise from a life of learning and growing alongside the young.

HOW TO APPROACH THIS BOOK

We begin with a humble, cautionary note.

There are kindergarten teachers who spend their days with the same twenty-four students. There are part-time art teachers who may come in just two or three days a week to work with a rotating group of students. And there are full-time high school Spanish teachers who work with 172 students in five different sections. There are teachers who have been in education for several decades, and there are those who are relatively new to the profession. There are teachers in small communities with barely enough students to comprise a full fifth grade class, and there are teachers in overcrowded urban junior high schools.

For some of us, the issue may be pressure from parents to get their children set up for entry into the top colleges. For others, the parents may be almost invisible, too preoccupied by their own difficulties to fully support the daily lives of their children.

Some of us give homework, and some of us don't.

Some of us work in thriving schools with an abundant sense of support, and some of us don't.

The bottom line is that each situation will be different.

As we approach this book, we recognize that there are broad concepts that affect every classroom. We have naturally tried to focus on these, but just as energetically, we want to include those more specific techniques that apply to narrower bands of the educational spectrum.

As a result, specific parts of this book or particular examples will inevitably not apply to each and every educator. We recognize this. Those who work in a nursery school may wisely decide, for example, to skip a section on homework.

In other situations, the examples we cite may somewhat miss the mark of what would make the most sense for your particular school culture, subject matter, or age group. To some extent, it may be possible to extrapolate or imaginatively sense how a proven strategy might be adapted to your own situation.

We know that not every unit will be of equal value to every reader. In the end, however, our hope is that the sheer variety and richness of this book will offer more than a sufficient reward to those who know what they are looking to foster in their own personal and professional arenas.

In terms of how you can get the most growth possible from this book, we envision three possible approaches:

1. Compelling narrative: *The Great American Teacher's Handbook* is designed to be read cover to cover if you should desire to do so. In crafting this volume, we have worked to replicate the sequence that has proven most effective in the countless workshops we have led over the years.

2. Practical resource: This book has also been designed to offer specific, valuable recommendations for those who are looking for guidance in a particular area, such as discipline, lesson planning, or difficult conversations. If you are facing an immediate problem, you can go directly to that section.

3. Long-term reference: The needs of a teacher in one situation at one time in his or her professional life are different from those at later points with different groups of students, colleagues, and parents. The scope and depth of this handbook has been created in response to

questions and concerns from teachers at myriad points in their careers. It is our hope that this book will not only prove to be valuable during a first reading but that it will become the kind of resource that will prove to be of enduring value as one's perspectives, needs, and aspirations change over time.

In addition—and we know this from our own lives—sometimes what is as important as learning something new is the opportunity to be reminded of things that matter. Many of the books that I have come back to again and again haven't been undertakings that are purely breathtaking, earthshaking, and groundbreaking. Like the power of praise and the enduring value of listening to each of our students, sometimes the issues raised herein are designed to bring us back to a sense of priorities, the issues that matter, and the things we may have known but somehow lost track of in the demanding, distracting drumbeat of our days.

In the end, however you choose to approach this book, know that it has been created with deep respect and admiration—for all of the hopes and concerns, for all of the trials and triumphs, for all of the challenges and revelations that are an inevitable part of the teaching profession. In education, there is no arrival at some Olympian peak of educational omniscience. Part of the wonder and the ongoing excitement of education is the fact that if we are to remain effective and fulfilled in our work, then we must continue to grow alongside the students we teach. In a world in which so many professionals plateau in backwater places within vast organizations, those of us in education are privileged enough to be continually challenged to grow and to have the chance—each and every day—to make a difference.

It is common for those on Wall Street to speak with great facility about "growth" industries. To us, with an apology to those same mavens, we would suggest that there is no other profession more truly and directly devoted to growth than education.

Thank you for being an active part of this process. Thank you for continuing to care about the growth of the young and inevitably about your own ongoing development as a professional. And finally, thank you for placing a little trust in us. We hope that some of the work we have done over the years and some of the work we are sharing here with you will make a lasting difference along the way.

PART 1

Creating a Positive Tone

Chapter 1

THE IMAGE OF AN EFFECTIVE TEACHER

It was my last day of kindergarten. My mother and younger sister had come to the steps of Grove Patterson School to share the final moments and to begin summer vacation together. Mrs. Routzahn, whom I will remember forever as a large and florid woman with a warm and jowly smile, bent low and gave me a hug. My mother thanked her for the year. Our final good-byes were exchanged.

On the quiet walk home down Drummond Road, I looked up at my mother and said with a quiet finality, "She never wore them."

With some perplexity, my mother asked what I had meant. Incredibly, I can still remember the pink coral earrings I had so eagerly picked out for Mrs. Routzahn as my first Christmas present to a teacher. I had apparently spent the rest of the year checking her earlobes every morning as soon as I had hung up my coat in the cloak room.

She had never once worn the earrings I had chosen with such eager anticipation.

It may be unusual to have taken such notice of a gift given. It may be no less unusual to remember that episode over the course of the passing decades, but that wasn't the only small schoolish moment remembered from those early years. I can recall Miss Freeman scoffing to our third grade class at the *very idea* of toothpaste and telling us all that the only "dentifrice" that really made a difference was Dr. Lyon's Tooth Powder. Sure enough, over the sighing objections of my mother, our family purchased a pale blue can of Dr. Lyon's Tooth Powder. Miss Sonnenberg had lived in Germany right after World War II, and she told us about the brand new stockings her neighbor had been so proud of, stockings that had disintegrated in the blast of a bus's exhaust. That image sometimes still arises unbidden when I see a woman crossing behind a bus idling at the corner.

Children are so impressionable, so open to experience, so touched by the look or the tales of a teacher along the way. I can remember every one of the educators in my life—their foibles, their warmth, and their mannerisms. To me, this just seems natural. They were a daily part of my life and a powerful influence on who I became and how I saw the world.

The fact is that children are affected by their teachers day in and day out—for good and ill—as they move through their lives as students. Occasionally, they are recognized and praised. More often than not, they simply feel that they are one of the crowd, one of the many. Through careless comments or at moments of reckless insensitivity, a teacher can turn them off, embarrass them, blunt their hopes for success, and make them feel hopeless as artists, as mathematicians, as students in general. And yet through conscious, touching efforts, those same teachers can make them feel noticed. They can awaken hopes of mastery. They can uplift secret aspirations. They can open images of lighted pathways to the future. They can make students feel good about themselves.

What makes the difference? Who are those educators that children remember long after they have left their classrooms? What are the characteristics of a truly effective teacher?

At each of our workshops, we first instruct the educators and participants to gather themselves into groups, share their memories of one truly effective teacher from their past, and then distill a set of characteristics. When the task is complete, we share these lists. The result is often a fairly godlike (or goddess-like) description.

There are often apparent contradictions in the way we see effectiveness—one person citing careful planning and another citing a wonderful sense of spontaneity. One made each child feel special. Another made every student feel equal. I suspect that these aren't inherent contradictions, that there is a secret pairing in each paradox, that the careful planner could afford to follow up on more spontaneous and teachable moments, and that before one is able to trust a teacher enough to feel special, there has to be an essential quality of fairness in the classroom.

The lists that emerge from each of the many workshops we have led are vast and yet largely parallel:

- Those most effective teachers were passionate and knowledgeable about their subject.
- They loved their subject, and they loved to teach.
- They came to class well prepared and well organized.
- They made us laugh.
- They understood boundaries.
- They knew who we were, and somehow, we knew who they were.
- And even when they must have been tired, we sensed their underlying energy and their abiding enthusiasm.

Sometimes, to their collective surprise, the teacher whom these young educators remember as being the most effective doesn't turn out to be the one who was the most fun or the most immediately popular or the easiest to get along with. Often, they were a little intimidating—maybe even a little "scary" at first. But time and time again, we collectively discovered that we deeply valued those teachers who set high standards, and as long as they were fair and consistent, we didn't even mind if they were strict in holding us to those standards. Sometimes, in doing so, they inspired things in us beyond our own expectations. They not only brought out the best in us but also the things we didn't even know were there.

A relatively complete set of characteristics, collected from our most recent series of workshops, is contained in its entirety in the appendix. We open this book, as we do so many of our workshops, by highlighting such a list for two reasons.

First, we have shared this list to encourage everyone to reflect on their own styles. The value in this might be to help us recognize and reinforce our strengths and perhaps even identify areas that we might want to work to develop more fully.

Secondly, there is value in visualization.

Christine often tells the tale of when she first moved to New York during a time when crime was far more prevalent. Because she was an attractive young woman not from the city, her husband was concerned about her traveling long distances on the subway by herself, so he gave her an interesting piece of advice: "Pretend you're an undercover cop."

With a self-deprecating laugh, she shares how that idea, that visualization, actually had the power to change her attitude, her focus, even her posture. She was ready. She was on the lookout. She was poised. And that one image really did help to transform her outlook and even her confidence.

Even before the first students arrive, visualizing ourselves as the embodiment of our most effective teacher—organized, energized, and knowledgeable—can make a huge difference in how we approach our work and how we see ourselves.

We fully recognize that this list of educational virtues can be a little intimidating. None of us is omnipotent; none of us is perfect. The purpose in sharing this list isn't to suggest that each of us must try to be all things to all students. Some of us, for example, are naturally more spontaneous, while others are naturally better planners; however, that doesn't mean that the more methodical planner can't quietly and consciously begin to cultivate an ability to sense and seize that spontaneous, unplanned teachable moment or that the more spontaneous among us can't learn the power of thoughtful and effective planning.

One of the greatest rewards of this profession is that, as we grow in teaching, so often we grow in our own lives, too. A new openness to spontaneity or an emerging orientation to planning might just stay in the classroom, but such explorations have the power to transcend the professional and become part of our more personal lives. If education is truly focused on growth, it may be important to recognize that it is not only about the growth of the young. If we are teaching well, if we are moving ever closer to images of ourselves as effective teachers, then lessons learned along the way may well have the capacity to become part of the experiences that enrich us as adults even when day is done and the classroom is left behind.

Chapter 2

"WE'RE ALL IN THIS TOGETHER"

We're all in this together.

It is a statement. It is an image. It should become an unshakable conviction. From the very beginning, from before that first morning in September, it is vital to believe that we are united with the class in a compelling, shared adventure.

Being able to state this, to envision it, to believe it is quite simply one of the most pivotal factors in establishing a positive relationship with a class.

If there is one thing that serves to undermine a teacher, if there is one telltale characteristic we have come to believe is at the root of any deep-seated struggle, it is the teacher who—knowingly or unknowingly—isolates him- or herself from the class.

Students of any age will test us as teachers. Before we ever dare to enter that first classroom, we need to anticipate that testing—not as a possibility but as a certainty, and not as something to be avoided but as something to be welcomed. This point cannot be overemphasized. The testing will come in many different forms, and each of us should welcome it.

What, then, is the most important component of our response to that testing?

Stay united with the class.

What does that mean?

We're all in this together.

Stay focused on that statement, visualize that image, feel the strength of it as an unshakable conviction however tempest-tossed you may feel from time to time. Together, we are embarking on a year-long journey, and students want—deservedly—to have some genuine confidence in their guide.

It is vital that we stay united with the class.

* * *

You may think, *Well of course I want to stay united with the class*. But the truth is that many of us unknowingly isolate ourselves from the rest of the class. If there is trouble, many of us succumb to the powerful and unintended temptation to isolate ourselves—but how?

- We scold the entire class.
- We take it personally.
- We sense the eyes upon us and unconsciously accept a me-versus-the-world mind-set.
- We turn what may be a few unpleasant snickers into an entire classroom now leaning against us.
- We use an unconscious lexicon that separates us from the students—even from those who may be quietly rooting for us to succeed—to pass the test, and get on with the journey. We use a very singular "I" and a very collective "you," as if the two are separated by an unbridgeable gulf. "You kids having fun yet?" "You are just out of control this morning." "When you act like this, I don't know how to teach you."

The "you" in each case is a disastrously all-encompassing pronoun destined to distance, to insult, to betray those who may be quietly on our side or even just those neutral ones who are waiting to see what happens next. We are wrong—critically wrong—to lump them all together. And in the end, if we castigate them all as one, if we blow hard and lose heart and see no distinction between the reckless pretender to the throne and the simple bystanders, we will have succeeded in *making* it us against them and them against us.

And beyond that lies an often vicious downward spiral. We grow so defensive, so conscious of survival, so wary of their power that we lose track of our own. We cut back on the very praise that will draw them in. We stop going to see them in after school plays and games, where our presence might make a wonderfully positive difference. We don't stop them at the end of class or in the hall for informal, friendly one-on-ones. We give up on forging bonds, getting to know them as individuals, and letting them get to know us.

* * *

The testing can and must be faced. The challenge can be defused. The testers can become vital parts of the shared journey. Students—even those who thrive on the role of court jester or murderous upstart—ultimately want us to succeed.

If there is a child in class who is testing us, we generally have two choices. We can either isolate ourselves or isolate the child and the act itself. The best choice is to isolate the test—and the tester—as much by our manner and presence as by our own internal assumptions.

From that first morning in September, students are watching us, sizing us up, trying to figure out what makes us tick. At first, the challenges may be indirect, slight, and surreptitious. You may hear a smart-aleck response from somewhere in the back of the room, a nasty remark about your plastic shoes, an unseemly comment on your ancestors.

What to do?

We can overreact like so many do. Just as destructively, we can pretend we didn't notice. But a little humor or a little sharp-eyed response is probably what they're looking for. You may give a smile that reflects a certain so-what-else-is-new bemusement, eyes that catch the tester clearly in the crosshairs, a slight pause in our manner. We heard. We saw. We noticed. We aren't going to overreact. And we aren't going to wish it away. We knew it was coming. We expected the test. We aren't shaken by it, and we are ready to get on with the lesson. And we are ready to deal with more of it—and more strongly—if it really comes to that.

So if little Stanley shoots a spit wad at us as we're about to launch into our lesson, we face myriad choices of what to do.

What should you *not* do?

- Go nuts, as if we can't believe that anyone would ever dare challenge us. It may be easy for us to "know" in advance that a test is coming, but when it really happens, we may completely lose our cool.
- Lecture the kids on things they already know.
- Spend four minutes berating someone for a thirty-second interruption.
- Take it personally. "They really don't like me." Don't dare even think there's a "they."
- Project it into a bleak and unalterable future. "This is never going to work."
- Challenge the kid into a defensiveness that will only escalate. "What was *that* all about, Stanley? You think you're tough? Huh? Huh? You think you can disrupt my class with a little piece of paper? We'll see who's boss!"
- Pretend it didn't happen. This is so crucial. So many teachers are so floored that kids would dare to test them and so uncomfortable exhibiting any kind of strength that they just look away day after day after day.
- Say, "You kids are really out of control this afternoon! All of you—settle down!"

That last point is key. It is vital to monitor how we phrase what we say. There are many elements to passing the test, but without question, the most important one is to remain united with the class—or at least the rest of the class. It is vital to avoid condemning the entire class. The rest of the class may be chuckling or even snickering, but they inhabit a kind of waiting space, a role as watchful observers with unclaimed loyalties. By something as simple as a word choice, we can verbally link them with the upstart. Don't.

So what should you do?

A little power, a little humor, and a little cool go a long way toward diffusing a testing situation even if deep down inside it feels as if we're faking some of the confidence. Fake away. But do the right thing. Keep it strong. Keep it understated.

Let them know with your strength, your eye contact, and your weary bemusement that you knew what was coming. And you would just like to get on with the show. Let your eyes linger on the perpetrator. Let him feel your stern resolve. And perhaps as you look up, share a brief look of warm bemusement with others about the room. Remember, we're all in this together.

Then push on.

Make it a great and promising journey with a strong and good-humored guide, and they will follow. In time, even the upstart may find him- or herself quietly returning to the fold.

The fact is that all of us test the authority figures in our lives—or we ought to. Don't hold it against your students. Don't dread the possibility. Pass the test and get on with it.

We will go into greater details on how to go about this in the unit Establishing Discipline. In the meantime, stay positive. Stay connected. You and the class are embarking on a great journey together. Don't let one (or four) wisenheimers turn it into a twenty-four-against-one situation. It's up to you. Through your choice of words, your internal imagery, your confidence in the journey, and your abiding belief in the better angels of their nature, you will be able to create an enduring sense of teamwork and unity.

Isolate the act. Isolate the actor. Stay united with the rest of the class. Keep yourself aligned and united with the hope and promise of the unfolding journey ahead.

Chapter 3

THE POWER OF PRAISE

Just last year, out and about in the neighborhood where I teach, I passed a student on the street with a smile and nodded hello. Ten paces later, I stopped and turned back to him.

"Ray," I called. He halted and turned around slowly, suddenly watchful and even perhaps a little apprehensive. What was *this* going to be about? He gazed at me with those pale, long-lashed eyes, wondering what was to follow.

"I'm really glad you're in my class."

Now please understand that Ray was a popular and well-adjusted kid to whom things seemed to come easily. He was an eighth grader who (like most eighth graders) put on a great show of keeping his thumbs in his belt loops and being immune to the effect of adults, but there was no mistaking the sudden, startled warmth in his eyes. He took an involuntary step toward me, blinked with surprise, and smiled. He didn't know quite what to say. "Thanks," he finally managed.

"Thank *you*," I replied.

And I watched him walk away with a lightness of step that made me wonder why I so rarely took the minor moment aside to tell a kid how I felt.

Praise is one of the most powerful, and certainly one of the most underutilized, tools in any teacher's repertoire.

Several Septembers ago, I convened an open faculty meeting by asking each of the educators with whom I worked to recall the one teacher who had most singled them out, who had made them feel special, who had really noticed some special talent or characteristic in them. I turned them loose to talk with each other about such teachers and to recall the power of such an experience. My goal was to begin the year with a fresh recognition of the power we have to make a lasting impact on the lives of young and impressionable students.

When I called them back together to share their recollections, I was in for a dismaying surprise. Here among adults who had chosen education as their calling in life, half of the teachers said that they couldn't remember one teacher who had ever really singled them out for special praise.

Those who had been luckier could still remember. In some cases, they shared, almost shyly, the impact of such praise. Somewhere back along the half-vanished years, a teacher had noticed. An educator had seen poetry, had sensed mathematical insight, had recognized artistry or special kindness, and had been conscious enough to share that recognition with the child. Such moments were not only remembered, but for some of them in the room, that moment marked a quiet turning point in their lives, too.

If there is one thing I have come to believe above all else in this life, it is that every one of us lives our lives undernoticed, underthanked, underhonored for who we are and what we strive to become. From that shortfall, there arises a powerful human hunger.

Students come to school each day with the unspoken, barely acknowledged wish to be noticed, thanked, and honored. Day after day, they arrive, carrying their homework and their other burdens, their goodness and their worries, their little hopes and perhaps a lingering sense that they don't really matter that much. In that very hunger, there is tremendous, life-size opportunity for those of us who want to make connections, who want to make a difference.

As humans of any age, but certainly as impressionable young people, we are confused about who we are. We harbor the quietest of hopes—that those private aspirations of becoming a writer, a dancer, a scholar, an athlete, or an actor will somehow find resonance in the outside world; that we will catch someone's attention sometime, somewhere, somehow; and that our secret dream, nurtured in hopeful isolation, will find recognition and reinforcement.

What power we have as teachers. And, if the results of that faculty meeting are any indication, how rarely we use that power.

Praise is a power we underuse in the best of times.

Praise is a power we tend to abandon when the going gets tough.

Praise ought to become our first, most reflexive inclination and act in both good and bad times.

THE VALUE OF PRAISE

We should praise, first of all, because it feels good. Secondly, we should praise, because it *is* good. Beyond that, though, think about what praise is capable of achieving.

Praise can certainly be used to single out some quietly dazzling accomplishment or characteristic. Let me change that. Praise *should* be used to single out such things. As teachers, we should attune our very beings to moments that deserve such recognition.

How many teachers simply nod or move on to the next question without any acknowledgment when a correct answer is given? But we certainly elaborate when the answer is off-target, inattentive, or wrong altogether. What if we responded just as energetically to great, insightful, focused, beautifully worded answers from our students? What would happen to the mood and the atmosphere in our classrooms? I suspect we all know how the posture might change if these hungry, hungry students knew that we were doling out morsels of warm and genuine recognition.

In addition to the power of responding more enthusiastically to specific answers, praise can be used to honor the long-term steadfastness of the child who works tirelessly to fulfill his or her responsibilities as a student. So many of us allow the quiet, dutiful, and hardworking student to become invisible in our eyes—eyes that are so readily distracted by the war whoops from the back right-hand corner of the room.

Well, isn't such a dutiful child getting a pretty steady stream of good grades? Probably. But is that really sufficient? Is that all she deserves? In the end, is that all we can do? For that child, a good grade is perhaps so standard that it's almost meaningless. It is a letter ink-jetted onto a transcript somewhere.

What if we did something different? Imagine this scenario:

What if, in the middle of the period, we were to ask that same quietly dutiful child—let's say a child named Caroline—to stay a moment after class.

She is rarely in trouble. She may never have been in trouble. So with ten minutes to go before class is dismissed, she may be ransacking her memory for what it is she could possibly have done to displease us.

The period ends. The classroom empties. She is standing before us, a little worried. We break the silence. "Why do you think you're here?"

"Because you asked me to stay."

"And why do you think I did that?"

"I have no idea."

"Well, let me tell you. Because while I have been spending a lot of my time and energy working with some of the kids in this class who've been involved in mischief or who haven't turned in the kind of work they should, you've been an absolute star. I don't have to talk to you much. And I don't want you ever to think that's because I don't notice or because I take what you do for granted. You set an example in here of precisely what every teacher is looking for. Has anyone ever told you that?"

A look of blushing, startled relief accompanies an almost imperceptible shake of her head.

"Well, they've said it to me. Your past teachers think the world of you. And you know what?"

Another shake of the head.

"So do I."

A gulp of pleasure at last, a flash of teeth, and only the barest moment of eye contact.

"Caroline, have a wonderful evening."

She starts toward the door, trying valiantly to contain her inclination to burst. "And Caroline?"

She turns. She can't wait to get home, maybe to tell her mother or maybe just to sit in her room with this feeling.

"Don't ever think we don't notice. We're busy with other things, with other kids who demand our attention, but we notice."

And then, she is gone.

Too corny? An exaggeration?

Perhaps for some of us. But I believe—deeply and sadly—that the best of our students become somehow invisible to us. Statistics reveal what we know in our hearts to be true, that 80 or 90 percent of our conversation as teachers is about kids who are in trouble or cause trouble. And mostly what we mark on their papers are errors, as did our own teachers and those teachers' teachers before them.

But we have the power to set our own tone in our own classes. Yes, of course, we'll have to "correct" papers and shut down tomfoolery and all of the stop-stop-stop stuff we do as teachers, but we have a power that goes beyond all of that, a power most of us use far too rarely. And it is a power that may outlast anything else we ever do in the classroom.

It is true that we may feel beset by kids who won't work or won't behave or that we are endlessly being tested by rowdies or troubled by our own self-doubts; however, whatever else may have gone on or gone wrong that day, think of how Caroline will feel as she enters her house that evening. Remember her. She embodies our values. She is worthy of honor. Praise matters. Praise illuminates. Praise reinforces.

There is a hunger out there. And no one, not even parents ("Aw, Mom, you're just saying that!"), has the influence that we do. We represent the outside world, the "real" world. And what we notice, what we dare to see and say, provides the kind of nurture that so many hunger for and so many are forced to do without.

THE UTILITY OF PRAISE

Is that all praise can do? Just make us feel good for a moment?

Hardly.

More than any other tool available to us, praise can be used to build—or to change—an individual reputation.

Picture the kid who's been a persistent thorn in your side. He's a little unsteady in his skills, or for that matter, he may come across as hopeless in your class. And the challenges he confronts you with may be a distraction, designed to keep the attention away from his failure.

Wait for the right opportunity, but anticipate it. The next time he offers something constructive in class, the next time he turns in homework with *anything* worthy of congratulations, ask quietly to see him at the end of class.

He'll no doubt be expecting the usual put-downs, some remarks about getting himself under control, lectures he's heard countless times from countless exasperated teachers (read: "dumb adults") before you.

He'll no doubt wait with a long-rehearsed what-do-*you*-want leer, weight all on one leg, very Brando—or try slipping out the door unnoticed—when the period comes to an end.

"I wanted to talk to you about the paper you turned in."

"Yeah?" *What was wrong with it?* he's thinking.

"I loved what you had to say about Thomas Jefferson. Nobody else in the class seemed to really get the point that without a war, he managed to double the size of the country." Pause. Pause. Let the silence reinforce the surprise. "You *got* it. That was terrific."

He was likely ready for anything but what he just experienced. He's probably so accustomed to adults only talking to him about his shortcomings, gotten so used to having his defenses up that you've completely floored him. He's likely speechless. He may even give a disregarding snicker. He may grab the paper and turn to the door, as if it didn't matter at all. Don't be surprised, and don't you believe it. You've caught him red-handed, doing something well.

It may be that he'll intentionally self-destruct and turn in a paper next time that is perversely, completely rotten. Call him up to your desk at the end of class again. Give him a wry smile. "You and I both know that you can do better than this. You've got a good mind for history." Resist the lecture. Let him leave, and stay in touch.

You've spoken to him in a way that he's probably rarely heard. You've praised him. You may even have begun to create the fabric of a new identity—as someone who *got* Thomas Jefferson, as someone who's actually *good* at history.

The tough guy may still saunter out, as if nothing has happened, but he knows that you have seen something good in him. He knows that your expectations of him are higher than he's used to. He may never quite give in to you. He may never really let his little light shine. After all, inertia is inertia is inertia, and everyone else seems to take his bad reputation for granted.

But somewhere deep inside the darkness where he lives, a small light has been lit. And I suspect we each know, cynical or not, that there is a chance, a slim, candle-in-the-wind outside possibility that he may suspend disbelief, that he may be open to that possibility, and at the very least, that history won't be his least favorite subject. He may even begin to think of himself as "not bad" in history. Opportunities don't always reach fulfillment, but there is always the possibility for transforming an old, established, crummy reputation if we are attuned to it and have our eyes on the hungry, sometimes hurting child within.

USE THE POWER OF PRAISE TO UPLIFT AN ENTIRE CLASS

They may have gotten on your nerves from the get-go.

Any other teacher who has seen your class roster in the early days of September before the first class may have rolled his eyes, shaken his head, clapped you on the shoulder, and wished you good luck with *that* crowd.

We've spoken about praise as just something good to do.

But praise as a tool? There may be no tool in your arsenal more powerful for leveraging the transformation in an entire class. Catch them red-handed, doing something well.

From the start, go out of your way, stay totally attuned to finding those moments in which they outdo themselves, in which they (maybe accidentally!) do something well. It doesn't have to be major. It can be as brief as a five-minute interlude in which the discussion actually took hold, in which they actually seemed to be listening, to be thinking.

"Wow! Did you feel that? That was a great exchange. Tommy, go on."

Too sappy?

Don't you believe it—or if so, cast it in your own words. But catch them. Highlight those moments. Illuminate the tiny instances that have the chance of becoming the foundation for a new, radically more successful reputation.

The kids have turned in papers. Quietly ask two of them after you've read their papers if you can read sections of their papers aloud. They were *that* good. You'll no doubt get a bewildered, embarrassed, shrug-it-off response, but stay with it. Read it without giving the name if the kid really refuses the public recognition, but read it nonetheless. And ask the class what they liked about that particular passage.

Don't brook *any* nonsense. You've got a kid's paper, and the kid may feel vulnerable about that. Get warm, rich, specific praise—or if they won't provide it, if they're that ironclad, go ahead and give it yourself.

The quotation was perfect. The example was exact. The topic sentence served as a gateway for the rest of the paragraph. Whatever. Whether or not you are allowed to mention the student's name, make it clear that some *good* work is being done in this class, and there may just be a possibility that some of the kids (nothing is transformative for everyone—give up that illusion) may take a little more care with their quotations the next time.

And then broaden it.

"You folks are starting to really produce some *excellent* work."

Now it may be that only four of the twenty-four papers were actually excellent or anything close to it, but no one will know that but you. The kid who knows he did a slinky job on it will maybe—just maybe—begin to think he's in the minority, and the class itself, perhaps for the first time in a long while, will have heard something positive.

Praise is the greatest reinforcer of excellence. Praise is the guidepost that points to higher terrain. It is one of the most effective tools in creating and deepening a vision of higher expectations.

And notably, even in a class that is miles away from excellence, where the morale is bad and few kids seem to work, it can serve as a source of illumination for those students who do try and those moments where things actually click.

Praise can be co-opting.

Praise, in general, is pure good. But there can be a powerful Machiavellian side to it.

Let's go back to the kid who's been a thorn in your side, the one who wrote about Thomas Jefferson. In the example before, we focused on developing his skills, on changing his self-perception, on getting him to possibly begin believing in his own chances for success.

But there is also a serious possibility that your praise may gradually begin to neutralize him as a negative force in your class. Each of us is hungry for recognition, and when that recognition comes—and in this case, at the end of such a long wait—are we really so willing to bite the hand that feeds us? The praise-starved child needs to be fed, for no better reason than the fact that he's hungry. But those whom we have surprisingly fed after periods of protracted hunger may be a little less inclined to pull down our statue in the classroom town square, especially if we have been the one teacher in years to notice and highlight the good in him.

Beyond the individual child, the class that has felt the glow of rare and specific praise often finds it harder to forsake a new allegiance to the teacher who noticed. It is a tale as old as mythology; one shoots the messenger who brings bad news. I think that the converse is no less true. There is, in the praise-giver, the potential for deepening, life-affirming bonds with an individual or with an entire group, particularly if the praise is warm, honoring, specific, and true.

Praise reinforces your values in the classroom.

Unless we are in the throes of some particularly morbid funk, we're probably not likely to say, "Maybelline, I liked how hard you pinched Rufus to get the Play-Doh away from him!" What we praise should align with what we value.

What do we value in our classrooms?

If something is truly a value of ours, we need to be on the lookout for it, attuned to it, and ready to highlight it with praise. There is nothing that provides greater reinforcement of our values than the celebration of examples of those values in action.

It was a cool autumn morning in the garden behind the school. The kids were at recess. A group had gathered in the central area to play soccer.

Suddenly, there was a breakaway. Jamaal had stolen the ball and was hurtling downfield with it in an exhilarating four-on-two. A goal looked certain.

Just to his side, Henry collided with a player from the other team, and both of them went down in a tangle of limbs.

Jamaal stopped in his tracks. He let the ball dribble away. One of the players from the other side, sensing salvation, eagerly took over the ball—until he saw what was happening.

Jamaal was crouching over the fallen boys. The impending goal—even his potential status as team hero—was less important to Jamaal than making sure his classmates were all right.

I went over to join him. The boys were shaken up, but as they donned suitably macho expressions, they were up and dusting themselves off, ready to play again.

I stopped the game and called everyone in. I asked Mike to hand me the ball while we spoke.

"Did you all see what just happened?"

There were frowns of confusion. Of course they had. Two boys had fallen down.

"No," I said. "Did you watch what Jamaal did?" Now Jamaal was fidgeting with grinning embarrassment.

Together, we spoke of the decision he had made, the choice he had taken. And when I turned them loose and tossed the ball back out to them to begin again, there was—ever so slightly—a different, gentler spirit in the game.

If you value it and you see it in action, freeze-frame it. Underscore what matters to you as a leader of children. Emphasize what you believe in, and let the kids see it, not just as some vague platitude but as a highlight laid out before them, specific and active and real.

Even in more minor matters, reinforce those behaviors that build teamwork and trust. If you wonder why the students are late and are troubled by it, notice that not all of them are late and begin to thank and praise those who make the effort to be there on time. And yes, notice and praise those who seem to be making an effort at being more punctual.

In the younger grades, it's possible to get away with direct statements like "I like how quickly Savannah Mae put the tarantula back and went to her seat when she saw that it was time to start our next activity."

The same sentiment might play a little poorly with a sarcastic cabal of high school sophomores, but honesty and recognition do have the potential to make a difference to students of every age. "We've had some difficulty getting started on time. I was really impressed with the way so many of you came in and got right to work. We had more time to go over tonight's homework. That may make it possible for you to get finished with it more easily," said with a wry and twinkling smile can make several points. A lesson leveraged with praise is one more likely to be listened to than any lesson alone.

If it is kindness we are looking to foster and support, it is vital that we begin to notice even the little acts of kindness—someone holding a door for another student, someone sharing a book without being asked. Praise them because they deserve it, and praise them because the class needs to know what matters in your classroom.

Praise defines our values. More than that, it reinforces and promotes those values in our classroom and in the wider school community.

Praise has a profoundly unifying effect on the culture of a class.

In classrooms characterized by a negative undertone, there tends to be a great deal of caution about taking risks and about even speaking up at all. Fearful of snickers and undersupported by the teacher, students tend to become minimalists. They're all looking out for themselves, watching their own backs with a kind of collective isolation the teacher could have prevented.

My father once told me the story of a summer camp he went to where, incredibly, the head of the program actually authorized an annual campwide vote for one of the children to be "camp goat." That child was deemed fair game for bullying all summer long—even a little limited torture and taunting from the counselors and the head of the camp himself.

As dismaying as that may seem, most of our classes enter our rooms with predesignated goats. It's the kid who talks funny. Or the fat kid. Or the kid who's ridden with anxiety and easily provoked. Or the kid without an ounce of social grace. Often, it's the one kid who's already got enough trouble without having to serve as fair game for others. And too often, it's a kid who is genuinely hard to like, even for teachers.

The kid's life has probably been a protracted experience of torture—or at least its ever-present possibility. It may be that the taunting and put-downs have been limited to the locker room and the lunchroom and the bus stop, but there is at least a possibility that somewhere along the line a teacher or coach who really didn't care for the student gave tacit approval to his designation as the class goat.

But a failure to intervene establishes our values, whether we intend it or not.

A failure to intervene allows the culture to be claimed and defined by the reckless and predatory. A failure to intervene fosters an environment in which there are goats galore and in which their lives are perpetually compromised. In a culture in which victimization is permitted, everyone—the predators, their prey, and the supposedly innocent bystanders—are all tainted by the same poisonous spirit.

A classroom environment in which teasing, taunting, and even the subtlest sighs or eye-rolling are off-limits is one that can foster growth and risk-taking. When everyone feels safe, when everyone is protected, a true sense of closeness can flourish. The development of a true sense of team spirit depends on everyone being on the same team—*no one* left out.

THE CULTURE OUTSIDE THE CLASSROOM

Some teachers would suggest that they only need to deal with the classroom, that what goes on in the hallways or the cafeteria or the locker room is none of their business. Others would never admit as much, but their action—or rather, their inaction—says it for them.

If we are really to make a difference in the lives of students, if we are really to make a difference in the

A Brief Note on Sarcasm

In our classrooms, sarcasm has to be off-limits for students and for all of us. Sarcasm can parade as easy humor, gathering a ripple of laughter in its wake, but sarcasm always has a victim, its own goat, if you will. Sarcasm used against one student puts the others on alert that they may be next. Sarcasm used by the teacher gives tacit permission to students to use it against that person themself. Sarcasm undermines trust, and sarcasm is almost always articulated as praise that suddenly whipsaws into derision.

If you want to build a class reputation and spirit based on praise, you should never resort to sarcasm, because by doing so, you create a distrust of even the most well-intended praise. If there is something that needs correcting, say so directly. Particularly considering the human hunger for praise, sarcasm is a cruel and merciless weapon that, as novelist John Knowles once observed, is truly the voice of the weak.

culture of the schools where we work, our turf must extend beyond the classroom door.

We have probably all seen teachers walk right past cackling gangs of students. They might be inclined to stop and intervene on behalf of a "school rule," but if it's "just" a case of cruelty, they might well walk on.

We have probably all seen teachers who would pick a student up by the scruff of the neck for saying "Shit," but who would walk by without a word when overhearing that same student taunting a classmate, calling him a "fag." It is often easier not to intervene—even when there is a clear-cut victim. It's out in the hall. It isn't our business. It isn't our problem.

But our inactions, like our actions, define who we are and what our true values are.

Just as recognition can support our values, so a lack of recognition can forever undermine them. The fact is that students notice what will make us wheel around and what we just pass by. Our inaction is as much a testament to our values as our action. Students may try to find camouflage in their "bystander" status. As adults in school culture, we are never bystanders. If we hear, if we observe, if we witness something and do nothing, we inevitably become implicit, active supporters of that behavior.

To a very real extent, we create our own worlds in our classrooms and our schools by the sum total of our actions and inactions. What we notice, what we honor, what we praise—along with what we actively stop or choose not to notice—eventually defines the nature of those worlds.

TWO WONDERFUL BENEFITS OF THE MODERN AGE

It is commonplace to bemoan modern society. Thus, it gives me special pleasure to highlight two ways in which modern society makes life easier for us as teachers.

Every example of praise I've discussed so far has been spoken. There is great value in that. It is personal. It is direct. It has the sense of proximity and meaning. But it is also temporary, and it might well never reach home.

There are two solutions for this:
- The phone call.
- The handwritten letter.

The fact is that we are all insanely busy, so that means if we're going to use this "praise thing," it had better not take much time.

Nowadays, with so many parents working, there is rarely someone at home, and almost everyone seems to have some sort of answering machine. I keep my students' home phone numbers (and addresses) in my roll book, and when someone deserves to hear something great—perhaps in front of Mom and Dad—I can just lift the receiver, dial, and leave a message.

> *"Ms. Rutabaga? I just wanted to take a minute to call. This is Mr. Eggplant from school. Earlier today, the class was squabbling a bit about what to name the new guinea pig. Half of the class had its heart set on Josephine, and the other half absolutely wanted to name it Spike. Your little Eustachian Tube listened to both sides. She's a very good listener and a really sensitive, thoughtful girl. And she's also quite creative. She stepped up and suggested that we call the guinea pig 'Spike-ephine.' And everyone just loved the name. The battle ended. The new pet had a new name, and little Eustachian Tube had saved the day. She's a pretty great kid, and I just wanted you to know what we think of her."*

Click.

What did that take you? Seventy-two seconds?

And Ms. Rutabaga's reaction when she gets home? She'll hear that there's a call from school, and her eyes will probably darken in grim anticipation. What *now*?

And oh, the light in those eyes.

We've all heard how negative phone messages have a way of *mysteriously* getting deleted before the first adult has the chance to hit the play button. The phone message of praise works—those never get deleted.

The second tool you now have is the handwritten letter. You may say to yourself, "What? The handwritten letter isn't a modern tool!"

Exactly.

Email and computer-generated form letters have become so prevalent that the handwritten letter has become something of an endangered species, so when a letter genuinely, painstakingly written by a human being (with an actual hand and an honest-to-goodness pen) arrives, it tends to garner special notice.

For this reason, I keep a small stack of note cards on the side of my desk for the purpose of sending a handwritten note of praise home. When I write a short letter home—even the briefest, handwritten note—to a child singling

A Note on Specificity and Praise

Praise each student—and each section you teach—for what they are truly good at. The more specific the praise, the more meaningful and memorable the connection forged. An "A" may no doubt feel good. "This is a great paper!" will feel even better. "The power of your verbs really brought this paper to life!" is far more specific. It is far more likely that the student may reread the paper and see the verbs for their musculature. And it is more likely still that the student will be able to replicate—and expand upon—the success of the paper with the far more specific compliment than with the more general.

Similarly, it is important to remember that an "A" is generally about the paper. The student's selection of verbs is about the student.

him or her out for some achievement, some act of kindness, some modest success after a difficult stretch, the result is often a shy, quiet thank you in the hall or an email of surprised pleasure from the parents.

I can fill such a note card with what? Seven sentences? It probably takes me less than six minutes to write, start to finish. And yet, more often than not, I would judge that it *has* lit a small light in a child's uncertain darkness—that someone recognized something good about them. And beyond that, I know that some of those note cards have been photocopied and sent to grandparents. Others have been stuck to the refrigerator door for some weeks to come.

A FINAL NOTE

Praise is worth it just because it is a human good, but as teachers, we are in a unique position to affect the lives of our students with such recognition.

When a mother tries to honor a child's success, she is likely met with an exasperated, "Oh, Mom!" As teachers, we straddle the tenuous gap between the warmth of the dedicated parent and the chill of the outside world. Our voices, our recognition, our praise can make a telling difference. Despite the startling absence of such recognition in the lives of half of those faculty members, there was a second half that *had* experienced such moments. And how they spoke of them—even years and decades later—was incredible.

There is such a human hunger—yes, for notice, for thanks, for honor. It is time we ended the famine. It is time that we saw and recognized—either privately or publicly—the dreamer in even the most cynical and challenging of our students.

The reasons are intensely positive. The reasons are—if we are being honest here—also intensely practical.

Really look for the good and the growth in each section and in each student, however difficult it may be. Giving up will only reinforce those difficulties.

It may take time. It may take a certain amount of faith. And it may take persistence, but in the end, we have the capacity—as no one else does—to help each student and each class emerge from the cocoon of a smaller, more confining, perhaps more negative self-image. We have the power to enable each of them to begin to build a bigger, better, more positive self-image and reputation. Teachers who expect trouble with little Wernley Cupid III or from their sixth period hypochondria class are likely to find it. Little Wernley and the sixth period section tend to know they are trouble. They tend to fulfill their own reputations.

If we truly want to help a struggling, troubled individual or an entire, despised class to succeed, we must refuse to accept their long-term negative reputation. We must look beyond it. We must catch them in what will almost certainly be fleeting moments of success. And over time, with vigilance for anything praiseworthy and a self-serving determination to bring out the best in them, we may enable them to develop a greater sense of promise, purpose, and possibility.

Particularly for the student no one cares for and for the section everyone dreads, here is where we can truly make a lasting, pivotal difference. And in the end, it may be that if we don't do it, perhaps no one ever will.

Chapter 4

TEN WAYS TO PRAISE

We intentionally began this book with a section on establishing a positive tone. Even knowing that many young teachers may have been inclined to rip the book open to the section on establishing discipline, it has become one of our fundamental convictions that the greatest priority in any class is to begin to build a positive self-image for the students in the class. And while many of us do reinforce such an image, we have become aware that sometimes we limit ourselves through a simple lack of imagination in regard to *how* we deliver praise.

Sometimes opening just one additional channel for fostering this enhanced reputation can make a telling difference in the way a class comes to feel about itself and their educational leaders.

Before focusing on these potential channels, we would like to focus more deliberately on the *size* of the praise.

It is vital to keep praise believable. One can focus on a specific **act**, on larger, **overall progress**, or on the **identity** of the class or child. It is precisely because children begin to doubt the credibility of their parents' objectivity that parental praise grows somewhat dubious at some point along the way, so praise that is overly grand for a minor act can cause students to question our credibility.

Whenever we can up the ante and expand our praise from noticing a specific act to recognizing greater growth or larger improvement, we have come closer to shifting the child's self-perception. When we can further deepen the dimensions of a child's self-perception by touching his or her very identity, we may have shifted something deep and enduring within the child.

What are we talking about in terms of act/progress/identity?

- "I am so excited by this poem!" "Perfect paper!"
- "I am so excited by how much your writing has improved!" "You are growing by leaps and bounds in math this year!"
- "I am so excited by the writer you are becoming!" "You are becoming a real mathematician!"

Each set of statements above will feel good. The first are more localized and temporary. The second are meant to convey a sense of progression and a teacher's recognition of growth, improvement, and progress. The third are almost a whisper to the hopeful child within: "I see you. I see real talent. I see what you are capable of and capable of becoming."

Now let's look at ten specific ways you can deepen positive connections with each of your students.

1. Share lingering eye contact.

A child has just given a wonderful answer.

The simplest and perhaps most personal way to honor that child is to pause and share warm eye contact. We know that human eye contact has a deep sensitivity to time. We inherently recognize the typical passage of a teacher's eye contact across the classroom.

It takes only a moment or two longer, a pause that deprives the rest of the class of nothing, in order to let a smile shine deep in a student's heart, to honor the student who day after day is responsible by saying a silent, "Wow," to let a student who rarely participates know that she is seen and that her contribution matters, to let an outlaw realize—without the embarrassment of having you actually *say* anything in front of his sidekicks—that you are offering a warm welcome whenever he is ready to come in from the cold.

2. Give brief, spoken praise.

It can be so short as to go unnoticed—seemingly. But a sudden, sincere, and heartfelt "Brilliant!" may not only make a child's day but it can also awaken a dormant hunger in other strivers in the classroom to wrest such recognition.

3. Highlight the moment.

"Did you all hear that? Taylor, can I ask you to repeat what you just said?"

She does. You look around the classroom, nodding, warmly watchful.

"What I loved about what Taylor just said was that it shows she has been there thinking about the question for maybe the last few minutes. And what she had to say shows how deeply she's been thinking about it."

It not only honors Taylor, but it whispers a message to the impulsive to hold off a bit and to those who hang back to not count themselves out by rehearsing a thought to death.

4. Have a one-on-one after class.

"Ghengis," you say as you and the class are gathering up your things at the end of the period, "Can I see you for a minute?"

No matter how golden he is, there is almost certainly a twinge of unease, a flush of vulnerability, a deepening of his defenses *and* his impressionability. You wait for the last student to leave—or if there is another class waiting, you take the conversation into a quiet niche in the hall.

"What you said about the fourteenth amendment/number of trilobites found in the Midwest/the times when *y* doesn't change to *ie* before you add the *s* was *spectacular*."

Let the moment linger. Let the predictable aftershocks, the successive realizations that this isn't going to be bad, that it's actually good, in fact, that it's *great!* run their course. Let the sweaty, shocked, joyful smile emerge. Let the warmth of your eye contact highlight the moment.

This is such a great, underutilized possibility.

If once a week, every Thursday, for example, we committed to noticing the best statement in class—and committed to expanding the circle of students we noticed—what a difference we would discover within a matter of months.

5. Write a more encompassing note on a paper before you hand it back.

Is it just a great paper? Or is it dramatically better than that paper would have been in October? Or does the child actually show promise (with encouragement) to become a really good science student or scientist? Whatever the case, write it out on the paper. Your thoughts beyond the regular "Good Job" will mean so much to them.

6. Highlight excellence for the class.

Of course, in some class cultures, it can be tricky to make too much of the student who actually *tries*. Even then, we encourage you not to accept all anti-intellectualism at face value.

Post real excellence on the bulletin board. Ask the child ahead of time if he would read the paragraphs you've highlighted in his paper to the class—or if not, if he would allow you to read them.

Let him know how good you think it is. Let him feel the flush of academic leadership, and let the rest of them see a demonstration of excellence and of your glow in response to such a performance.

7. Tell the child's adviser, homeroom teacher, or another person who teaches this child.

Okay, sometimes we *are* the child's adviser and/or homeroom teacher, but in every other case, tell the other person. And please encourage them to pass it along.

Let the child know that things have gotten so good that people are actually talking about him or her.

8. Tell your supervisor.

Ask your supervisors to please single out the child the next time they see him or her. Ask them to seek out the child so that they think, *What I said was so great even the principal knows!*

9. Call the parents.

Parents don't tend to cross-examine teachers about praise. They might start out the call feeling the same way as the child does being asked to stay after class—on alert, defensive, uneasy, vulnerable.

But then you can deliver your praise. Be specific, and consider beforehand whether you want to limit the praise to the act, the revelation of growth and improvement, or the indication of some deep and inner talent.

Imagine the parent looking at the child when he or she comes home. Imagine how much easier it'll be when you have some more difficult news to share with the parent and how much less suspicion and defensiveness there may be between you two.

10. Write to the child.

Keep those family addresses and a stack of (correctly) stamped envelopes on the corner of your desk. Five sentences, one lick, and a drop in the mailbox on the way to the car, and you've softly changed that child's world and likely the number of things hanging on the refrigerator door.

There is so much that is difficult, stressful, and time-consuming in our lives as teachers. In the end, though, perhaps the most powerful and positive things we can set in motion depend on simple consciousness and simple acts.

Chapter 5

SETTING HIGH EXPECTATIONS

He sat at an aged desk. His forehead bore the creases of a life of scowling. His hair was thick and dark and swept back and parted down the middle, as if he were posing for an old daguerreotype. His glasses were thick enough to complete the image of an unforgiving schoolmaster. One sensed that the hickory stick could not be far away, that its snap would sting, and that it would be readily put to use. And to top it off, his name was Adolf.

Not a pretty picture.

But when I think back on the teachers who brought out the best in me, he stands right near the top. He was as unforgiving as he was unrelenting. We students graded each other's homework assignments, and if one of us couldn't quite read or find a classmate's answer, he would roll out a sentence, thunderous in its understated quiet, that I can still hear after all the passing decades: "When in doubt, mark it out!"

And how did we respond?

We made absolutely sure that our answers were clearly labeled. He was one of those math teachers who was fanatic about proper units. It took us maybe three nights into the school year to learn that we had better put "square feet" in neon lights next to whatever feeble little number we'd come up with.

After years of math courses that allowed me to get a little paunchy and self-satisfied, this was one serious boot camp, and this was one serious master sergeant. But we loved it. Contrary to all of our generic expectations, this was as far from a cool guy as we'd likely ever find, but we'd go any distance to earn his respect.

No one ever dreamed of crossing him or even questioning him. Why? I think there were probably three real elements that mattered, three elements that have continued to resonate with me as the keys to his success.

First, he brooked no nonsense.

When I think of Adolf Nelson and discipline, I can't even remember a single instance in which he actually had to punish someone. He ran that tight a ship. From the moment of entry into his room, one sensed that he wasn't there to make nice. He was there to teach. He had no favorites, no chosen victims. He was strict, but he wasn't mercurial, moody, or capricious. He wanted us to learn. He treated everyone fairly, and no meant no.

Secondly, he was there because he loved mathematics.

He thought algebra was just incomparably cool—those functions and slopes, that incredible quadratic equation, derived by some long-lost genius, those things that have caused fear and trembling for so many of us in our lives. To Adolf Nelson, they were absolutely inspiring, and in his presence, in sensing his energy as he would unfold himself from the desk and rise to take chalk in hand, all of us knew that he was in touch with a source of mysterious power.

We watched the numbers play out. We saw the variables glisten. We witnessed the most barnacle-encrusted of equations emerge with an x alone on the left and an incontrovertibly simplified answer gleaming just beyond the equal sign.

He loved his work. Every class mattered. Every moment among us glistened with a sense of streamlined urgency.

He believed in his subject as if he were imparting to us the oral history of how to find our way to the Fountain of Youth, and any misstep, any inattention along the way would leave us aged and haggard wrecks. There was that kind of energy. There was that kind of urgency, that sense of mission. A mastery of mathematics *mattered*.

Finally, algebra mattered so much more than his own popularity.

Thus, it wasn't long before we all came to like him, the ungainly, nearsighted tyrant that he tried (so easily!) to be. In addition to the frown lines of a man who likely worried a lot, there were the crow's feet of a man who laughed and frequently found delight.

Oh, it's true that he was stubborn in refusing to let us see when and how we might have surprised and pleased him, but what Adolf Nelson did for everyone in that room was to establish from the very first class, from the very first contact, a clear sense that mediocrity was simply not permitted. If we had ever dared to convince ourselves that we had worked hard, been thorough, really tested ourselves in the past, we were in for a rude awakening. Boot camp wasn't easy. Every good grade wrestled from Adolf Nelson was an earned grade. Whatever the intellectual equivalent of elbow grease might have been, we knew we'd learned to use it. We'd been required to use it.

This was academic toil, the kind that led to the development of a kind of intellectual musculature that only arose in the presence of a teacher who set uncompromisingly high standards, who was there alongside you every step of the way to achieve those standards, and who was there to greet you at the finish line with a grin of welcome and homecoming.

* * *

But not every teacher needs to be like Adolf in order to set high expectations.

I still remember that first day. Jenny appeared in the classroom, young and attractive, brimming with a busy confidence that seemed to mask a certain vulnerability. We knew that she was young and new to the school, and she was assigned to teach eleventh grade English to a fairly rowdy group of us kids. We didn't know that she was also new to teaching and that we were her first class.

She strode across the room with a large straw purse at her side.

"Here," she said, wheeling about like a magician and reaching inside her bag. I can still remember precisely what it was that she pulled out. It was a fairly modernistic metal bust of a woman, set on a wooden platform about eight inches in height. Over it, she had pulled and tied a thin, translucent plastic bag, the kind one got one's drying cleaning returned in.

To me, it looked vaguely sinister—this intriguing sculpture of a woman's head and shoulders now shrouded, almost asphyxiated in plastic.

"Write," she said.

Now I will tell you in no uncertain terms that I didn't fancy myself a writer. While a half dozen classmates got dutifully to work and several began peppering her with obstructionist questions ("How long is it supposed to be?"—of course), I sat there, a little frozen by the open-endedness of the challenge. At that point, I was a proud math-science guy. If asked to write a poem, I generally could come up with the one every student seems to fall back on—the one about autumn leaves and their symbolic parallel to death ("brown" and "down," you know it; we've all written it at some point).

But there was something different here. I liked the provocation she had set up for us. I can definitely confess to being intrigued; however, I didn't yet trust myself, and I didn't yet trust her.

Oh, and there was a week or two of testing. She was young enough and lighthearted enough that each of us (the guys particularly) seemed to take turns testing her mettle, but her humor, that incredible twinkle in her eye amazingly diffused it. She had *known* that we were going to test her, and she had responded to each volley with a sharp return and a look in her eyes that said, "Oh, isn't it fun to be immature?"

She came across as wonderfully unfazed and somehow began to convince us that while it might have been fun to be immature, it was much more exciting to grow. And if we were willing, she would help us along the way.

It was a powerfully compelling image that she held in her imagination and projected out across that classroom—accepting us as we were but daring to imagine us (and allowing us to imagine ourselves) as we *might* be.

She didn't actually say she had high expectations for us, but how she responded to the testing made it clear that in her own mind, we were letting ourselves down. We were capable of so much more.

Jenny was as different from Adolf in style, in looks, and in obvious coolness as possible, but both of them believed ardently in the power of the journey and the opportunity to bring out the best in us. By the end of that very first class, as a few students read what they had written, her eyes shone with smiling, surprised delight at the work that handful of students had done. All of us—even the most cynical of the testers—wanted to earn her smile. More than any of us who entered that room, she was convinced that we each possessed a deep and secret talent, a buried treasure she was determined to uncover. Through her absorbing, eyes-on-the-prize steadfastness, we came to understand that by goofing off and giving only a halfhearted effort, we weren't letting her down. If we weren't ready to embrace the challenge, we were letting ourselves down.

We weren't even capable of isolating her—in large measure, of course, because she refused to isolate herself. And the fellow—whoever he was—who tried to offer some macho little test was met with such eminent patience and disappointed power that he just sat there with a sort of foolish grin on his face, isolated in the testing but welcomed back to the journey, if and when he was ready.

By the end of the year, it was fair to say that Jenny had transformed my life, and in all likelihood the lives of countless other students over the years. We were writing for her but discovering ourselves along the way.

* * *

Adolf Nelson. Jenny Hankins. Light-years apart, but each richly, enduringly effective.

Each successful teacher will use his or her own style. No matter how we might dream, no matter how long we are in the profession, no single one of us will be able to touch every life. There were undoubtedly students who didn't respond to Adolf or to Jenny.

But when we come to class each day committed to reaching what is best in our students, when we know that the test is coming and we can face it with our eyes on the prize, then teaching has the power to become the engaging, illuminating, and rewarding journey we imagined for our students and for ourselves.

Chapter 6

AN UNSHAKABLE SENSE OF TRUST

We have spoken of teachers and coaches who have allowed themselves to indulge a class's inclination to harass a designated "goat." And yet, there are teachers who seem just as sure to support the flip side by fostering a spirit of favoritism. Those favorites may well enjoy a special status in their class. The adult may get angry with others, but at worst, he will chide the favorite, most likely with a knowing and forgiving twinkle in his eye.

Is it really wrong to have favorites? Isn't it an inescapable part of the human experience? Aren't there just some kids it's easier to like?

Of course. Just as it is obvious that there are some kids it's almost impossible to like. But that is precisely the reason why this issue is so important. Let's take a look at the reasons.

EVERY CLASSROOM MUST BE A LEVEL PLAYING FIELD

Students recognize full well the teacher who holds the star to a different standard, who unconsciously responds one way to one student and a different way to another. They know the teachers who hold boys to one standard and girls to another. They may know it and recognize it much more clearly than the teacher does him- or herself.

Every one of us probably can recall a teacher who, like Adolf Nelson, was tough as nails but still earned the respect of the students in the class, because he was tough as nails with everyone. And every one of us can probably also recall a teacher who just seemed mean, who gave strictness and discipline a bad name, because enforcement was decidedly uneven, unpredictable, and inconsistent. Whether that teacher went after someone may well have depended equally on which student had done something or which side of the bed the teacher had gotten up on.

It is incumbent on us to do more about our own unconscious responses to students. We must be deeply and genuinely reflective and constantly vigilant: *Do I expect more excellence or more trouble from the boys in my class? Do I let some of the students get away with things that I take others to task for? Do I really hold each of them to the same standard?*

If we are really trying to establish the kind of trust that builds bonds and fosters growth, then it is essential that we be open-minded in our expectations and evenhanded in our willingness to praise and discipline.

TRUST DEVELOPS MUTUALLY

There must be a single standard in the classroom.

A teacher who hopes that the kids will give her a break must be willing to sometimes give the kids a break. The teacher who takes kids to task for being late to class must set the example by always being there on time.

The teacher who likes to wisecrack and engage playfully in a little stand-up comedy (don't be shy about it, for humor is a great tonic for all of us) mustn't always cut short the kid who wants to get an occasional laugh.

Just as the kids will know if we are allowing Jennifer to get away with something that Jack cannot, so they will know if we are allowing ourselves to do something that they are not. They may not say anything aloud, but internally, perhaps even unconsciously, they will begin to withdraw.

BE WILLING TO BE HUMBLE

We must be able to admit that we are human, that we don't know everything, and that we sometimes make mistakes.

We must be willing to apologize if we've snapped at a student.

If we don't know the answer to a student's question, then pretending we do, inventing an answer, or deflecting the conversation may fool some of the people some of the time, but how much better is it to be able to say, "That's a great question. Let's see (together!) if we can find the answer."

And when we mess up a computation at the board or read the wrong answer out loud or mismark a student's test, how much better is it to laugh a little at ourselves than to pretend or blame or hide the fact? If we are truly hoping to encourage a spirit of risk-taking adventure in our students, it is fundamentally important that they get to see how comfortable we can be with our own limitations.

BE OPEN TO THEIR FEEDBACK

This can be as simple as an opening, "So how was homework last night?" Don't argue with them if they say it was too hard or too long or too boring. Be open to hearing what they have to say. Ask follow-up questions. Feel the openness of a real dialogue.

If they're not really allowed to complain, if they're never allowed to tell you that the homework was way too hard or that the test way too long, you may not hear about the mild resentment, but not talking about it won't make it go away, either.

If the students you teach are old enough and if you're comfortable with the very prospect, ask them for feedback on your teaching style. "What do I do that really helps you? And—*gasp*, yes—what do I do that annoys or frustrates you?"

It clearly takes a certain amount of confidence to be *this* open, and some of what we hear might startle us a bit and even hurt our feelings or dent our self-concept a little; however, isn't it much better to get the issues out in the open than to leave them to simmer behind the eyes of those who watch us (and perhaps resent us) each and every day?

If we really want to grow as educators, we must ask ourselves: Who knows more about what we need to know than the students we are commissioned to serve?

If we are open to the idea of soliciting such feedback, then we must put certain cautionary structures in place. No one wants to let loose a feeding frenzy, particularly with one's own blood in the water. Don't make it homework, and don't make it a class discussion. The first encourages phone call or email coordination of answers. The second encourages spontaneous piling-on.

Hand out 5 x 7 index cards. Ask four questions:

1. What do I do well that works for you?
2. What do I do that frustrates or annoys you?
3. What do I need to know about your learning style in order to teach you more effectively?
4. What do you wish I knew about you?

Tell them honestly that this is important to you. You value what they have to say. Tell them to please be respectful but honest, too. No one has to sign the card, either, and they can disguise their handwriting if they want.

Collect the cards before the end of class. Read them at home that night. Think about what irresistibly valuable information those little cards might contain.

And in the morning, report back. You don't need to go into every detail, but addressing the things that they seemed to think you did pretty well and addressing one or two issues that they want you to work on can be incredibly liberating, relieving, and bond-building. After all, you spend much of your energy as a teacher showing them how to improve. What greater model for openness and mutual respect can there be than the opportunity to allow them to do the same?

* * *

In the end, one of the most telling characteristics of deeply respected, truly effective teachers is the extent to which they are able to build bonds of trust with the students with whom they work.

Trust doesn't mean equality. You are the one in charge. Their education is your responsibility, your challenge, your job. When tested, you may well need to invoke all of your authority. As the testing begins to disappear, you can relax into a more natural role as guide for the intended journey. And as the year progresses, if you have truly succeeded in building trust along the way, there is the chance that something close to kinship may develop around the late-night campfire at the end of another day's journey.

Chapter 7

KNOWING THE WHOLE CHILD

I remember as a student feeling as if my teachers only knew one side of me. My English teacher knew me as a writer. My math teacher knew me as a mathematician. And when we had a dance teacher for a while, she emphatically knew me as a klutz. And that was okay…as far as it went. But I never really felt that they knew who I was beyond the single dimension they saw through the lens of their particular subject.

It almost always makes a profound difference to me as a teacher to see a student who struggles in my class in an entirely different environment—in the arcing lunges of a basketball game, reading a particularly poignant memoir in English class, on stage in a musical production, or being picked up at the end of the day by his father because his mother is struggling in the throes of chemotherapy.

Of course, it's possible—it is done all the time—to teach our students as if they have little relevant existence outside of our particular classroom. But if we are truly attuned to the richness that education can be, if we hope to make a difference in the lives of the students we teach, it is incumbent upon us—and it is happily rewarding—to begin to see who they are and how they function, what they dream of and what their lives are like outside of our class.

How do we do that when we are already so busy? There are many ways.

1. Letter from home

At the beginning of the year—perhaps even before the beginning of the year—some teachers write a letter home to the parents, inviting them to write a personal, private letter back about their child—what they are concerned about, what they want the teacher to watch for, and what their hopes are for the coming year.

While it's true that not every parent responds, the great majority, given the opportunity to speak openly about their child, do so with great energy and care. Knowing some of the child's past issues, recognizing some of the parents' concerns, and getting a sense of the child's family can add immeasurably to our understanding of who the child is and might grow to be.

2. Self-description

Early in the year, some teachers also ask each student to create a one-page autobiographical portrait as a homework assignment. Each child is encouraged to write about things that they love, things that they hate, things that they're good at, what they like to do with their free time, and so on. And if the age and spirit of the class lends itself to such a possibility, the assignment can even become a riddle by withholding the name of the child and concluding with the question, "Who am I?"

Whether or not the assignment becomes a class-wide game doesn't really matter. The real purpose of the exercise is for the teacher to enhance her understanding and appreciation of certain unseen dimensions of the student's life.

3. School files

Each child in a school customarily has a file containing all sorts of information. Some teachers prefer not to look at these until the school year has begun in order to allow for their own impressions to form without prejudgment or prejudice from the past records. Other teachers prefer to see the files before the start of school so that they can begin with a fairly clear sense of the composition of the class they are facing. Either works well.

But those teachers who never once refer to the files, who may go through the entire year without realizing that a child has been adopted, that a parent (or sibling) has died, or that the child has a diagnosed learning difference is depriving him- or herself of valuable, enriching information and is directly allowing the child to remain more one-dimensional than any child deserves to be.

We strongly encourage you to take the time—make the time—to look at the files. There may be only a handful of students who stand out and who make a new and deeper impression after such a reading, but it is highly likely that it is precisely those students who may be the most in need of such awareness and sensitivity.

Above all, know the family situation. Increasingly, there are families of divorce, of single parents, or of foster parents, with two mothers or two fathers. Increasingly, too, there are families wherein one parent is legally forbidden to see the child. Don't get caught failing to understand or appreciate the central, critical, and confidential importance of all of this information.

4. Medical records

Most schools will make a point of sharing the list of students with important medical issues with their entire faculty, particularly those students with serious allergies. Typically, this is done early in the year when we are all overloaded with massive amounts of new information. In some cases, it is not done at all.

Before you take a class trip (unaware or forgetting that a student is to be given medication twice a day), before you take the class out on an exploratory walk around the neighborhood (unaware or forgetting that a student is critically allergic to bee stings), before you allow a student to bring in birthday cupcakes made with peanut oil (unaware or forgetting that a student is critically allergic to nuts), it is vital that you keep these facts in mind, perhaps storing the list in a place where you can readily reference them.

If your school is responsible enough to share this information with you, recognize that you are probably on overload, so record it in some abbreviated code in your grade book.

If your school does nothing to alert the staff to these issues (and virtually every class has at least one student with a serious health issue), take it upon yourself to consult with the nurse, and make sure that your own records are accurate and up-to-date.

5. Guidance counselor

The same needs to be said for the school's guidance counselor. He or she will likely have important information on at least one or two of the students in each of your classes. We encourage you to treat this information with considerable understanding and confidentiality. Again, there may not be vast numbers of students who will be included in such reports, but each student you learn about in this context will be that much more likely to be well understood and well served by you.

6. Journal writing

Not every teacher can make time for private journal writing. A high school Latin teacher or a middle school physical education teacher may not choose to make use of this option, but many teachers who work in a self-contained classroom and many English and health teachers have conducted powerful, thoughtful, and enlightening dialogues with their students through the use of private journals.

7. Getting-to-know-you games

"Tell us one thing we wouldn't know about you by looking at you," you might say. It is a simple game, perfect for that period that winds down with eight minutes left. Rotate through the class. Begin with a student who is something of a risk-taker. You and the rest of the class may begin to find out some fairly remarkable things about each other. And don't forget that you need to take a turn, too.

8. Student birthdays

Make note of each student's birthday, and make yourself a chronological calendar of all of them, including perhaps half-birthdays for those students who celebrate summer birthdays when school in not in session. You don't need to buy presents or have a three-tiered cake. Simple recognition and perhaps some minor privilege ("Anthony, since it's your birthday today, you get to clean the tassels on my golf shoes!") will suffice. It may be minor, but herein lies a simple opportunity for an enhanced connection with your students—one by one by one.

9. Extracurricular events

If your students are old enough to be in school plays or sporting events, or if they are young enough to be in dance or piano recitals, there may come a very special opportunity to see them outside of the classroom. You will not only learn from the experience but will ever after see them in a new, more three-dimensional light. Beyond that, you may well connect with them and leave a warm and lasting impression.

10. Finally, keep a central record of this information.

Most grade books I have seen over the years simply have the student's name and list of grades (and possibly attendance figures). There is powerful communicative value in having contact information in grade books—a family address, phone number, and email account. Having at least one confidential (stapled closed in the back of your roll book) page with critical information about each class may save you considerable time in the long run. More than that, it may save you from potentially serious oversights. If you have ever seen a child in the throes of an anaphylactic reaction to a serious allergen, or if you have ever stayed late with a deeply frightened mother, knowing that an unstable father has illegally come to collect his daughter, you need not be reminded of the central importance of this information.

* * *

Our responsibility as teachers reaches well beyond the content of the text-books we use. It is only with a thorough understanding and appreciation of the special qualities and needs of our students as individuals that we can best support their learning.

Chapter 8

THE CULTURE OF A CLASS

You call on Stephen. Or Miranda. Or Kaleem. Or Ishmael.

There is a squirm of discomfort. You know how much they struggle, how difficult this subject is for them. You want to build their confidence. You wait until there's an easy one, and you lob a soft pitch right over the plate. And somehow— perhaps it is a lapse of attention, perhaps they really don't know the answer, perhaps it is that they are frozen in the headlights of the oncoming class—there is a silence or a blurted out wrong answer.

And from somewhere toward the back of the room, there is a snicker. Or an intentionally audible whisper. Or maybe just an exchange of glances that Stephen or Miranda or Kaleem or Ishmael knows is out there and senses, just as a small, exposed animal does, the breath of a predator.

Deborah raises her hand—perhaps the only hand raised in the class. As she delivers just the right answer, both you and she are aware of the psychological knuckled fists of hostility hitting her sharply between the shoulders.

If Deborah is a girl, she may just be disliked for her insistence on those lonely A's. If it's a Nathan, chances are he'll have a quiet hell to pay in the locker room or a hard time looking for somewhere to sit at lunchtime.

Each school is different. The culture coming off the streets is different. The tone set on high is different. But in any school or any situation, it may be more lastingly important than the subject we are expected to cover that we teach our students shared, vital, living respect.

The fat boy with the porcine eyes, the homely girl who picks at her acne scars, the child who keeps trying to fit in but hasn't a social clue are customary outcasts in the Darwinian jungle of the school's social mix. Too often, truth be told, we as teachers aren't particularly fond of them, either.

Sometimes the parents ache and come in with a helpless plea. The child hasn't had a birthday party invitation or even a phone call all year long. Sometimes, perhaps most damningly, the child has always been a source of frustration to the parents—impulsive or depressive or just not what they had in mind.

Our classroom may well be a tiny, circumscribed world, but within its confines, we have enormous influence.

We have the power to recognize. We have the power to reach out. We have the power to engage in quiet one-on-ones when the rest of the class is gone. We have the power to forestall the bullying and support those who spend their days on the receiving end of torment.

It is within our power, if we have but the heart, imagination, courage, and willingness to reach out, to be the champion such students have rarely had or dreamed might exist.

There may be little we accomplish in the course of a year that affects a life more than a meaningful outreach to a child who spends his or her days in chronic isolation. We aren't trained psychologists. We aren't faith healers. We are teachers, and it is in that role, with simple empathy of spirit and generosity of heart, that we have the chance to touch young lives. First, however, some natural questions need to be addressed:

IS IT REALLY ANY OF YOUR BUSINESS?

Many others simply feel a kind of helplessness in the face of another's social pain. Teachers feel that a student's loneliness is none of their business. As they walk down the hall on the way to the cafeteria, they manage to ignore the kid being jammed up against the locker, the mocking lilt of the cool girls taunting the lonely one for her K-Mart clothes, the student who is told, "Seat's saved," as he's about to take a lone empty place at the end of the bench.

Even back in their own classrooms, there are teachers who seem almost to conspire with the class, perhaps in a shared twinkle of eyes following a very apropos jest at the expense of one of the loners. More often, there is a pretended ignorance or a heatless look of "oh, come on now" to the offender, while the laughter goes on.

Anything short of direct, strong, and supportive intervention provides pernicious, passive permission for the persecution to proceed.

ARE YOU WILLING TO MAKE A DIFFERENCE?

This isn't about psychology. This isn't about religion. This isn't even about counseling.

This is about education. This is about learning.

Who among us doubts that the boy with the jaw-aching stutter struggles to focus on French as long as there is a drenching downpour of laughter every time he speaks?

And what of the pale third grader who comes from unknown chaos at home and who flinches at unexpected moments? What are his chances of being able to focus sufficiently on decoding so that he ever learns to read? Or how about the fifth grade girl who is already five feet eleven inches in her slope-shouldered, don't-notice-me crouch? How is she likely to fare in a math class where a teacher ignores the taunts of "giraffe"?

You may not be able to make an immediate difference in your school's prevailing culture, particularly if the administration turns a blind eye. You may have to settle for giving them a single period in the day where they can count on a safe environment for learning, but you will make a difference. Many of them will quietly, gratefully remember you ever after.

So how can you help? You start by identifying who needs help.

WHO ARE THE OUTCASTS?

Take up your grade book. Look at each name, and think about who each one of them is and how they likely experience the day—the isolated class clown who hides a terrible self-esteem problem behind a haze of tomfoolery, the buck-toothed girl who probably has serious, undiagnosed learning issues, the boy who is just plain, achingly alone from the moment he arrives in the morning until he heads for home when the day is done.

AND WHO ARE THE VICTIMIZERS?

Chances are that the victimizers' self-esteem, at least beneath the surface, isn't too great, either, because one thing we know for certain is that students don't need to behave badly if they are feeling good about themselves.

But you can do two things for them, if you are wise enough and willing.

You can put a serious end to their sordid self-aggrandizement at someone else's expense, and you can perhaps help them to find a way to feel good about themselves that isn't at someone else's expense.

HOW CAN YOU HELP THEM?

It starts by recognizing that you are the only grown-up in your class, that you are responsible for more than going over your subject and going home, that you are responsible for the culture of your class.

Everyone in the class will quickly sense what you will tolerate and what you will not. Turn a blind eye or share a pair of half-bemused eyes in the aftermath of a jest at another student's expense, and they will understand that you are giving up part of your rightful authority and that they are the ones who get to set the social guidelines in the room.

Picture this situation: "Nice one, Giraffe," laughs the kid in the back corner when the tall girl stumbles in her reading.

First of all, that student should never again be allowed to sit in the back corners of any class. The backseats are always prospective sniper nests, the favorite perches of those who want to keep everyone else aware that the teacher is far away and that there is a bull's-eye on each student's back. Change the seating, and move him right up front. Reverse the pattern.

Secondly, stop cold as a stone, your ears pricking up like a wolfhound finding a scent on the wind.

Close your book, keeping your place with your index finger. The lesson is suddenly on hold. There is a larger lesson to be learned.

Close the distance between you and the sniper. Stand above him. Look him square in the eyes, even if he—and as long as he—looks away for conspiratorial solace.

"Mr. Davis," you say, calling him suddenly by his formal surname. Your voice is quiet and seriously authoritative. You pause again and make him look up at you.

"This room is a safe place for learning. No one gets mocked. No one gets teased. Wrong answers and taking risks with learning are allowed. Is that understood?"

And wait until he responds. Then briskly snap open your book to the appointed place and move on. The point is to put him—and the entire class—on notice.

In this room, during this time, there are no victims. Everyone has a right to be respected, to be wrong, to stutter, to be just who they are without the ever-present danger of public derision.

One-on-ones as the class departs are also useful.

> *"Can I see you for a minute, Lucius?"*
>
> *Lucius looks stricken, uneasy, half-glancing back at the final students out the door.*
>
> *"That comment you made about the circulatory system/the dative plural/the experience of a soldier in the trenches…it shows to me you've really thought about it."*
>
> *A warm moment, as he looks up to you. Perhaps, if it feels right, a very light, very brief hand on the shoulder.*
>
> *"Just wanted to tell you. I know you're a thinker, and I like it."*

How long will he remember that moment, that relief, that possibility?

WHAT ARE THE EFFECTS OF INTERVENTION FOR THE REST OF THE CLASS?

In classrooms that truly are safe havens where teachers establish and enforce clear guidelines for student behavior, there is something of a sigh of relief, a breath of fresh air—and not only for the chronically victimized.

Virtually everyone becomes defensive and preoccupied in an environment where the teacher abdicates responsibility for establishing norms of behavior. Students will respect not only norms as they apply to students' treatment by the teacher but norms as they apply to students' treatment of each other, to the emotional safety of everyone in the room.

Some may see this as a humanitarian mission, just one more responsibility in an occupation that has more than enough responsibilities. The fact is that it's not only the right thing to do, but it is sound education, too.

Students who are preoccupied by the constant threat of ridicule—even if they know that they aren't likely the victims—have far less emotional energy for learning and growing than those who work in an environment based on community and mutual trust.

In the scheme of things, a classroom is a very tiny universe, but you are the ruler of that universe, for you are a teacher. Show what kind of universe you would run, given the chance.

Because you *have* been given the chance.

Chapter 9

FINAL THOUGHTS ON CREATING A POSITIVE TONE

Many of the teachers with whom we work are more preoccupied with classroom management than they are with creating a positive tone, and by classroom management, they implicitly mean having meaningful rules and establishing discipline. Discipline is vital—an essential foundation of any successful educational journey.

But we have opened this book with this unit on creating a positive tone for a critical reason. It is eminently possible (as we will discuss in the next chapter) for a teacher to unleash a reign of terror across a classroom that alleviates almost all disciplinary problems and that at the same time absolutely precludes the kind of interactive, trusting relationship at the heart of great teaching.

First and foremost, if we are to achieve what we aspire to do as educators, it is vital that we not lose sight of establishing that positive tone. Beyond that, if we have opened the year—and even each period—with high expectations, with praise, with a determination to raise the reputation of each student and every class we teach, we will have gone a long way toward establishing the trust and legitimacy of our authority. Fear alone may force a kind of unwilling compliance, but it doesn't foster powerful, positive educational experiences.

The teacher who begins first with praise and who can steadfastly hold onto a vision of the better angels of each child's nature has taken a first, essential step in developing the kind of relationship with a class from which greater, more meaningful growth will emerge. **Effective discipline is a necessary but insufficient aspect of classroom management.** We must begin the journey with a sense of where we are bound, an abiding commitment to the betterment of each student, and an unshakable belief in excitement and value of that journey.

PART 2

Establishing Discipline

Chapter 10

ESTABLISHING DISCIPLINE: OVERVIEW

Alice Idealist stands at the front of the classroom on her first day as a teacher. She has prepared a series of lessons designed to inspire. She looks like a soprano in the choir, one about to sing to the angels. She has no idea what the kids have in store for her.

Colonel William "Old Take No Prisoners!" Westwallace (Retired) stands at the front of the classroom on his first day as a teacher. He is wearing a camouflage flak jacket and a malevolent scowl, and he carries a rubber truncheon visible to all. He has the flushed look of someone who loses his temper easily. The kids have some idea what he has in store for them.

Alice imagines that her students will be grateful to her for choosing education, having thereby given up her chance for fame and fortune. She hopes to be loved. She dreams of making a difference. She was very likely a good and dutiful student herself, and she has entered her first classroom with the expectation that her classes will be filled with replicas of the young Ms. Idealist.

Colonel Westwallace knows full well that kids are going to test him, and he's come in ready to bludgeon the tar out of the first little whippersnapper who gets out of line. He believes that fear is the only force that can really motivate these savages they call students. He is determined from the get-go to drum that fear into these little miscreants. He'll make them work. He'll make them toe the line.

Students *will* test a new teacher. It is—not even regrettably—part of human nature. As adults, we may be more sophisticated about it, but we do test our doctors, our mechanics, and certainly our parents. Most of us likely remember with some chagrin the way we tested—not to say tormented—our substitute teachers when we were young. We can only hope that karma is a concept that doesn't always apply.

Alice has all the right instincts, all the hopefulness and good intentions one might wish for in any beginning teacher, but she is simply asking for trouble if she doesn't expect to be tested. She may ignore the challenge until it is so apparent, so monumental that she has no choice but to respond, and then there may be overreaction or the simple, excruciating pain of self-doubt and self-recrimination. She'll likely wish that she could have found a teaching job in a school that had only good and respectful students, students who would never dream of testing a teacher.

There is no such school. Anywhere.

Alice is right—absolutely right—to enter the classroom with high expectations, with the ambition to inspire, and with the hope that great collective energies will be mobilized in time. But she is wrong to enter the classroom with such heavenly expectations. As a result, she may spend a good part of the year in her own private hell, wondering what is wrong with the kids, with the administration, and tragically with *her*.

Alice is someone we see in the workshops we run for young teachers. Unfortunately, we often don't see her until after a year or two of frustration and dismay. I wish we had seen her before her first day.

Alice's intentions are absolutely correct. She believes in her students. She wants there to be a positive tone in her classes. What she doesn't know on that first morning is that *wanting* a positive tone is simply not enough. She has to *set* the tone, and to do that, she will have to learn to be comfortable—truly, deeply, biologically comfortable—as an authority figure. She will have to learn to be strong in her willingness to discipline. The students will have to take her seriously, not only as a potentially inspirational and caring force in their lives. Like it or not, they will have to take her seriously as someone who is comfortable—even forthright—in setting limits.

Alice may come to question whether or not she has the charisma and strength of character to be an effective teacher, as if such a quality were something genetic, innate, and inborn. But we have learned that the power to lead a class has to be learned and practiced before it can become ingrained, second nature, almost as a reflexive part of who we are and how we operate as teachers. As we have observed in case after case after case (and this may be the most important single statement in this book), **effective classroom management is based upon an eminently learnable set of skills.**

Let us repeat that.

Effective classroom management is based upon an eminently learnable set of skills.

The problem with Alice isn't that she is congenitally weak, too much of a wimp to ever run a classroom. The problem is that teachers are rarely prepared for the testing that will come, as surely as a string of blue-sky days will give way to rising humidity and the sudden, ominous turmoil of thunderstorms. And the second problem is that once we are alone in our classrooms, our ability to learn from others and watch successful teachers in action is drastically limited. We are left to our own reflections.

The good news (as Christine and I have observed time after time) is that Alice—that *any* Alice—can eventually become a strong and powerful teacher who will be able to inspire, whose lessons will matter, whose caring will affect lives. She has all the right intentions, the creativity and caring, the ideas and idealism. What Alice—or any openhearted teacher—needs to learn is the practical and eminently learnable skill set for classroom management.

While Colonel Westwallace may well withstand the test, he may never manage to convert that success into anything other than a year of pleasureless tension. He may, in fact, teach them Latin or math or whatever his subject specialty is, but as long as he stands at such remove, as long as he is lactose-intolerant to the milk of human kindness, he will continue to resent and distrust the students. And they will almost certainly come to feel the same about him.

★ ★ ★

As they are entering their first classroom, teachers (and even startled veterans in their first years at new schools) need to be aware that they will be tested, but for those who are prepared for it, who are willing to be strongly authoritative, even firmly disciplinary, the world of education, of interaction, of sudden wonder and shared journeys lies beyond.

Because the test can be passed—and the testing will pass.

Strength and authority and integrity are essential, as they are for doctors, mechanics, and parents. Kids are more comfortable—they can relax and get on about their lives—in an environment in which the limits are clear, the limits are real, and the limits are unselfconsciously reinforced. Kids in an environment where the limits are stated but wavering, where their moms set one limit and their dads set another, where the parents set different limits depending on their moods, their fatigue, and their own uncertainties ultimately become preoccupied by the limits themselves and constantly push against the walls, eager (almost desperate) for them to hold.

We are absolute believers in empowering students, but all of us—students as well as teachers in our own careers—want to know what is expected *and* what is allowed.

In the course of their education, students will experience strict and lenient teachers, teachers who demand work by a deadline and those who forever rescind those deadlines, teachers who are comfortable being the confident adult and those who try to establish a kind of palsy-walsy equality that is, in the end, uncomfortable and unnatural for everyone. Consequently, you must set your limits and stand by them.

Games have rules. When they are little, perhaps we will let children take a turn over or have four strikes (or twelve), but there comes a time when a child who never loses, who always gets an extra turn, or who is allowed to blast back to a teacher without consequences simply needs to learn that there are rules and that there are those who will apply them and enforce them.

We need to stand for simple, clear limitations in order to establish our comfortable authority in the world. We need to be willing to establish a sense of order and discipline in our classrooms (and this may be the second most important statement in the book), **because students are hardwired to test, and they want us to pass that test.**

Beyond that testing lies the far more meaningful tone of a class—a warmth of care, a spirit of inspiration, and a sense of control that makes every space more comfortable, more fertile for genuine growth. This section is devoted to how young teachers, how *all* teachers can establish the sense of clear expectations and firm discipline that will allow everyone to relinquish the need to test and move forward on the journey of education.

Chapter 11

HOW TO BE THE MARSHAL OF A WILD WEST TOWN

With your indulgence, we'd like to borrow a page from the old Western films.

The town is in an uproar.

Chaos and uncertainty are palpable on the wind blowing in off the prairie.

A bad guy moseys into town, with a gun-toting couple of cronies. They haven't shaved in weeks, and they smell like horses, sweat, and whiskey.

Rumor has it they've shot down more than their fair share of lawmen in their time. Their poster is prominently placed in the town post office, their ugly mugs glaring out at the camera under the black, stenciled word WANTED.

They spit a lot.

They push back the swinging doors to the saloon, and the crowd goes silent. The piano player grabs his hat and bolts. They order drinks they'll never bother to pay for.

Finally, one of them takes the toothpick out of his craw and gnaws out a question to the trembling barkeep, "So who's the marshal in this town?"

And everyone is deathly silent.

But the desperadoes follow their gazes.

Who is the marshal in this Wild West town?

You are.

Whereupon the barkeep suddenly ducks for cover.

All right.

Got it?

So there are three important points to be made about this particular town at this particular moment.

The first.

You may look suddenly around, as if there must have been some ghastly mistake.

Who would ever have appointed *you* marshal?

Well, somebody did, and evidently, at the time, you wanted the job.

Well, come on now. Can't you just take off the badge, plunk it apologetically down on the table, buy everyone a round of drinks, have a good laugh about it, and bolt for the door?

Not bloody likely.

Every one of the townspeople scattered about the tavern is looking straight at *you*. It's your job. Somebody's got to do it, and it's pretty clear none of them want a piece of it.

Beyond that, it seems mighty clear that the baddest of the worst has suddenly taken a shine to the likes of messin' with you.

Every eye in the place is on you.

What do you do? *What do you do?*

The fact is that this is your job. This is your town. This is your challenge. This is what they've been paying you for during the halcyon days when everything was peaceful. This is where the real work begins. This is where the real money is earned.

You may feel a lot less like some sure-handed Gary Cooper than like Don Knotts in *The Shakiest Gun in the West*.

This scene itself may be a caricature. You may never have to have a shootout with a reckless gang, and your classroom may never much resemble a saloon; however, when the threat is real, the test is looming out there, and the challenger has made his presence felt, there are only two real choices.

One is to beat it out of there and hide behind the rain barrel, waiting anxiously, frantically for June when you're going to be on the first stagecoach out of town on your way back to the job your Uncle Thaddeus offered you, chiseling tombstones in Dodge.

The other is to slide your chair back real slowlike and let yourself rise to your own true stature. Likely, those desperadoes wouldn't have been able to tell how tall you really were with you sitting down all nice and cozy like that.

But challenged four-square like that—on your own turf of all places—you let yourself rise and keep on rising. Before long, mouths come open. You're tall—yes, even the rookie teachers among us who can barely see over the countertop on tiptoe—taller than you had ever imagined.

By this point, the wicked grin from the bar has turned into a dumfounded, jaw-dropped gasp of repressed, "Great golden gophers! Would you look at *that*!" And his sidekicks have taken cautionary looks at the exit.

By the time you have uncoiled to your true, majestic height, you don't even have to say no, for the bad guys are quickly paying for their drinks and asking the barkeep, who's magically reappeared, if that's enough, tip and all.

And as you continue to blaze them with the blue-light acetylene torch you've fired up in your eyes, you feel something close to pity.

Because throughout the animal kingdom, even though there is a deep and well-established pecking order in almost every species, actual antler-to-antler, horn-to-horn, claw-to-claw fighting is rare. Power is something that is sensed. Power is something that is radiated. Power is something that can be learned.

Feel your power.

Project your power.

Send the bad guys packing.

Don't you dare take off that badge. That is the first point.

And who knows, maybe come June, those bad guys will have come back— this time as peace-loving, teeth-straightened, law-abiding townsfolk ready to welcome newcomers on the very next stagecoach.

And here is the second point.

The drama may feel as if it's all one powerful electric disturbance between the reckless renegades and you.

But look all about you.

There are good citizens, gulping audibly, glad that they're not in your shoes, wanting nothing more than to see you lay down the law. They want to get beyond the testing. They want to go on about their daily lives without the constant threat of gunplay and the exhausting waste of time that endless testing can become.

In that moment, when all eyes are on you, when you know deep in your heart of hearts that not one of those good people is going to lift a finger on your behalf, it can feel as if you're all alone.

"Larry?" you whisper. Maybe your old fuzzy-haired friend will really come through for you this time.

Dead silence.

"Moe?" you suggest.

Just the wind.

"Curly?"

A wild *woo-woo-woo-woo* before he hightails it out of there, clanging his head on a hollow pipe.

In that moment, the challenge tick-tick-ticking and not a soul coming to your side, it can feel that if they're not *for* you, they must be *against* you.

When in fact, stepping out of role for a moment, you know in that same heart of hearts whose side they're really on.

They want you to find it within yourself to meet the challenge head on. They want the renegades to be put in their place. They want you to pass the test. They want to get on with their lives, to get on with the lesson, to get on with their learning and growth.

I will never forget the moment when I had to enter the class of a gifted, veteran teacher who had all but given up on the relentless lawlessness of a handful of scoundrels at the back of her class. I opened with a pure, ice-cold silence and then began very quietly to tell them their time had passed. There was a pin-drop stillness when I had finished.

And the only thing that broke the silence as I headed toward the door was a single student whispering with relief, "Thank you."

Don't ever assume they're not on your side.

It's surely from their midst that the test will arise, but don't ever give up on them. Don't ever mistake their silence or intimidation or even their nervous snickers for a wish that the bad guys will win.

All eyes will be on you. There will be a test. <u>And they want you to pass the test.</u>

GATHERING YOUR DEPUTIES

The third point is more of a trick, but it's a good one.

And if there's really any doubt in your mind that classroom management is something learned, I will openly admit that I spent the first seven years of my teaching career having no idea about this nifty little technique.

I'm a man. I've got a big voice. I can shout down a runaway train. I can certainly talk over the hijinks of a restless group of third graders.

It wasn't until my seventh year of teaching that I walked into this particular teacher's class and saw her in action. It was a late Friday afternoon in the dog days of whatever month it was, and the kids were verging on out of control.

Instead of trying to bellow over the hubbub, she stepped quietly into the center aisle and knelt. I couldn't tell what she was doing—I've never been certain—and I kind of like it that way. I'm not sure, but she seemed engaged in a pretty skillful babble of double-talk—just random syllables spoken almost under her breath. In every other pseudo-phrase or two, there was a key, ear-pricking word like "homework" and "important" and "on the test" and ultimately "final grade."

By that point, she absolutely had the class's attention.

And what, in fact, had happened?

Had everyone noticed simultaneously?

No.

But here and there about the room, kids who had noticed were suddenly doing what? *They* were the ones quickly trying to shut the others up. There was a sibilant hiss of "shh-shh!" that spread like whispered wildfire about the room.

And when it was truly quiet, the teacher rose and repeated what she had said, almost as quietly, as if nothing had happened.

But something *had* happened.

She hadn't had to invoke her power as marshal at all. She let the deputies do it.

It wasn't only that I had learned in a thunderclap twinkling that whispering is at least as powerful as bellowing but that I had seen the power of deputizing them or allowing them to deputize themselves.

Oh, it'll undoubtedly be you out there on your own in those critical moments when the big challenge comes, but this scratchy-scratchy Friday afternoon was certainly no big challenge. It was just kids being restless kids and needing to be brought back to center. You don't always have to go it alone.

Enough of the kids want to get on with their lives and their learning. The desire for mastery is part of the human condition. Next time the kids are performing like monkeys in a fun house, consider the whisper. If that doesn't work, you can always go back to playing Zeus on high and let fling a few well-chosen lightning bolts.

But I think the lesson goes deeper than that. Students can be "deputized" in a rich variety of ways. If there is a kid who has always been an outsider, make it a quiet part of your mission to bring him in from the cold.

If you teach in the upper grades, try to find a moment, a reason, or an excuse for a conversation about something he or she has done well. Find out about a hobby or an interest, and softly, naturally, as if you're just chatting while you hang up your holster for the night, bring him or her into your world. The student may not wear a badge or stand by you when the bad guys come to town, but next time, he or she may not be so inclined to snicker with them, either.

And if you're someone who teaches the young, put the little rogue in charge of something grand. Invent a job for him, one with panache, and maybe even give him a title like "Chief Irrigator." He'll learn a new vocabulary word and save you the trouble of watering the plants. "Mr. Clean" gets to go down the hall and bang the erasers together in a wild whirlwind of chalk dust. "The Pony Express" runs the attendance down to the office for you. Look at the little jobs you have to do all day. Make them big career opportunities with important-sounding titles, and suddenly, as quietly as the sun comes up, you've got a roomful of deputies.

Once I had one of those students who had previously been every teacher's nightmare. I faced the first day with a certain understandable trepidation, but when I designated the seat right beside my desk as his, I didn't do it with the sense that this was the marshal's office and his spot was the jail cell. I quietly, unspokenly made it the "most important seat" in the room, and from that first morning, I treated him like my special assistant, my go-to guy, the one I'd ask for help, the one whose opinion I'd solicit, the one I'd send to the main office for index cards, always telling him that I needed them "on the double." He'd come racing back to class (yes, he'd probably committed the unpardonable sin of *running in the hall!*) panting, out of breath, and proud, as if he'd returned with a vital message from headquarters, having made it through intense enemy fire. And I, perhaps as no other teacher ever had, projected *pride* in what he was capable of.

At this point, it may not need to be said, but the restless young outlaw gradually and gratefully became one happy little deputy, madly loyal to his marshal.

★ ★ ★

In the end, the experience will feel like a narrative, a story that may be sometimes scary or unsettling, but the experience is as old as teaching—and perhaps even as old as parenthood. It can also be broken into clear, discernible elements:

- The test will come. For each age-level, the test is different in its manifestations. Four-year-olds look nothing like seventh graders, and seventh graders look nothing like high school juniors. Fortunately, none of them look anything like the outlaws depicted above in the threat they pose or the precise way they will test us, but each and every group of students we face will test us in their own raw and rudimentary ways.
- We may wish the test away. That won't happen.
- We may wish for allies. They are there, but they won't emerge when the chips are down. By definition, the test will pit us alone against what feels

like the entire class and perhaps the entire seething horde of our own nightmarish imaginings.

- The allies won't appear when we need them, but it is vital to remember and keep at the forefront of our understanding moving forward that they are there. We are working to restore the domestic tranquility in the classroom as much for them as for anyone.

- It is vital, essential, and inescapable then that we own the power ourselves. No one else can give it to us or do the job for us, but the immensely possible flip side of this fact is that, just as no one else can give us the power, *no one else can take it away from us.*

- The power is ours to claim, to aver, and to affirm. Standing up to the test is one of the most difficult, most challenging, and ultimately most life-affirming things we can do, both in our professional and personal lives.

- Don't add to your own isolation. Remember the mantra, particularly when you are feeling most alone: *We are all in this together.*

- Own the power.

- Practice owning the power. There are countless little tricks along the way for immobilizing the opposition and bringing the townspeople actively into your deputized inner circle. We are here to help, as is every teacher who has ever slung on a holster and looked out at the town square in their own version of high noon, but ultimately, you will have to choose the moment that you meet the challenge and summon the power on your own.

- Remember what is hardest to remember when the chips are down, when the guns are drawn, and when it seems as if the whole world is rooting for you to fail: *They want you to pass the test.* Once the test has been passed, it is possible at last to undertake the true, uplifting journey that is education at its best.

Chapter 12

THE POPULARITY TEMPTATION

For many young teachers, particularly those working with older students, there may be a powerful and abiding temptation to be cool. It can even happen with teachers of younger students.

I remember all too clearly watching a physical education teacher playing Nerf football with my third grade class. The self-appointed quarterback, he faked a pass, wheeled and spun past their outstretched hands, evading their attempted tags, and broke into the end zone for a touchdown. Even though he was a teacher in his late twenties against a gaggle of nine-year-olds, once in the end zone, without apparent self-mockery, he spiked the ball in a flurry of masculine triumph. In the strangely juvenile daze of that moment, he seemed to lose any overriding sense that he was a *teacher*. I confess that I never quite thought the same of him again.

THE DANGERS OF FLIRTATION

With older students, particularly with young-looking twenty-somethings teaching high school students, there can be a tremendous undertow to appear cool, flirtatious, and casual with enforcement of the rules. For many of us, too, we have barely outgrown a kind of antiauthoritarianism, and now it feels a little strange (but utterly necessary) to actually become that authority. The effects, beyond any transient ego-boost, can be damaging in the extreme. Subtlety in such circumstances is only in the eye of the beholder. Everyone knows, and it will get out. Ultimately, you may have to get out as well.

Many of us can remember the arrival of a cool teacher, a teacher we secretly had a crush on, a teacher who seemed more of our generation than the creaky, salt-and-pepper administration of the school, and there can be a certain worthy sense of connection in that proximity of age in advising, in counseling, or simply in listening to a teenaged student in distress.

However, the risks outweigh the rewards, and they must be recognized and handled with extreme caution. For many of us relatively new to the profession and emerging from our own smoky adolescence, the idea of having a class of twenty-five students in our thrall, focused on us as they never were when we were a student among them, can awaken great yearnings. Now is our long-awaited chance to be truly popular!

There may be a temptation to flirt with or to respond to the flirtations of a student in the class. The damage wrought by even partly harboring this fantasy can derail a career. More than that, we are allowing ourselves a comfort-able—and destructive—naïveté if we think that other students and colleagues won't notice or get wind of it. In a situation in which the ions actually are streaming—if only from the student's one-sided interest—there is a significant danger for the young teacher. Any inclination to reciprocate, however playfully, any inclination to soften at all will be sensed and will lead to a class in which favoritism and alienation become endemic.

A teacher teaching four or five sections of even twenty students is dealing with up to a hundred students, perhaps fifty of whom are of the preferred gender. The teacher may be somewhat attractive, and students love to play head games with *any* teacher. Who among us hasn't tried to figure out the way into a teacher's good graces? And who among us hasn't at least watched as a classmate tried out his or her charms on someone in power?

For many young teachers, their reaction to the sometimes flirtatious probing of the students is seen for what it is—as another variation of the test with which students will naturally confront relatively new teachers. It is a test, like all tests, that students want you to pass. Though the tactics and sophistication of a high school boy or girl may be far more flattering than the wisenheimer chicanery of a clan of seventh grade boys or the ballyhooing impulsiveness of a group of third graders, it must be seen in the same light.

That this is a test to be passed is never in question. The very capacity to be taken seriously as a teacher is at stake here. And it is the ability to be taken seriously and to earn respect as an educator that must remain the primary focus of every young teacher. If there is any chance that you look almost young enough to be mistaken for one of your students, dress it up. Wear clothing that accentuates your authority and reinforces the boundary between you and the students. If you're a male, put on the first tie you've worn since the interview. That means no more jeans. Wear a blazer. If you're a female, this classroom is no singles' bar. Mute your fire. Dress it down. Make it unequivocally clear that you're the adult and that you're not trying to hide that fact.

From interviews with countless students and observations of countless classes (and even from teachers' recollections of their lives as students), we have come to understand that *popularity is almost always an indirect outcome*. Teachers who *try* to be popular and who want students to think they're cool almost invariably find themselves struggling to regain a modicum of respect, not only from the student in question but from everyone else in the class who knows exactly what's going on.

We are responsible for creating an effective learning environment for our students. As much as we might like to bring some collegiate persona into the classroom and flout that very authority we are now supposed to become, we are being paid to teach. It is not only our responsibility but also our job. It is our chosen career. Those of us who are tempted to engage in ego-boosting by-play with the cheerleader or the quarterback (or even to the sensitive, misunderstood poet in the room) have failed to comprehend the most important lesson of great, popular, even cool teachers.

Such teachers have no doubt about the necessary distance between the adults they have become and the students they are paid to teach. As a result, students come to trust that they will act their age, enforce rules consistently and fairly, and treat each student as equal members of the class, regardless of physical attractiveness, adeptness at flirtation, or the depth of his or her temporary infatuation.

If there is someone in the class with eyes for you as a new, young teacher, keep three things in mind. Chances are that you aren't the first on whom they tried out their powers of flirtation. Secondly, everyone will be watching to see if even this nimble, suggestive advance can send you badly off your chosen course. Finally, once your magnetic compass has strayed even slightly from true north, some form of reckoning will come, and the chance for earning their respect will almost certainly have been lost and, with it, the chance to be truly liked and admired, as only an effective, undistracted, and fair-minded teacher can be.

Chapter 13

THE POWER OF "NO"

There is a powerful myth that there is something innate, something inborn, some sort of animal charisma that gives certain "chosen" teachers immediate control of a classroom, a quality that dooms the rest of us to a bitter, uphill battle against our genetic inadequacies.

This is one of the most destructive myths in education. It humbles young teachers, and it probably was responsible for sending Jennifer Longley packing at the end of that lonely June afternoon.

We've said it before, and we'll say it again: All of our observational work with teachers of every stripe and all of our consultations over the years have confirmed again and again that effective classroom management is built upon nothing more subtle or magical, nothing more genetic or metaphysical than an **eminently learnable set of skills**. Inevitably, some of those skills come naturally. Others must be learned along the way.

The ability to be taken seriously by a classroom of students is something that doesn't necessarily come easily, but convincingly projecting that kind of power is a skill that can be *learned*. In the end, it must be.

We have seen teachers—truly inspired teachers—who wonder why they can't control a class, and when we have watched them being tested, they pretend that the test isn't real or that it isn't happening. They try to exert their authority with averted eyes. They unconsciously flash a self-protective smile when they're frustrated. Their voice is unsteady. They keep their distance or perhaps even take an unconscious step back away from the challenger.

But there is an answer. Even for those teachers who have all but given up hope. We have to learn to say **no**—and to mean it.

When Liza, my eldest daughter, was three, I was settling her into bed one night when she suddenly blurted out, "Monica always takes my things!"

I was a little caught off guard by the statement. I asked her what she meant.

"Monica always takes my things," she explained.

Now Liza wasn't exactly your conventional three-year-old kid. While others in her nursery school class were involved in the sandbox or the block corner or the dress-up closet, Liza was likely to have happened upon a neglected twig in the playground. She might be whooshing it around and having the finest time imagining it as a witch's broom or a magic carpet or—who knows what?—perhaps a flying twig.

As Liza told her tale, I could see Monica looking up from the sandbox and thinking there must be something special about that twig. She'd get up and just come right over to Liza and yank it unceremoniously from her hand.

I asked Liza what she said to Monica when that happened. She gave me an uncomfortable shrug and said, "Nothing."

I thought for a minute while she chewed intently on her little fingernail.

"Liza," I said, "the next time that happens, I want you to do this. I want you to say to Monica, 'Don't you ever do that again.'" My voice was firm, and I shook my finger in warning as I spoke.

Liza blinked up at me, a little wide-eyed. This was definitely outside her comfort zone. I told her to practice, to let me hear her say it, then and there. Not quite taking her moist fingertip from her mouth, she muttered, "Don't you ever do that again."

I chided her. "Come on. That wouldn't stop anyone." She tried it again. It was only a little better this time, although she actually did wag her finger. I eased her out of bed so that she could put a little body English into it.

By the time I had tucked her in, kissed her good night, and headed back downstairs, she had managed to say it with all the conviction a three-year-old could muster: "Don't you ever do that again."

Four nights later, as I was again putting her to bed, she murmured as matter-of-factly as she could, "Monica stopped taking my things."

I resisted the urge to exult with her. I didn't even look back in her direction.

"Oh?" I said. Then, with a soft smile, I added, "I'm glad."

You can likely guess what happened. Monica had come up to her and snatched something else, and instead of turning her woeful eyes on her, Liza had summoned her pent-up, three-year-old righteous indignation, shaken her finger, and told her off. Monica had evidently been sufficiently taken aback that she dropped whatever she had taken on the spot.

And apparently, it never happened again.

We have learned from a lifetime spent in education that the ability to say—to really say—no is perhaps the most telling characteristic of a teacher who's going to be successful. That certainly may not be a glamorous or inspiring fact of life. It's just true.

I used to dread public speaking. Now I relish the opportunity, and it isn't because I was a natural born speaker. In my first public speaking class, the teacher commented to the class after my initial speech, "Richard has shown us almost exactly what not to do." Needless to say, I was mortified, but I came back, determined to learn. There is no gene for comfort at a podium. The *only* difference between then and now has been experience and the willingness to take a risk—as I did giving my second speech—gaining that experience.

Experience, in this case, in saying no. Experience reinforcing the limits, no matter the cost. The cost of failing to establish those limits is more of the same—failing to gain control, to be taken seriously, to achieve the real satisfaction that can arise from leading an educational journey with a sense of confident control.

The same principle applies to the comfortable ownership of your own authority. There's no gene for classroom management. In the end, the difference is experience. If this feels like an area you haven't yet fully mastered, it is vital to practice. At first, it may be that you can only summon the strength of will to do it alone in front of a mirror. Later, there may be a colleague or a loved one (or at least your bewildered little Mexican hairless) who would be willing to sit while you try it out. (When your Mexican hairless hightails it, yipping and yowling, out the back door in response to your no, you may feel that you've graduated to the next level.) Throughout it all, be honest with yourself. Only speak as you really would be able to speak in front of a class full of students.

Try it.

"No."

"That's enough."

"Mr. Steinmetz."

It doesn't always have to be that mighty two-letter word. It simply has to convey that enough is enough, that an indelible line has been etched in windproof sand.

Nothing more. Nothing less.

FEELING THE POWER

What does it feel like when you've done it well? Is there a moment of deepening, serious silence while you summon your determination? Are your eyes locked unflinchingly onto the student's? Is the set of your jaw as grim as the Reaper's? Are you truly willing to unleash your no and listen as the thunderclap rolls against the walls of the room and echoes back to you? Do you *really* mean business?

In truth, it looks like this: It is definitely not angry. It doesn't have to be loud. In fact, it shouldn't be. If it's done well, if it's done right, it should be so firm and forceful that it will *seem* loud to those who remember it. Then, let the silence linger.

Keep your eyes steady, locked, and loaded. If you are really present, if you really *own* the resoluteness of your voice and posture and expression, a few seconds will seem like a power-shifting eternity. In those few seconds, a limit can be set, and every member of the class will know it. The chatter and the snickers and the tomfoolery may resurface from time to time, but the most fundamental question in that classroom will have been answered: Who is in charge here?

You are.

Do you really mean it?

Absolutely.

Do the kids really get it?

Just look at them, their hair slightly askew from having been blown back ever so slightly. They may finally take you seriously. They may finally respect you.

More than likely, they are finally ready to get on with learning and growing. The most important lingering question—that lingering, telltale doubt that you would ever be more powerful than the saboteur in the back of the room—has finally been answered. The deepest feeling in the room, beyond the whisper of papers settling back into place on the bulletin boards, is one of simple relief. The classroom is safe. The standoff is over. The rightful leader has emerged.

And gradually, from this point forward, the clownish, testing immaturity may finally begin to wane.

A TELLING TALE

Knowing that you can say no and that you can call a halt to the tomfoolery without hesitation, backpedaling, wavering eye contact, or trembling discomfort is perhaps the most essential element in your developing skill set.

We know a young high school teacher who was challenged about a grade by a big, burly hockey player who dwarfed her in size. He was used to throwing his weight around—on the ice *and* in the classroom. The challenge quickly sharpened into a real high-noon face-off in the center of the arena, with the crowd hushed, riveted in silence by the one-on-one they were watching unfold.

Finally, the hockey player, in a show of throwing-down-the-gauntlet arrogance snapped, "What gives you the right to give me a grade like this?"

She looked at him hard. No apologies. No wobbling skates. This wasn't ice. This was a classroom. This was *her* classroom.

With a self-assured wave of her Bic and the coolest of eye contact, she took a single step toward him and said calmly, "I'm the one with the red pen."

And the puck shot past him and went into the net.

Power in the classroom has nothing to do with height or weight, age or brawn, genetics or experience. It has to do with firmness, confidence, and conviction. These can be practiced. These can be mastered. These can be (and must be) part of who you are and how you feel when you enter the classroom each day.

Chapter 14

THE POWER OF SILENCE

We've just completed a discussion of the power of the spoken word, and that word consisted of only two letters.

So what could possibly be more brief than no? Dead silence.

We are a gregarious species. Silence has the capacity to make us uncomfortable. In certain circumstances, silence can be as unsettling as entering a crowded elevator and continuing to face the rear. In some cases, it radiates an energy field that can be almost unnerving.

Resorting to such silence takes a certain determination, a determination that misbehavior must end, that inattention must refocus, that order must be restored.

And if you are going to unleash it, the silence must be heartfelt. It should be stony. It should have mass. It should endure. And you must completely own it, standing tall, filling the vacuum in the space that silence consumes.

THE POWER OF SAYING NOTHING

So how do you use silence effectively? It might be that you turn to look out the window with a gaze that could shatter glass. It may be that you stop a student cold with a look of contained volcanic heat.

Silence—but only if it is truly owned—can utterly halt and transform the prevailing atmosphere in a classroom. With a slow and crinkly demise, the racket will gradually disintegrate. With a magic, all eyes will come front and center, as if silence was visible. As if their grim but very nomadic consciences had just reappeared in the door of the classroom, the students may well come back to dead-center focus.

Oh, someone, some smart-aleck who hasn't yet caught on to the fact that you're comfortably in charge may let go a wisecrack that eddies out a ripple of uncertain laughter. Ease your eyes slowly into this student, and let the kid feel the weight of the silence. Let everyone take note of which one of you blinks first.

Then begin again, very softly—a lesson at lullaby level. You have quietly yet firmly brought them home again without wasting the breath of the lecture.

Proceed quietly, firmly, resolutely. Then wait another moment longer before you call on anyone. Then with perhaps a twinkle in your eye, simply whisper the name, and let them get on about the business of learning.

Chapter 15

PREVENTATIVE DISCIPLINE: SEATING ARRANGEMENTS

We have spent the opening chapters of this unit establishing discipline, focusing above all on a kind of *stance*, an *outlook*, an *attitude*. Ultimately, the quality of control in your classroom is established in that stance, that outlook, that attitude.

Assuming that you have internalized this sense of yourself as one who is genuinely comfortable as the authority, what else can you do to control disorder in the classroom? You can take steps to *prevent* it.

Notably, we're not talking about avoiding confrontation. We're talking about cutting the number of such confrontations dramatically ahead of time, before the kids even get there. One of the most effective ways to do this is through seating arrangements.

AN OLD DOG REMEMBERS AN OLD TRICK

I had been teaching a solitary math section in a room that belonged to another teacher. I was dismayed and more than a little discouraged by how chatty the students in the class were. It felt that it was open season on chatterboxing after every pause, and that I constantly had to draw them back in.

This went on for weeks. I felt I had tried everything. They weren't being "bad" exactly. They were just noisy, slow to focus, quick to squander time and my patience. After a time, with a regretful shrug, I was beginning to accept that this was nothing more or less than a critically chatty class.

And then it hit me.

The room we used was one of those classrooms that was great for doing projects, with the kids sitting in groups of six around large tables. At any given moment, half of the kids were facing away from the board, away from me, or away from whoever was talking. As many kids were facing the back of the room as were facing the front.

And *all* of them were facing each other. No wonder they were chatting.

Had it been my own classroom, I would have rearranged the tables. As it was, I had four choices:

1. To leave it like that and live with it (no thanks!).
2. To ask the teacher whose room it mostly was if we could change the seating plan. (But he really liked projects. He liked the teamwork around a table. And he honestly didn't seem to mind the chatter.)
3. To do a quick rearrangement of the tables at the beginning and end of each period. That would have been fine. Harness the kids. Put them quickly and effectively to work at the start of each period. Energize them. Work together. Make it right. Had option four not been available, that is exactly what I would have done, and it would have worked.
4. As it turned out, I was able to trade rooms with someone. I traded for a room with a lot less sunlight but with desks arranged in a horseshoe. No one had his or her back to another student. No one had his or her back to the board. Everyone was facing each other, the action, the focal part of discussion, demonstration, and debate.

And guess what? It turned out it wasn't such a chatty class after all.

There are classroom seating arrangements that work well for some teachers but not for others. Having students facing the front or semicircled toward each other helped facilitate, focus, and encourage dialogue. These structures alone obviated the need for constantly telling students who otherwise have their back to you to stop talking.

FILLING THOSE SEATS

The next question concerns how you fill those chairs after they've been arranged.

We have been approached more times that I care to remember by teachers who have all but given up on controlling a class and who genuinely claim that they've "tried everything." And yet, when asked if they use a seating chart, they say no. There is often a certain grimace of disdain, as if seating charts are only for megalomaniacs who hold kids in perpetual contempt.

But each of these individual teachers has been willing to suffer through mayhem and let some significant percentage of every class be frittered away on stuff and nonsense rather than identify what is really in the best interests of each student.

Let's face it: kids will rarely pick the best spot for themselves. Where does the most utterly distractible kid like to sit? Right behind the whirling dervish. Will the wisecrackers ever choose the spot by your desk? Not hardly. And aren't the terminally quiet ones mysteriously able to sense which area of the classroom will best allow them to live in perpetual and unbroken silence?

Left to their own devices, kids are almost hypnotically drawn to precisely that place that will bring out the worst in them. Time and time again, as if they are trying to solidify whatever reputation they have earned, they will choose the one place in the room that will reinforce their most primitive characteristics.

What if the willfully invisible were placed absolutely, inescapably in the center of the action? Mightn't their hands finally (albeit hesitantly at first) lift skyward, particularly once they've seen that you are smiling upon them, noticing them, beckoning them forward, and welcoming them into the discussion?

And what if all that Denise Distractible had to look at in front of her was the board itself? Mightn't she be incrementally more able to focus on the algorithm that's up there in black and white?

What if the best and the brightest were positioned at the back of the room, where the power of their engagement might somehow radiate forward through the class like a freshet of wind?

But it goes beyond that, too. As someone who has spent considerable time notating the interactions of a class on a grid of the seating chart, I can verify what we all suspect. The kids who want attention know just where to sit, and those who want to slide away know just where to disappear into the drifts of a teacher's cold zones.

THE UNCONSCIOUS MAPS OF A CLASSROOM

And it isn't only about the front and back of the room. For right-handed teachers who spend a fair amount of the time working at the board, the hottest zone in the classroom is to their *left* as they face the room. In such cases, you know who will gravitate there and who will mysteriously choose the right rear of the room. In the quick interactions of a classroom discussion, how often does a teacher working at the board truly pause to stand up and wheel about to include those seated directly behind him or her? How much easier, swifter, and more fluid it is just to call on those—again and again and again—in his or her foreground vision?

And even when the teacher has put the chalk down, the dialogue is already engaged. The eager beavers have warmed up, rehearsed, gotten into the flow. Even in a lesson where the teacher isn't using the board at all, established patterns will prevail, and patterns, established early, tend only to deepen as the year unfolds.

Ask kids where a teacher's hot and cold zones are, and they may not be able to articulate an answer on the spot. But they know. Each and every one of them knows.

As much as we might be inclined to dismiss a seating chart as either hopelessly archaic or essentially negligible in tangible result, the skillful and willful positioning of the students in a class can have (and has had time and time again) a compelling impact on the amount of learning, the quality of the interactions, and the number of those who are engaged.

If we really believe in building a team spirit in a class, we certainly aren't going to succeed if we allow our students to fragment into the same divisive little cliques that hold sway in the lunchroom. We have the chance to develop a new, dramatically more positive culture and instead promote an environment that is truly individualized and customized to the long-term benefit of each and every student.

At some point in your career, the practice of arranging students in appropriate classroom desks may become more second nature. Even then, it shouldn't be casual, and it almost certainly shouldn't become laissez-faire. The simplest and most effective system we have seen is one in which each student's name is written on a small Post-it sheet, color-coded by gender. On a grid with the desks outlined, try placing each student in turn, beginning naturally with those students who really have to be in the front of the room because of their distractibility, penchant for mischief, or unspoken desire to disappear entirely from view. Next, beware of poor combinations—students who like to chatter or simply show off for each other. Finally, place the remaining students, alternating between genders as much as possible. Briefly go over the pattern again one student and one cluster at a time. The fifteen minutes you invest in orchestrating an optimum classroom setup—and perhaps the grumbles you may hear when students first walk in as they discover that they can't just sit in their chosen zones—will be eminently worth the investment of your time. Feel free to make necessary adjustments as the weeks unfold. And be explicit and honest about the reason, because there is work to be done, technique and information to be learned, and growth to be achieved after all. There is no reason to be self-conscious or uncomfortable moving students about to minimize the chances of tomfoolery and maximize the opportunities for progress.

Chapter 16

ISOLATE THE INDIVIDUAL: THE PRIVATE VERSION

There are going to be times in which you are challenged or times even more frequently when there is simply someone who doesn't seem to understand that you are in charge and that there are classroom guidelines. In the chapters that follow, we propose a graduated set of steps by way of response. We will thereafter guide you through the possible escalation of disciplinary challenges.

We begin with cases in which the challenge is more indirect. In such cases, we encourage you to begin working quietly and privately to reassert those guidelines and bring the student back into line. The goal is to do so without a public standoff and without shaming the student in question. The goal is to isolate the individual, lay down the law, and do so privately. It may be that it's just a kid who can't sit still or who likes to yodel from the alpine heights down to his (imaginary) friends in the valley. He isn't out to get you, but he's being a pill.

You don't want to challenge him to a duel. You don't want to alienate him, but you do want him to get the message. You make a note that when this period is over, you're going to have a little talk with him. You don't say anything in class. Let it be private.

When the class ends, you slide out the door into traffic, right alongside him.

Quietly, so as not to draw unnecessary attention to yourselves, you state his name.

"Knuckles?"

He blinks and looks around. He could be eight or sixteen, but he'll blink. He'll look around, as if maybe you meant a different Knuckles.

You stop in your tracks. Chances are that he will, too. If not, you repeat his name a little more pointedly and nod toward the wall where he's supposed to join you.

Now it depends on the culture of your school. There are schools and cultures and kids with whom such a confrontation needs to be carefully orchestrated. Distance, namely personal distance, is culturally determined.

For most circumstances in most schools, it's fine to stand there and wait for him to set his back against the wall. He may give you a look. He may polish his fingernails. He may look to see who's watching.

All of your attention is on him, and your eyes are neutral. Your voice is deeply quiet. "Do you know why I want to talk with you?"

Of course he doesn't, but let the silence linger. It's on your terms. This kid isn't a bad one, and this pointed comeuppance isn't a shoot-out at the OK Corral. This is just a kind of early warning, but you want him to know you mean business, too.

"Do you think you've been paying enough attention in class?"

"Do you think you're doing your best getting your homework in on time?"

"How do you think that comment made Teresa feel?"

It doesn't matter what the question is. Whatever disturbed you enough in class to want to have the conversation, that's what the opening question should concern. The key point is that it's got to be a question, and even though you know that he probably won't answer, you're asking him anyway. Quietly.

He shrugs or he gives some goofy answer or he honestly expresses a resolve to try to do better. Let the silence tick briefly, just enough for him to make decidedly uncomfortable eye contact.

"You're a good student, Knuckles. I want to see you paying better attention tomorrow. Understood?" Again, let the silence gather in the stillness after the question. Ask him if he understands. Questions, the resulting silence, and waiting are powerful.

Then, surprisingly, thank him, with a quiet smile and strong eyes. When he nods and starts off, know that he may do so with a snort of face-saving derision, but know, too, that he probably heard, that you put him on notice.

That's all. That's it. It took maybe twenty-one seconds. It was quiet, understated, relatively private, but it delivered a message.

Open with a reputational compliment about how you believe in him as a person. You know he's a good student. You see him as a good kid. Then set his behavior in class as sharp, self-defeating evidence against that claim. This is a possible first step in confronting a student who is causing trouble, but it can deliver a low-level warning with private and powerful impact.

Chapter 17

ISOLATE THE INDIVIDUAL: THE MORE PUBLIC VERSION

The next step is more powerful and more public. This time, the dialogue in the hall may have a little more steam to it. The "Understood?" may be cast with a little bit more of a barbed hook. There may be less a hint of a smile, and you may not say thank you at the end.

What's the reason for the escalation? There hasn't been any improvement. Or this may be a first real challenge from her, but it was observed by everyone in the classroom. It's gone beyond the private word-of-warning. Everyone in the class is wondering how you will respond.

You will still give her the benefit of the doubt, the offer of privacy in the hall. It will still just be a one-on-one, but this time, you're not going to be completely private about it. She was being a snide little turkey, and if you don't do *anything*, the class may end up thinking that you have let her get away with it. And you have no intention of doing that.

"Turkey Jo, I want to see you at the end of class."

You're still not going to confront her in class in front of her peers. This is the last step, a gently respectful willingness to remain private, but you're making it clear to her and to every bystander on the farm that a line has been crossed and that you intend to follow up on it.

And be sure you remember at the end of class that you have a little twenty-one-second rendezvous out there in the hall. Don't let her slide out of class in a gaggling group of gobblers. Call her back if necessary.

Make it private, but make it public that you're making it private.

Chapter 18

SENDING A STUDENT TO THE OFFICE

One of the most important considerations in the life of a teacher—particularly for a teacher relatively new to a school—is to develop an effective working relationship with one's supervisor. The issue is important enough that we have devoted an entire section to it later in the book. For now, though, we want to focus on how to handle discipline with your supervisor and your students.

USING THE DISCIPLINARY HIERARCHY

When it comes to the issue of discipline in the classroom and dealing with an especially difficult student, we are often presented with the fundamental paradox of our relationship with our supervisors. The job of the supervisor in almost every circumstance encompasses two largely competing and sometimes conflicting roles. On the one hand, the supervisor is there as a master teacher, as an experienced educator, as a prospective mentor for all of us relatively new to the profession or to the school. At the same time, they are the ones who hold our careers in their hands.

What do we do then when we want to share a concern about a student with them?

If the supervisor seems at all supportive and accessible, the answer is to make effective use of them. If there is difficulty with a particular student, chances are that the supervisor has had to work with the student before or that he or she at least knows the student can be difficult.

But even if that is not the case, even if this is a new student or a student who has been previously presented as a model citizen, it is vital that you know what you need and be proactive about seeking it out.

Let's say that Johnny Trombone regularly makes enough uproar in your class to qualify as his own brass section in the classical music ensemble your classroom might become. You have already taken each of the recommended preliminary steps:

- You have initially found something praiseworthy about him and tried to establish a positive relationship from the beginning.
- You have been strong and firm with him, met his eyes, and called him to account.
- You have spoken with others who teach him, as well as those who have taught him before, looking for ways to connect and ways to bring out the best in him.
- You have gone one-on-one with him after class.
- You have even called and spoken with his mother, who was (choose one) equally discouraged/angry and defensive/indifferent as Marlene Dietrich with a migraine.

And still he is there, unhushingly loud, brutally disrespectful, unwilling to perform, and tinkering with the spit valve instead of doing his lab work.

You've done all that can reasonably be expected. It's time to raise the stakes. **It's time to make use of the disciplinary hierarchy.**

The hierarchy is there for a reason. During the years in which I have served as a school principal, I have intentionally made use of the shadowy, unsettling connotations of "the principal's office." Students who were brought there understood that this wasn't a favored destination on any of the student's tourist maps.

The hierarchy is also there because we simply don't necessarily want to invest the time to deal effectively with a protracted problem with a student in the course of a class period.

The hierarchy is in place because it holds a symbolic value. A parent who receives a concerned call from a teacher is likely to sit up and take note. A parent who receives a concerned call from a principal is likely to recognize that the issue has now reached an institutional level.

It is worth noting that school cultures vary widely, and it is worth making sure that it is an acceptable strategy in your school to send a child to the office. If not, ask your colleagues how the administration prefers to deal with escalating trouble and follow that pattern.

UPPING THE ANTE: FOREWARNING THE SUPERVISOR

Assuming that it is a convention in your school to send the occasional student to the office, there is something you can do that is even more effective than the spontaneous deportation of the student in question. That is, you can enlist the support of the supervisor preemptively and proactively. Confer with the supervisor *in advance* of the exile.

As with so many initial conversations, the best opening line we know (with your supervisor and with many others) is simply, "I need your help." It is collaborative and respectful in tone. It suggests that there is a problem and that you would like to create a solution together. A supervisor who is approached with such a statement is likely to recognize that he or she is being asked for counsel and that you are requesting his or her assistance. Except in the most abstruse of cases, supervisors—and most people, we have found—are pleased to be asked for their advice and assistance in solving problems.

Next, state the situation. List the comprehensive steps you have already taken to deal with this issue. (Except in extreme situations, we don't recommend a trip to the office without a background of serious, low-level efforts to remediate the situation.) This cataloguing of what you have already done may well make the difference between your appearing weak and unable to deal with the situation and your coming across as a strategic professional who has a clear disciplinary framework and who is now simply invoking the next step in a staged response.

You tell the supervisor that the problem has been persistent. You have warned the student that if it continues, he will be sent to the office. And here you tie the knot. You ask the principal to make it clear to the student, if and when he has been sent, that the two of you have already been in conference about the issue. It is that serious. It is critical enough that out of all the students under the supervisor's influence, he—Johnny Trombone—has personally and individually been singled out for expressions of concern.

Promise that you will select as the pivotal occasion for the dismissal from class a crystal clear, open-and-shut case. **As always when you send a student to the office, make sure that you appear there promptly at the end of the class.** Otherwise, students who suspect a teacher won't follow up will almost inevitably claim that they have no idea why they were sent to the office, that they were simply laughing (along with everybody else) or reaching for a pencil (along with everybody else).

All of this is not to say that you can't be spontaneous in your decision to send a student to the office. Sometimes, it is just the right thing to do. It is a call for the artillery when the infantry has flagged. It also serves to remove the student from the flow of the class so that the violas and guitars at last have a chance to be heard.

Finally, it sends a message to the rest of the class that the extent of a single misbehavior or the duration of a chronic undertow has become unacceptable. It will serve as a warning to others and a source of private relief to those who wish to get on about the business of learning.

AFTER THE ENCOUNTER

As follow-up to sending a student to the office, it is (as noted above) vital that you get to the office before the student leaves. It is also vital that you place a call home, if the supervisor has not called already. The parent deserves to know that things have escalated. If they are not informed, the truly responsive parent will have no idea that the trouble has deepened, and if he or she is not informed, the truly unresponsive parent now has an excuse as to why nothing has been done (i.e., the teacher failed to communicate). The blame is thereupon deftly shifted from the parent's failure to yours, and you should never let that happen.

As you and the student leave the office together after a brief summit, it is important to have a word together—a strong, firm, prohibitive word: no. But keep in mind, particularly in this perhaps overwrought situation, the impressive power of building a positive reputation.

"You are (choose one) such a good/bright/conscientious/positive kid. I expect more from you."

Don't say something you don't believe. Find the positive about the child that both of you know is true, even if it lies buried and wounded. Because you are not gaining all that you might gain if you simply prevent the bad behavior. There is the potential—now with the supplemental, supportive heat of the attuned administrator—to use this raised temperature to transform the relationship and tone in your classroom.

Finally, when Johnny slides into class the next day, turn to him with a significant look—not one that's threatening, hair-trigger angry, or embarrassed to have sent him out, but just a gaze that lingers long enough so that he takes your meaning. And if *anything* in his performance that day can be seen as positive—or at least as less negative—don't miss the opportunity to build a positive connection. Warm, approving eye contact that lingers just as long, coupled with perhaps a subtle nod in his direction, can underscore that you notice him more than simply when he's being a scoundrel. Even if it is over his mighty, years-long resistance, you are determined to help him build a new, more positive and productive reputation.

Chapter 19

ENLISTING PARENT SUPPORT

The incident was sufficiently serious. This is big enough that it's not something to be handled without support. You've tried all the techniques listed in the previous sections to no avail.

It's time to reach out to the parents.

WHY CONTACT THE PARENTS?

The parents may have influence on a child's behavior that transcends our abilities. After all, they see the child many more hours per week and per year than we do. They may have heard the same things before and have a sense of what works.

Secondly, contacting the parents provides notification. It creates a pattern of communication so that the parent in question cannot complain to you or your supervisor that they really had no idea Thumbelina had so persistently been failing to turn in her homework. Parents, particularly defensive parents who may be looking for a way to excuse a child's behavior, may well and fairly go after the teacher for a failure to keep them up-to-date.

Finally, we owe the parents the courtesy of timely information. There shouldn't be any surprises at the end of the quarter. If we're going to lower a student's quarterly grade, if we're going to complain about a certain behavior in a written comment at the end of the term, **this information should not come as a surprise to the parent**.

WHOM SHOULD WE CONTACT?

Because parents may differ in their approach to school communications, it is a good idea to consult with colleagues for advice about how to maximize the chances for a positive connection when you call home. Some parents are known to be overly defensive of their children. Some parents may be known to be furiously retaliatory with the children. Still others may yawn when you call, indifferent to whatever someone from school might have to say. In some cases, a mother or father (or grandparent or aunt) may be known to be more receptive and responsive. Do what you can to find that out in advance from your colleagues. Make each call count. It can be deeply valuable to know in advance what you may be facing on the other end of that phone line.

WHEN SHOULD WE REACH OUT?

Unless the incident is starkly bad and warrants a call home based only on that isolated behavior, there should already be an established pattern of trying to solve the problem with the student. The call home should follow failed attempts to resolve the problem on your own (again, except in the more extreme cases).

If the matter is serious or chronic enough, it is prudent to notify the supervisor of your intentions before you call home. He or she may have important information about the family situation that will help with your

Please understand that there may well be times during which we have just begun to feel that there has been a downtick in a student's performance or behavior. In such cases, the call home may be more of a consultation, a thought-you-ought-to-know early warning. In this case, the supervisor probably doesn't need to be informed. In fact, if we are inclined to make regular use of home contact—which we should—it might be overwhelming for the supervisor to be notified of every contact.

communication. Particularly if there is potential for uproar from the parent, your supervisor should never be caught flat-footed and uninformed.

Finally, although it asks even more of us as teachers, the best time to reach out to a parent is in the evening. Many parents, even those who routinely provide an office phone number, work in locations where there is minimal privacy. To receive a phone call from school, however open-ended and information-only it may have been intended, can awaken tension and discomfort, either because personal calls are forbidden or because talking about a child's problem in front of colleagues is simply embarrassing. The call home in the evening (after dinner but before bedtime) allows the parent the opportunity to speak with the student before he or she goes to bed.

HOW SHOULD WE MAKE CONTACT?

Unless we are in an ongoing dialogue with a family, email is not the best form of communication to convey negative news.

Email is notoriously capable of being misread—for tone, attitude, and an estimation of the seriousness of the issue. Email also precludes the possibility of on-the-spot dialogue, of asking questions, and of clarifying points. Email, like all one-way communication, almost invites a family to ignore it or to overreact.

The best first step in contact is almost certainly by phone in the evening.

The phone enables us to be heard, not misheard, as can happen with unidirectional written information. It allows us to ask questions, to modulate tones, and to listen to both what is said and *how* it is said. Finally, because it requires mutual communication, it is dramatically more likely to foster a partnership than an email that pops up ominously on a parent's computer screen.

That said, there are certainly times in which we need to create a kind of "paper trail": documentation that parents were informed or, in more serious cases, that they and the student were put on notice about certain behaviors. Even in these cases, however, we strongly recommend the initial phone contact with a follow-up thank you by email, summarizing the nature of the conversation, the information and possible consequences, and any prescribed plan moving forward. By using the phone and following up in writing, we can arrange a two-way conversation and an adaptive dialogue as we provide a paper trail for the student's file.

Notably, unless we have called and called in vain, it is not a good idea to leave a voicemail. The voicemail may "mysteriously" be erased before the parent returns—leaving us uncertain as to whether the parent never received it or simply ignored the message. Beyond that, a voicemail left at, say, 8:00 p.m. may inspire a parent, returning home late in the evening, to call you (out of responsiveness or anxiety) at some untold hour of night. But in either case, it is better to leave a message than to ignore the problem altogether.

WHAT DOES SUCH CONTACT SOUND LIKE?

We refer to our preferred opening a number of times in this book, but it is genuinely and consistently a sound approach.

We begin with a simple statement, "Ms. Turnbull, this is Joanna Lamplighter from school. I teach your son histrionics, and I'm calling because I need your help."

Such a statement opens on an invitational note, asking for their assistance. It engenders a sense of partnership. It opens respectfully and asks for counsel and advice. This is a dramatically more positive, dialogue-fostering approach than one that begins with a saturation bombing of all of the child's misdeeds. One encourages openness and dialogue, and the other almost guarantees a defensive shutdown of a parent's sense of shared concern and participatory problem-solving.

Next—and it is so easy to forget to do this—note something positive, some way of seeing the child that you and the parent are likely to agree is the child at his or her best. This almost inevitably brings the parent to your side and prevents them from dismissing you as someone who has never seen anything good in his or her child.

Detail the concern or objectively report the incident. Don't generalize. Don't make subjective judgments. Don't assume. Don't suggest, for example, that the child "needs to study more," because he or she is failing tests. The parent may have honestly observed the child studying for four hours on Sunday afternoon. In fact, the notes the child had to study from may have been the flawed and incomplete result of a serious auditory processing problem. Assigning cause to a situation nets us little and may alienate the parent. We need to limit ourselves to reporting the particulars.

When you have finished the brief, objective reporting, it is wise to ask questions: Does this surprise you? Have you heard similar things in the past? Has your child told you about the trouble he or she's been having in my course?

This stratagem allows—even encourages—the parent to speak yet almost certainly precludes an attack on you and your forebears. It prompts the dialogue we should seek in every such communication, if there is to be effective development of a partnership between school and home.

Listen to the responses, which may go on to include more emotional baggage. Try not to interrupt. Try to sense and acknowledge the underlying feelings of the parent. Parents are almost always intimately tied to their children emotionally, after all. Most parents would rather hear bad news about their own lives than their child's. As aggravated as you might be by a child's performance or behavior, a neutral, nonjudgmental, listening approach can relax a parent's deep-seated anxiety or hostility.

If there is a need to respond to an implicit "so what" in the parent's statement, couch it in the same terms recommended for dealing with misbehavior in class. Don't make it a challenge to you or your authority. Present it as interfering with the progress of the class or, more pointedly, with the child's ability to make the progress you know they are capable of. Present it, if necessary, as detrimental to the spirit of the class. Tell the parent the relevant facts: "Too many of his classmates are now beginning to fear his sharp tongue, and in the long run, it's going to affect how the other kids see him." Maybe the child's behavior is preventing him or her from being ready for next year: "After failing to turn in this many homework assignments, we're concerned that, no matter how hard she decides to work next year, she simply won't be successful in French III." Or perhaps the child's self-esteem is suffering: "I know that she believes she can do the work; however, I watch her when she reaches out for a test I've graded, and she really seems to be dreading the results."

If at all possible, work together to codesign a concrete strategy, a set of consequences, and a goal for the child in question. The clearer the plan, the more readily it will be possible to provide follow-up and feedback.

And if follow-up has been promised, it is imperative that we follow through. The result of promising follow-up ("I'll contact you at the end of next week to let you know if there's been any progress") and then failing to reconnect not only deprives the parent of vital information but also may make you look like an inconsistent, unreliable source of information. If necessary, put the timing of the promised follow-up into whatever you use as a calendar.

If the conversation goes badly or unsteadily, if there is an evident disconnect or a need to draw in either the other parent or the supervisor, be swift to encourage a face-to-face conference. However it concludes, work to end the conversation with a genuine, unsarcastic, "Thank you, Ms. Turnbull. I care about her. I am concerned, and I appreciate the chance to talk."

If the matter is serious enough that it needs clarification and follow-up as part of a growing paper trail, write an email summarizing the situation that prompted the phone call, the exchange that took place, and any prescribed follow-up. If the conversation went badly enough, against all of your natural instincts, be sure to notify your supervisor in the morning. It is far better to warn your supervisor unnecessarily than to let him or her be caught unaware by a call from an irate parent.

THE POWER OF ONGOING COMMUNICATION

Most parents are naturally more invested in their child's growth and success than we who teach for only a fraction of his or her life. They need and deserve accurate information—regardless of what they choose to do with it, regardless of how they may react at the time. The consequences of not having informed them promptly and accurately can have potentially serious ramifications for us and the student alike. Let them react however they want, but never let them criticize us for failing to issue fair warning or failing to enlist their support as parents of the child in question.

Almost every parent harbors deep-seated love and high hopes for his or her child. By breaking through the silence and becoming a real, caring force in the child's life—even if we're nothing more than a voice at the other end of a phone line—we have the capacity to build a vital partnership in support of that child. And in that partnership, where adults are working together on a child's behalf, may lie the best hope for the care and growth of that child.

Chapter 20

THE SOLO INTERVENTION: ENOUGH IS ENOUGH

We probably all have images in our head of a classroom that is truly out of control. Like a bad dream, it just keeps getting worse. It is easy in such moments to give up hope. It is also unnecessary—and wrong—to do so.

Situations are *always* salvageable.

The class seems to be sliding inexorably away. Whatever hopes you may have had for the year are increasingly being replaced by hopes of just getting to June. It may not be awful, but it's not what it could be or should be.

The operative norm in the class remains (or has become) unproductive enough that you suspect even the students may be relieved to have it addressed. You yourself may well have come to wish you'd started the year more firmly. You may now want to realign the desks and assign seating for the first time. You may want to create a brisk new routine for the moment they arrive. You may want to establish new rules and guidelines for acceptable behavior.

Isn't it too late? Doesn't the year already have a kind of unwieldy momentum? Can you change the rules and routines this far along in the year?

Absolutely. You *can*, and if you know it can be better, you *have* to. You don't have to wait until next September to achieve some measure of relief.

You and, perhaps more importantly, *they* deserve a new beginning. It's never too late:

- to declare that **today is the first day of the rest of the year** and confront declining standards of performance or behavior
- to summon forth the better angels (and harder workers and more respectful students) of their nature
- to raise the bar to demand that they reach higher, work harder

Whether you're deeply troubled or just really frustrated, it is time to act forcefully to take back your class. Either because it is at a less critical stage or because you simply prefer to handle it yourself, this one is yours to tackle.

So how do you do it?

It is vital that you meticulously choreograph your own intervention in advance. It is vital that you prepare what you're going to say and craft a bold, punchy, crackerjack home run of a lesson to follow immediately on the heels of the intervention, because the intervention shouldn't take long.

It isn't going to be a rolled-out lecture producing predictably rolled-back eyes in the students you face. It will begin, surprisingly enough, with a question, because what is important is that, at least in some measure, it is a discussion.

THE INTERVENTION

You arrive well before the first student shows up. That is essential. Cut the previous period short if necessary. Be there, standing in a stony, Rock of Gibraltar silence, as your students begin to arrive.

There may be some questions, some wisecracks, some efforts like those of children trying to distract the Bobbies at the Tower of London. Remain implacable.

When it is time for the period to begin, cross the room and ostentatiously pull the door closed. Latecomers will earn a protracted, silent stare on this particular morning, but even those who have arrived on time may come to sweat at least a little.

You stand before them. You scan them with probing eye contact like the searchlight at a crime scene. "This morning," you begin in a steely low tone, "we're not going to start in with the lesson right away. We have other things we need to discuss."

A long pause.

"What is it we need to discuss?"

The question is strong, like a sharp wind off the prairie. The silence will come back across the room, but someone eventually will speak up. It may be another wisecrack like "Why you're such a lousy teacher?" If so, give only expressionless eye contact, lingering, uncomfortable to behold.

Or someone will make an honest but wrong guess. "We're going to talk about the exam/the International Fair/the class play?" Your head should barely move to say no.

Perhaps there is truly dead silence.

Eventually, you speak. "Has this class been making the progress it should?" you may prompt them, if there really is no honest answer. A few heads will shake. A few eyes will go downcast.

"What's the issue here?"

A lingering silence again.

A hand goes up. "We've been bad."

Another silence as you linger over the statement.

"I wouldn't say bad exactly. Can you be more specific?"

Chances are that a few others may rise to the occasion.

"We've been goofing off."

"We almost never turn our homework in."

"We talk so much we hardly get anything done."

"We don't pay attention to you."

"We don't like this class."

Don't be thrown by the few who may use the opportunity to distract you from your purpose. After the statements have accumulated, however few or many, let the silence return. Don't feel hurried. Hold them in your regard, perhaps a little less sternly now.

"Do you like it like this? How are you going to be ready for next year? Are you feeling good about yourselves when you leave this class?"

Please note that there may be some seriously alienated kids in the class who couldn't care less about feeling good about themselves or admitting that they've been goofing off. You can't hope to appeal to every hidden angel, but there *are* kids in every classroom in the country who really do want to learn, regardless of the prevailing climate. There are kids who will be deeply grateful that you finally appear to be putting a halt to the nonsense.

Remember the early injunction. Don't isolate yourself from your students. Isolate those who would undermine the class. Stay united with what is best in the group, however silenced they may feel.

Here it is vital to understand the power of eye contact, especially at that moment when you might feel most like avoiding it. Look solemnly and gravely from student to student. Then begin.

"I have to take some responsibility for the fact that we aren't making the kind of progress we need to." This moment may well be a shocker—from kids who've only ever heard themselves blamed for a breakdown in communication. It's an admission, and it's probably at least partly true. This very admission is what allows you—what almost requires you—to be the one to intervene, to provide leadership, and to set a new course for the months ahead.

"From this point on—"

Tardy Thomas Foolery enters the classroom then, senses something is afoot, and clowns a big-eyed face. There are snickers around the room. He slides into his seat.

"Mr. Foolery, I'd like to see you at the end of class."

Pause. Beat. Beat.

"From this point on, anyone who doesn't have a homework assignment completed to the best of their ability in and on time will be required to come to my office at lunch to complete it. Every class period will begin on time. Anyone speaking disrespectfully to me or to anyone else in here will have me to deal with. And this is your last warning. I may have seemed like a pushover until this point. Don't try pushing anymore." The language is yours to choose based on the situation, the culture, and your own comfort.

Detail the new regimen you intend to put in place, moving the desks, having an assignment for them the moment they arrive, sending ne'er-do-wells to the office at the slightest provocation, arranging to have split-second, four-question pop quizzes at the moment the period begins (so that someone late enough to miss just two questions has at best the opportunity to earn a 50 percent). And stand by your plan.

"This is the first day of the rest of the year. All of us who want to feel successful in this class are taking back ownership of what goes on here."

"Is that clear, Mr. Excalibur?"

You turn to your extreme right and stand directly over the crumpled nonchalance of the boy who is now required to pull the sword from the stony silence. You wait for him to answer. He shrugs.

"Mr. Excalibur?"

He nods.

"I didn't hear you."

"Yes."

"Mr. Demetrios?"

Mr. Demetrios casts an uneasy glance about the room and nods. Before you can correct him, he speaks up and says, "It's clear."

"Miss Channing?"

And on across the windswept silence of the room.

You stand there once again after the last student has acceded to the clarity of your demands. You allow your eyes to thaw just slightly.

And then, having prepared that bold, punchy, crackerjack home run of a lesson, you roll it out with a crispness previously unheard in the soggy confines of that humidly human classroom. You show them what collaborative progress really looks like. You're not going to settle for anything less than their best.

More significantly for those who really want to have the class begin to make serious improvement, you show them what a terrific lesson looks like. You let them experience what a terrific lesson *feels* like for the first time they can remember. You are crisp and clear, conscious and conscientious, fast-paced, positive, and high-energy throughout.

And when the class is complete, you stop. No "I told you so." No crowing. No need to comment at all.

Let your eyes briefly convey what they all just observed as certainly as you did. They may not know how it happened exactly, but they know *that* it happened. Be certain you remember to call the tardy Mr. Foolery up to your desk as the rest of them head somewhat startled for the hall.

In the end, it will probably be uncomfortable—perhaps very uncomfortable—to lead such an intervention, but such an intervention can (and should) only arise from such cumulative discomfort that you owe it to yourself and those students who *do* care to say that enough is enough, that it is time for honesty. It is time for recognizing that we have all erred and lost sight of what education can become.

And even if this never becomes a class whose turnaround you will come to savor, if you handle it with openness and firmness, you may begin to awaken from the nightmare that a truly tough class can be.

Chapter 21

WHEN IT IS BEYOND YOUR CONTROL: THE MEDIATION

There are times when you've tried intervening on your own or when you just start believing that another dynamic is called for. We present two models of such joint intervention. This is the first.

His name was Ernesto Ventura. He was a veteran Spanish teacher of unrelentingly high expectations and uncompromising precision. There was something deeply warm in his spirit but something almost military in his approach to the classroom.

The students in the open, liberal school where he worked were on the verge of taking to the figurative streets in the face of his unflagging, unflinching demands that they master Spanish, that they devote so much time (too much time?) to the class work and the homework he assigned. There was a restiveness in the classroom. It was true that some of the students (even some who had never given up) had begun to rebel by giving up on even trying to meet his expectations. They would put up with his stern and stubborn disapproval. It cost less than the seemingly futile, massively time-consuming effort to put together another perfect two-hour homework assignment.

Perhaps he felt some righteous indignation. After all, nobody prepared his students better than he did.

He might also have felt as isolated as a czar. In a school where so many kids felt close to their teachers, they were tired of what may have felt like harsh, inflexible demands. It was deeply bewildering and discouraging to Señor Ventura. Now, even when he brought vocabulary games to class—activities that had always brought out laughter and spirit in his students—the hostile standoff continued. The work declined. It wasn't good. And there were months to go before they got to June.

Evelyn Reedy was a math teacher, one of the best, a veteran of more than twenty years in the classroom. No one who knew her, who knew how her students felt about her, and who understood the esteem in which their families held her would ever have suspected that she would come upon a class that she would come close to giving up on.

As early as mid-September, Evelyn had begun going home more perplexed and defeated than she had ever felt in her career.

As the year dragged on, the feeling had deepened. There had been frustration and sudden, almost dizzy spells of self-doubt. She was angry and troubled, and she was afraid that this far into her career, this far into her life, she had somehow lost her way.

Each of these experienced teachers had likely spent long nights gazing into the fire. Each of them had likely tried coming to class with fresh resolve. Each of them had likely experienced improvement and hope that proved to be only temporary, and then it was downhill once again.

Experience is no guarantee against chemistry that just doesn't work. This kind of breakdown in relations can happen to any of us at any point in our careers.

This chapter is a narrative of two lives, two moments in time when even the most seasoned teacher comes upon a class that tries them, challenges them, and tests their mettle, one that is on the verge of defeating the teacher's best efforts to regain control and momentum of a runaway class.

For each of them, there was the formidable assurance that they had been through years marked by success. They were surrounded by colleagues who had known that year after year, they had arrived in June for a victory lap. There was much to comfort them along the way, and in time, this year would perhaps become a head-shaking anecdote, a time of insecurity and pain they would remember with wincing regard but one that would be safely cocooned in the fabric of other, far more successful years.

Nevertheless, there *are* times when even the most successful of teachers may come upon a class that appears to be beyond their ability to master the situation.

If we are isolated, if we are too ashamed to admit the painful truth of the experience, if we are insufficiently supported by supervisors who understand their rightful role, then perhaps all that each can do is soldier on until June and then breathe a heavy sigh full of regret and angst before we move on to the next September.

For teachers early in their career, there is no bedrock of such assurance, no happier history upon which to place the ashes of such personal defeat. A year like each of these veteran teachers experienced can serve as a tremendous, threatening undertow for those ideals we aspire to, how we see our careers, and, if we're honest, how we see ourselves as effective adults in the wider world.

But if we are able to open up to administrators who understand that they are being summoned to fulfill a rare and powerful duty, the misdirected journey of the class itself can be saved.

In both cases above, the teachers and the classes they taught were in the same division. In both cases, the teachers were open enough about their dilemma to work with the same supervisor. Winifred (Winnie) Franklin was younger than either of them, a slight, sharp-eyed African-American woman with a deep sense of purpose and an abiding belief in her teachers. She was the principal of their school. In both cases, they worked together to define—with an almost choreographed precision—what was to take place and when it was to happen.

THE INTERVENTION: VERBATIM

In the case of Señor Ventura, they chose a class first thing in the morning two days later. Both Ms. Franklin and Señor Ventura were aware of the absolute necessity of getting to the classroom before the students arrived. They were standing silently at the front of the room as the students began to file in. Ms. Franklin stood a little more front and center. Her look was solemn.

"What's going on?" one of the students muttered as he took his seat.

Ms. Franklin said nothing. When the last student had arrived, she told him to close the door behind him. The static electricity in the air was enough to arc purple sparks across the stillness.

"Why do you think I am here?" Ms. Franklin began in a measured undertone.

There was silence. She prodded their silence with her own. There was no mistaking the seriousness of her intention.

At last, a hand and a voice rose from the side of the room. "We've been bad."

Winnie cocked her head, as if she were contemplating the word choice. "I wouldn't say 'bad' exactly. I don't think Señor Ventura would say so, either." She turned to him inquiringly. He thought about it and then shook his head. "Can you be more specific?"

"We haven't been getting along," a student suggested.

Ms. Franklin let the silence linger. "How many of you would agree with that?" Slowly, again with students' eyes darting cautiously, surreptitiously about, the hands began to rise.

"Thank you," she said. "Señor Ventura agrees with you. He came to me because he is concerned about the situation."

She looked at him. He was clearly uncomfortable, but perhaps now there was finally an action underway that would change the course of the year. He nodded.

"He has asked me to speak with you and not to scold you. That's not why I'm here." Another zip-zap of eyes about the room, distrustful, curious.

"In part, I'm here to understand what *you* are upset about. It seems clear that you've all gotten off on the wrong foot. Am I right?" Now there were a few more nods and a little more willingness to acknowledge the difficulty. "Who can tell me what one of the issues has been?"

The students looked uncertainly from one adult to the other. Señor Ventura was more than a little exposed in the corner. The students didn't know how free they were to share what they felt.

"I want to say something before you respond. Señor Ventura came to me and has told me how much difficulty he has had working with you. In part, he feels he has somehow let you down. In part, too, I would say up front that you've let yourselves down. You're all going to be in Spanish III next year. It is vital that you be ready. I ask you, at the pace you are going, with the quality of the work you're doing, with the number of you who sometimes just aren't even handing in the homework, are you going to be ready?"

This time the silence was answer enough.

"So tell me," Ms. Franklin continued. "Who can tell me what one of the issues is. Señor Ventura is being very open and very courageous to invite me in to hear whatever you might have to say. He's not in any trouble, and neither are you. The success of this class matters that much to him. He wants to finish the last five months of the school year with a very different tone in this class. He wants you to be ready, and so do I."

A hand at last went up.

"He goes too fast."

"What does that mean?"

"He's like only talking to the smart kids." There was a quick, self-conscious ruffle of laughter. "Some of us don't catch on that quickly."

"And," someone else now chimed in, "he gets impatient if we don't understand it right away. I'd rather turn in nothing than show him how much I just don't get."

Señor Ventura was looking visibly awkward and yet somehow intrigued, caught up in the conversation. It felt almost as if, despite the critical nature of the statements, he was at last experiencing some relief in hearing something concrete.

"How many of you feel this way?"

After a moment, more than half of the hands went up. Ms. Franklin nodded.

"What would help you?"

"He should slow down!" someone said, and the laughter of this simplicity seemed to brighten a little of the room's prevailing overcast.

"He should try more than one way to explain something."

"He's never in his office when he says he'll be."

"He tries to act like he's not, but he gets really irritable if we don't just get it."

A stillness came over the class.

They seemed to realize how much they had said, almost as if they'd gotten away with something indiscreet, something unthinkable. Señor Ventura, a good man, was standing with his eyes open, but his head slightly bowed. Ms. Franklin allowed him a moment to compose himself. He seemed to be finding some deep and resilient inner strength. Despite the public isolation he was experiencing, despite the hurtful confidences shared, he seemed genuinely relieved, finally engaged in a dialogue about a problem that had gone on for far too long.

"Señor? Is there anything you want to say?"

He had barely begun to speak and acknowledge that he sometimes was impatient, that he knew he needed to be more available, more genuinely helpful when Peter Tomlinson interrupted from the back of the class. Sometimes when one truly listens, sometimes from far away or very close at hand, one can almost sense the arrival of the better angels of their nature.

"Come on, guys," Peter said. "Yeah, maybe everything we've said is true, but come on. We've all been taking advantage of the situation. If we don't feel like doing the homework, we don't. If we don't feel like working in class, we don't, and we're blaming it all on Señor Ventura."

Peter was a sturdy, stalwart Tom Sawyer of a kid—anything but dutiful yet so purely open and genuine and honest that he transformed what might have been a one-sided landslide into a dialogue.

Ms. Franklin didn't even ask him to explain. She sensed that silence itself would continue to prompt him. "It's not just the Señor. He can be pretty grouchy if we don't get it." And Peter and Señor Ventura exchanged a long look that was surprisingly free of tension. "But every one of us knows we haven't been working as hard in here as we have in other classes."

Ms. Franklin let the moment take a two-beat rest.

And then she asked, "How many of you agree with Peter?"

Sheepishly but with occasional shy smiles of connection and accommodation, hand after hand went up. It is important to note that not all of the hands went up. What Peter had succeeded in doing was to acknowledge a powerful, underlying truth. He had not relieved Señor Ventura of responsibility, but he had accepted his own. And in responding to that remarkably timely show of maturity, others in the class had proven themselves ready to step forward, impatient to embark on a vastly more productive journey together.

Winnie turned to the man in the corner.

"Señor Ventura. I know what a good teacher you have been and still are, and I totally admire your courage in inviting me in. Have you heard what the students have had to say to you?"

He still looked pained, overloaded with information he would have to sift through, but there was a sense in him that the awful beginning of the year had come to an end and that a fresh and open start was at last within reach.

At the end of the dialogue, Ms. Franklin shifted roles somewhat abruptly.

"Señor Ventura has taken a great risk, being willing to listen to whatever you had to say, and in front of someone who is, no matter what else, his boss. And you haven't exactly held back in your criticism." Shy, uncertain smiles peeked about the classroom.

"I was here to listen, but I am also here to tell you this. That all of you had better be ready for Spanish III, regardless of what you think about this class or Señor Ventura or me or anything else. You have work assigned. You have work to do. If Señor Ventura isn't in his office when he needs to be, come back and come back until he's there, and don't you leave until he's found a way to teach you. Is that clear?"

Now there were more baleful expressions, more subdued looks, but a more genuine sense of mutual understanding.

"Get your work in on time." Ms. Franklin looked resolutely from student to student to student before she turned to the teacher. "Señor Ventura," she said, "I want the name of any student who doesn't have the homework in even once. Is that clear?"

She directed the comment to Señor Ventura, but the iron filings tingled over the magnetic scalps of every student in the room. They understood who was really being addressed.

"Señor Ventura, have you heard what they've had to say?"

He looked up and nodded. "Yes."

"And each and every one of you," she said, looking over them, "have you heard—loud and clear—what I've had to say?"

They nodded and thought that they were going to get away with that, but she wasn't finished. Ms. Franklin crossed to the student farthest from the door.

"Understood?" she asked. The first student, a boy, nodded, but she waited for eye contact before she moved on to the next student.

By the time she had finished, each of them had agreed to the new and mutual understanding in the class. As she strode sharply to the door, she appeared to soften. She turned to face the class and the teacher as she was about to leave.

"Every so often," she concluded, "a good teacher encounters a good class, and for whatever reason, they get mired in problems. That ended this morning."

She looked at them with reserved warmth, nodded to Señor Ventura, and closed the door abruptly behind her.

As they had agreed beforehand, Señor Ventura had planned an absolutely tight lesson, no-nonsense, clear-cut, well-paced that began with a muted thunderclap the moment the principal had departed the room.

So what happened here? There had been a disconnect. There were frustrations on both sides. The supervisor intervened. The supervisor solicited student feedback and listened. And the teacher was there, exposed, and strong enough to accept the responsibility of listening to their grievances.

In the end, the class was faced with a resolute mandate. That complaining about the teacher and using such complaints as an excuse for failure was too self-indulgent, too self-exculpatory. They had taken a clearly responsible hand in the breakdown. The teacher had listened. Now it was their turn.

Both sides must acknowledge their part in the problem. Both sides must willingly work to make the progress that is necessary for a successful completion of the year.

Chapter 22

THE INTERVENTION: MARTIAL LAW

In this second and final joint intervention, the issue is not that you have somehow contributed to the tension. The issue is not about you at all. It's about them, and it's about calling on the ultimate power of the school's disciplinary hierarchy. This one is stronger, sharper, and it's not a dialogue at all.

Two years have passed. It is now another class altogether. Ms. Franklin has worked through the choreography with Evelyn Reedy, the woman who has been teaching math for more than twenty years. In this situation, a particularly difficult combination of students has come together with what appears to be the express purpose of undermining a much-heralded member of the faculty.

The scripting is subtly but powerfully different.

The scene opens as before.

The two adults have made sure to be in the classroom before the first student arrives. Ms. Reedy and Ms. Franklin are standing together in solemn silence at the front of the room as the students began to file in. Ms. Franklin's look is deadly serious.

"What's going on?" one of the students dares to whisper as he takes his seat.

The two say nothing. When the last student has arrived, Ms. Franklin tells him to close the door behind him. The statement isn't friendly, and it wasn't intended to be. The sensation in the air is like that of a courtroom when it comes time for sentencing.

Winnie Franklin lets the mood linger. She certainly never sits down. There is to be no receptiveness on her part this time around. She strides slowly back and forth across the room, as if she is controlling her unrest, trying somehow to find the right words. She still manages to open with a question. She wants them to speak. She wants them engaged. They had heard enough lectures in their time.

"Why am I here?" she asks at last.

A wave of unsettled silence laps across the room and reflects back to the front. The seconds tick as Winnie Franklin waits. She has all the time in the world.

"We've been bad," someone finally suggests.

Ms. Franklin nods thoughtfully, not so much in agreement as in consideration. "Can you be more specific?" she asks at last.

This time, the atmosphere can only be described as a distant rumble at the heart of the standoff, like storm clouds brewing in the mountains to the west.

"We've been goofing off in class."

Ms. Franklin nods and looks out across the class.

"We've been giving her a hard time," another student mutters.

"In what way?" she finally counters.

"Some of us don't do the homework."

Another long, portentous spell of waiting. Winnie Franklin is comfortable with the silence. She can outwait them all. She can wait forever. She has been here before, and she knows that in such a situation, time is absolutely on her side.

"Some of us are just rude."

"Why?"

There may be no answer that anyone there can provide. As it happens, Winnie Franklin doesn't particularly care that they don't have an answer this time. It is enough to have prodded them to reflect. It is enough that the teacher has heard their confessions. It is enough to have grounded this visitation, this moment as the pivotal point in the year.

"You need to understand this," she says with a quiet that carries deep, deliberative weight. "There are more than two hundred classes that meet in this school every day, and yours is the only class I've had to visit like this all year long."

"I hope you're listening—each and every one of you—because it doesn't get more serious than this. I am here to tell you that every one of you must be on your best behavior from now until the end of the year. I don't care what you think about this subject or this class or Ms. Reedy herself. We have reached a point where none of that matters. I am here for one reason, because Ms. Reedy knows how smart you are. She knows—we both know—what good kids you are, but every single one of you in this room, if you're honest with yourself, knows that many of you haven't been working anywhere close to what you could or should be working."

Winnie Franklin looks out over the class, taking her time to make eye contact, taking her time to let the weight of this moment sink in.

"You have a year's worth of work to do, and so far, too many of you haven't been taking it seriously. You have homework assigned every night, and so far, too many of you haven't been turning it in on time—if at all. Time is running out. You're not going to be ready for next year's math class—even those of you who have been working all along—because of all of the time this class has seen fit to waste. You have ninety-six days left in the school year, and forty-five minutes each and every day until it's over." And here, she lowered her tone. "I hope that you're listening, because I'm telling you right now that you'd better be ready for next year's math class."

"From this moment on, you are being put on notice—each and every one of you. If you haven't turned in a homework, if you haven't been attentive in class, if Ms. Reedy just doesn't like your attitude, I am telling her here and now that she *must* send you to the office. I am not giving her a choice in the matter. Is that understood, Ms. Reedy?"

Winnie and Evelyn may well have gone through the proximate script before, but in the current setting, even Ms. Reedy is freshly awakened, aware of the power of the moment.

After a reflective pause, she nods unequivocally. "It is."

Winnie Franklin lingers briefly before she turns hard on the class. "And I am telling you—each one of you—that you can be sent to my office for goofing off in the hallways or the lunchroom or any other class you're in, and I'll be willing to listen. But if you're sent to the office from this class after this warning, don't expect understanding."

"You are bright, terrific kids, capable of so much more. This year has been a shameful shambles—until now. This woman," Winnie continues after she nods in Evelyn's direction, "has taught hundreds and hundreds of kids who've been grateful to have had her to work with. From now on, there are no excuses. This is the moment when it all changes for the better. This is the first day of the rest of the year."

And she looks at each of them.

"Is that clear?"

There is silence until she begins to move, slowly and deliberately, close encounters of the pivotal kind, from desk to desk, starting with the boy in the corner farthest from the door.

She looks at each of them with an unflinching gaze and waits until there is full, exposed eye contact.

"Understood?"

Sometimes it is just a heavy nod, but this time, she won't move on until she's heard it spoken aloud by each and every one. "Understood."

When she has come to the last of them and received that final "Understood," she pivots on her heel and heads toward the door.

At the door, she nods to Ms. Reedy, as if she is saying, "Take it away."

As they had planned it so painstakingly in the hours leading up to this moment, Evelyn Reedy is ready with the best, most upbeat, most fast-paced, most carefully constructed lesson of the year, and in the remaining thirty-two minutes, those students who are open at all to the change that has taken place begin to get a genuine sense of what this class can yet become.

★ ★ ★

Each and every teacher may someday face a class that represents an utterly confounding and frustrating challenge. It is far more common and far more damaging to the psyche to experience such a class in one's first years in the profession. Without a context of ongoing success, such a challenge to one's hopes and expectations can shake the very foundation of the images we've dared to form of our careers, our futures, and who we are and wish to become.

In the early stages of such a disconnect, it is vital to delve into our own inner resources or tap into the reservoir of a colleague's knowledge and experience, but when all else fails, each of us deserves a supervisor who is open to putting him- or herself on the line on behalf of the journey we have embarked on, someone who is willing to mediate a difficult but transformational dialogue, one who is willing to suspend the constitution and declare martial law on behalf of the greater progress of a class as it struggles to grow.

Some supervisors may be inexperienced in or uncomfortable with such interventions. They may genuinely need some guidance from the teachers in question as to what they are looking for, what they need, and what they are prepared to undergo. The supervisor may feel a little gun-shy about stepping in so forcefully. They may question whether or not such a step will prove to be disempowering to the teacher before them. They may question their own ability to face such a hostile constituency.

But by the time such mediation or intervention is needed or sought, it should be clear that the teacher who has gotten to that point has exhausted his or her own resources and perhaps exhausted what remains of his or her own hope and good will. None of us in the educational community deserves to suffer through the prospect of an entire year, as each of these good and worthy teachers faced. No set of students, however hardened and impenetrable they may appear, deserves to be cut loose from their moorings and left to the merciless, lowest-common-denominator vagaries of those who have tried to hijack the journey.

It is important and *vital* for the educational community to understand that supervisors must be willing to open such dialogues and support good teachers when things are going badly. Through Winnie Franklin's wise and careful orchestration, Evelyn Reedy was able to reclaim control of the classroom she had loved for so long, and Ernesto Ventura was able to find the courage and openness to listen because of the class's willingness to risk honest feedback. It is particularly noteworthy to focus on the results of that first intervention. It may be of interest to note that the members of Señor Ventura's class were ready for Spanish III by the time the year had ended. What may even have eclipsed the not insignificant fact of such achievement was the fact that, faced with a challenge, confronted with human emotion and power in an all-too-human situation, the students and the teacher had found a way to learn from each other, and what they learned may well have been even more important than the preterit.

We have spoken throughout the book about the need to own the power, to be the commander of the classroom, and to lead the journey that is education at its best, but there may well be times—not often, to be sure, but times nonetheless—during which the ability to turn around a class is beyond our power. The bad news is that it really can happen—even to veterans. The good news is that there are resources we can invoke even then. The disciplinary hierarchy exists for a reason—that reason being to reinforce the power of the teacher and the need for progress in the classroom.

There may be some teachers who are too readily inclined to call upon this higher authority. In all of our years of working with educators, we have rarely seen teachers who too readily acknowledge the need for this intervention. On the contrary, we have too often learned of teachers who have suffered for weeks or even months without invoking the disciplinary hierarchy, without turning to the supervisor in charge and saying plainly, coolly, and clearly, "I need your help."

If you have not exhausted your own resources, then by all means, stay the course, face the challenge, and pass the test. But if you feel that you have truly summoned all of the power you can command and the class is still restless, unsettled, and insufficiently under control, then it is time to put an end to the turmoil that all of you have probably been experiencing. Call for an intervention. Work with your supervisor to design something that is workable and comfortable for you both.

Teaching is challenging and difficult and even discouraging at times, but if those times are stacked day upon day and week after week, it is vital for your sake and theirs to call in the reinforcements and establish a new first day of the rest of the year.

PART 3

Structuring Your Class

Chapter 23

PLANNING FOR THE YEAR

How many of us have taken American history and had the teacher lead us down so many apparently irresistible little side trips into those unforgettable battles of the French and Indian War, the smoky ramifications of the Industrial Revolution, and of course the ever-irresistible Reconstruction that we ended up having to cover the start of the Cold War, McCarthyism, the Civil Rights movement, feminism, postcolonial revolutionary movements, postindustrial America, and the *end* of the Cold War in a breathless, if brilliant, blur one hot afternoon in June?

Now don't get me wrong. I've got nothing against history teachers. In fact, some of my best friends are history teachers, but they do seem to be the guiltiest of us all.

No matter what our discipline—or in the case of a third grade teacher who teaches all subjects—the goal of completing the curriculum must remain at the forefront of our consciousness as we map out the days and weeks of the year. Falling short or racing to finish is just plain uncomfortable, if not actually problematic, but allowing sufficient time for a full, thoughtful exploration of each phase of the curriculum can add immensely to the richness of the year's experience. If you are in your first year at a school, it will look mighty good if you manage to finish them both at the same time. Your department chair might just notice. Next year's teacher might be pleasantly surprised, and you might even feel a certain thumbs-in-your-suspenders pride at the achievement.

PREPARING FOR THE DAYS INEVITABLY LOST ALONG THE WAY

How does it happen that so many teachers—history and otherwise—don't quite end where they're supposed to? How is it so many spend those final hours in June making a hopeless mad dash for the finish line? Is it that each year's class is so much slower than the one before that everything just takes longer (not that they finished last year, either)? Or do they blame it on that snow day they had back in January or that particularly irritating special assembly on "Basket-weaving for Ingrates" when class was cancelled?

We all know that perfectly reasonable excuses are there for the taking, but in the end, whatever delays have begun to accrue in one's approach to the curriculum, they can't be blamed on the unexpected, because in the field of education, in the daily life of schools everywhere, the unexpected is…well, to be expected. Recognizing in advance how many days are *truly* available to you as a teacher will enable you to realistically plan for the synchronization of your curriculum with the calendar as it truly exists.

Of course, there will be snow days and community service trips and interminable, blindfolded whittling demonstrations from a class dad. Of course, there will be fire drills, sudden commemorations of unknown folk heroes, and the odd jamboree along the way (what is a jamboree, anyhow?). And of course, one has to account for the times when the teacher will take sick days and the substitute won't be able to make any headway.

Because we know enough to expect interruptions, we should allow for maybe fifteen days just lost—*pffft!*—to the predictably unexpected, but so many of us never quite seem to make this plan. As someone relatively new to the profession, it is *vital* that *you* know enough to allow for that much downtime. That has to be part of your planning.

Those who insist on believing that they have closer to two hundred days in the classroom are those who will almost certainly run out of time, rush through the final topics of the year, and become more inclined to snarl needlessly at those who, with purely good intentions, set up whittling demonstrations and jamborees along the way. It is vital to be realistic about the fact that time is finite and that it is vastly better for your planning process to underestimate than to overestimate the number of teaching days available to you in the course of the year.

AN ACTUAL—REALISTIC—COUNT OF THE DAYS AVAILABLE

Each school has its own calendar, and each has its own holidays, professional days, and inexplicably placed spring vacations. The actual number of teaching days varies pretty widely from place to place, but on balance, most schools have around 175 days.

Let's start right off the bat and count on losing fifteen days to the unexpected. If it turns out that you've overestimated the number of lost days, well and good—this will allow you more time for review, for having a day just for the start of the Cold War and (*voila!*) a separate day just for the end of the Cold War, along with those enticing little side trips that will now take place in June instead of November.

But let's be conservative.

You'll net, once those fifteen days are knocked out of your calendar, a neat 160 days of genuine progress. If you've got a three-hundred-page book to cover, does that mean it's safe to plan on covering two pages a day?

Not likely. Because even then, if you are someone who gives a test every three weeks, that's easily ten tests a year. Chances are that you won't assign new reading the night before the test, and chances are that the day of the test, you'll collect the student's papers and not even think of assigning more work that night. Suddenly, that's ten days knocked out of class time and maybe even twenty nights on which you're not likely to assign new homework.

Do you assign homework over holidays? If not, you need to knock out every day before a break as another one lost to homework.

Would it really be so tragic, so unrealistic, so unfathomable to accept the possibility that there might be, in fact, only a hundred truly meaty, mighty days of actual teaching in the course of a year?

If you have a three hundred page book to cover, you would be better off assigning three pages a day. Try to get 1 percent of the work covered every day.

One percent a day.

Now, of course, you may not be facing as simple a task as assigning reading in a single fat book. You may be a Spanish teacher who's got a forty-eight-chapter textbook and a spiffy little workbook and all kinds of auditory lessons and vocabulary drills that you must cover. Maybe you're a second grade teacher with a whole host of subjects to address. These complications naturally make it harder to count the sum total of all that you have to teach, harder to divide whatever you have neatly by a hundred.

But take the long view. Scan across the panorama of all that you're expected to cover. Total up the work you have to do, and then whack it neatly down the middle and know that the first half *has* to be completed during the first semester. Whack each of the semesters neatly in twain again, and you've got your quarters: seventy-five pages of a three-hundred-page book and 25 percent of the entirety of the year. Again, know that it is better to plan ambitiously at the beginning.

Then, map it out.

Don't just do this as an idle exercise in August, knowing you'll never be able to find your plan by Thanksgiving. Post it by your desk, where you won't be able to avoid its sullen, conscience-crushing stare. If you've begun to slip, if there was a special, unplanned "Fortnight of Fruitless Festivities" inserted into the year, then giddyap. The time won't magically reappear in June just because you need it.

Your supervisors may have only the vaguest impression of these more personal, meaningful connections. They *will* know if you're organized, if you show up on time for meetings, if you get your grades in on time, and if you finish the curriculum. It may seem like something far more earthbound than the astral music you rhapsodize in class each day, but it does get noticed.

Start with an assumption that interruptions are going to make off with approximately seventy-five of the 175 days the calendar claims you have at your disposal. Make each of the one hundred remaining days count. Preplan and check yourself ruthlessly against a calendar.

And if you should finish early, then finish lavishly. Finish the year with a history festival tying together recurrent themes from throughout the curriculum. Spend time on review. Actually allow the students two weeks to delve into civil rights. Take time to build a life-size replica of the Berlin Wall in the faculty lounge, and then celebrate the present by tearing it down on the last day of school. Let the calendar work *for* you by recognizing even before August turns to September that June will come, and those warm, welcome final days will be far more conducive to reflection, introspection, recollection, and a sense of direction and connection if they are well planned and unhurried.

Recognize time as a finite, disappearing resource.

Make the time work for you.

Map out the full year in August, and do so with an almost pessimistic approach to the actual number of teaching days you will have. Then don't just lose track of your plan. Keep it there before you—a long-term reference and conscience—as you map your way along the weeks of the year.

Chapter 24

THE POWER OF THE OPENING DAYS

The summer has come to an end. The opening faculty meetings have been adjourned. You've gone home the night before school starts with a clear sense of where you are headed. You may have trouble sleeping, but morning will come. You will shower and dress and maybe take a long look at yourself in the mirror. And then you're off…

I've been an educator for more than three decades, and yet I still feel a residual flush of excitement and a little case of nerves when I head off for school on that first day of classes.

There's the healthy and energizing sense of being part of the vitality of a school coming back together after a summer apart. There's the healthy and inevitable sense of anticipation any performer experiences when he or she takes the stage, because—let's be honest—we are performers, ringmasters, team builders, magicians, sermonizers and, yes, the cool-as-a-cucumber marshal of the wild town it is our job to civilize. There's recognition that, unlike so many professions that have no real seasonality, no genuine summer break, no annual chance to start anew, today we will be meeting a brand new set of students, and finally, there's the recognition of the pivotal significance of this first day—even these first moments—in which enduring, indelible impressions are made.

For those in their first years of teaching or facing their very first September as a head teacher, there may be a tendency to enter that first class either with a pretended blasé or caught in the throes of a full-blown panic attack. Regardless of whether we expect to go in with a suavely affected cool or an unnerved suspicion that *everyone* can hear your knee-bones a-knockin', it is vital to look beyond how we are coming across, because this first day is a one-time opportunity.

Miss it, and all year long you may find yourself wishing that you had set out stricter guidelines, clearer routines, and more explicit modes of acceptable behavior.

Capture it, and you will have done yourself and your students a world of good.

THAT MIGHTY, IMPRESSION-BUILDING FIRST DAY

No matter how finger-fumbling, stutter-stumped, and larynx-locked you might feel upon entering class on that first day, it is critical to understand that you are not the only one. The kids who encamp themselves before you will do so with their own set of apprehensions. As they never will be again, their antennae will be up, excruciatingly sensitive to every nuance of who you are, what you expect, how easy it will be to get around you, whether you are *really* going to make them work or not, and what you genuinely, seriously, absolutely, earnestly expect of them. On the first day of school in September, every student who enters—from the little dormice in the nursery school to the massive rugby thugs knuckle-cracking at the back of the high school classroom—is at an utterly predictable and utterly usable peak of uncertainty, anxiety, and, yes, vulnerability.

However young or old, however apparently winsome or hardened they may appear, they will never again be so uniquely impressionable. This is the time to make your mark. This is the time to establish the practices that will guide and streamline the rest of the year. This is the time to make it clear just what you expect, just what you will tolerate, and just what you hope to achieve.

If you begin by teaching, if you begin by moving directly into your subject

("Who can tell me what 'science' really means?"), you will have squandered the one most valuable opportunity in the entire year, namely to set high expectations, to imprint powerfully memorable daily routines, and to create the kind of tone and spirit with which you want to guide them on the journey you will share until the hazy days of June.

On that first morning, however brazen they may appear, the students are still fresh, probing for whatever your expectations might be. Don't make it a secret. Don't make them have to probe. You can carve your own ten commandments, your own constitution, your own set of classroom expectations into the wet cement of their consciousness, and the impression will take.

By the second day, it will take a strong and pointy trowel to make anywhere close to the same impression. Give them a few weeks to settle in, and it will take a jackhammer. Even that brief a time into the year, you may already be regretting the fact that you didn't lay down the law when they were eager to take your measure.

Recognize the unique power of that first encounter, and use it right then.

If you are already into your teaching career, begin to keep active track of things you *wish* you had said on that first day for next September, but if you are reading this during the summer, particularly during the summer before you first face your own class, begin to establish the priorities and practices you will demand as part of building the civilization that will come to inhabit your classroom.

PREPARING FOR THAT FIRST DAY OF SCHOOL

It was a morning in early September, the Friday just before Labor Day. I was about to head off for the long weekend. On Tuesday, the students—my very first class of students—would arrive.

It may have been something peculiar about me, particular to my own set of anxiety dreams, but Peg Zilboorg, the remarkably perceptive Head of Lower School who was my supervisor, seemed to sense my personal preoccupation.

"Richard," she said as I was about to leave for the day. I turned and looked at her.

"Overplan," she said.

I cocked my head—both at her ability to sense the source of my unease and by the specificity of her recommendation.

"Overplan," she repeated. "It's a half day. You've got three hours with them. Plan for six, and you won't have to think about facing the void."

I laughed in grateful recognition that she had come to know me so well in only a few weeks. As someone who had never lacked for things to talk about, as someone who was truly, deeply excited to welcome my first class of third graders, I knew it was irrational that I was so concerned about running out of things to say and do, but she was right. And I can attest that her advice was wonderfully sound.

Not only did I make plans over the weekend for the equivalent of six hours of time with the incoming class, but I came into school on that first post–Labor Day Tuesday with a list of so many things to do that I clearly stopped that particular anxiety in its tracks. Being less anxious, I was able to be more gregarious, more interactive, and more warmly present with the kids.

And the morning flew by.

In case any gaping holes did suddenly appear in the days that followed, I now had an entire atlas of plans that had gone unspoken and untried on that first morning.

In the years since we began working with young teachers, I have come to realize that my own particular anxiety was not so unusual. More than once— far more than once—I have been approached by teachers about to experience their first day as a head teacher, and the advice "overplan" has recreated the same whimsical, grateful, head-cocked smile that I experienced all those years ago when Peg Zilboorg seemed to fathom my insecurity and offer a simple and effective prescription.

Chapter 25

EXPECTATIONS SHEETS

An expectations sheet is a format for presenting students coming in on that first day of school with a kind of code of ethics or code of behavior for life in your classroom. These sheets should be both concise and thorough. Tell the students what you want, what you demand, what you expect on that all-important first day. Go over it with them. Make it the focal point of your opening session with them.

At Packer, where I worked for a century or so, every teacher is discouraged from doing any teaching on that first day of school. It is just too important a time. Instead, each is expected to use that most impressionable of days to set a crisp tone for the year and go over a customized expectations sheet with his or her students on that first day.

Some teachers present their expectations sheets as unfinished documents so that the students themselves can take part in creating some of the classroom norms. Some of the suggestions made by cool high schoolers ("If you got some smokes, share 'em already.") can be dismissed with a smiling, knowing nod. Some of the suggestions made by the kindergarten classes ("Don't ever poke anyone up the nostril with a blue crayon!") can be downright hilarious.

Eventual shared ownership of the document, however, can make it a process that breathes, and if the students themselves suggest that no one should copy someone else's homework, it won't be your rule that they're breaking when the situation arises. It will be **theirs**.

SAMPLE EXPECTATIONS

What kind of items are contained on a sample expectations sheet? Here are some possibilities to consider including in yours.

Overview and Goals

- Your own love of the subject
- The value of mastering the subject matter
- Your hopes for their own growing sense of enthusiasm and interest
- Main topics to be covered during the year
- Intriguing, big-deal events, trips, projects, fairs, or exhibitions expected to arise from their studies during the year
- The skills that they will acquire and hone during the course

Values

- What you expect (and require) of them—the principal values you hope to instill and uphold throughout the year
- Mutual respect—no put-downs
- Mutual support—no put-downs
- A spirit of teamwork
- Universal participation
- Punctuality—to class and getting assignments in
- Honesty
- A willingness to listen to the teacher and to each other
- Risk-taking and a willingness to be wrong
- A belief in themselves as students and learners

Routines and Materials

- Books and materials students will need for the course
- What they are expected to bring to class every day
- Examples of what they should do when they first arrive each day:
  - No one enters the classroom until you are there
  - No more "hall" talk—from the moment they enter the room, their focus is to be solely on the subject at hand
  - Grab a textbook
  - Give a high-five to the gerbil
  - Get out materials
  - Put homework in the inbox
  - Start to work on the "Problem of the Day"
  - How and when to get extra help
  - Office hours
  - The teacher's availability via email

Work and Grading Expectations

- Homework policy
  - How often, how graded, how much time to expect to take on it
  - What to do if they forgot the assignment or can't get number twenty-three
  - What to do when they are absent
- Tests
  - How often, how long, how cumulative
- Late policy
  - What happens if a homework is two days late? A major project is late?
  - What if I'm absent?
- Grading policy
  - What part of any quarterly grade is made up by tests, homework, participation, and other class work?

More Personal Issues

- Pet peeves
- No hats on in class
- No gum in class
- No mocking the guinea pig—he's got troubles enough
- No imitation biological noises

It's fine and almost helpful if there's a little humor embedded in the expectations sheet, but its presentation and its centrality to the life of the class should be treated with absolute seriousness and a sense of importance. These are the foundations upon which this class will be built. Let there be no mistake about its importance, and no one will ever say that they didn't hear any piece of it.

BRINGING THE EXPECTATIONS SHEET TO LIFE

We encourage you to treat the introduction of class expectations with the kind of reverence reserved for revealed wisdom and instructions at the start of the SATs. Begin with the solemn distribution of photocopies to each student, and then have them alternate in reading from the list while you pace the room, watching over them, making sure they feel the impression-deepening effect of your presence.

Ask for examples: "Let's go over that again. What are you expected to do about homework on a day you're absent from class?" "Give me some examples of respectful and disrespectful behavior." Make the document come to life. Even though it may have begun as a one-way directive from you, make the process interactive. Ask if there are any questions.

Tell them that this will be shared with their parents on parents' night, and consider making part of the first night's homework a requirement that they go over these expectations with their parents. Require that they return it the next day with a parent's authorized signature.

Post an enlarged copy in a central position in the room. Refer to it. Never take it down.

And then, if and when the expectations sheet has been utterly and permanently absorbed into their semipermeable consciousness, have something utterly cool and perhaps even utterly personal ready to share with them. Tell them why you chose to teach science, and share your feelings that first night you looked through a telescope and actually saw one of its moons rise over Jupiter's horizon. Tell them about how Sir Thomas More and Galileo faced the same terrible choice and how that dilemma was what really first brought history to life for you. Play twenty questions with them. Prove that two equals three. Show them how many English words have come from a single Latin verb, or let them find out on their own in a burst of academic energy coming back to life after a somnolent summer sipping laconic lemonade.

Don't try to teach. Entice.

If you are so inclined, give them the night's homework assignment. Don't make it a bunch of problems or a reading with questions to answer. Let this be one of the days the homework isn't about getting through the book.

Ask them, perhaps, to write—and limit it (no more than three paragraphs)—on how they'd like to feel about the year in your class by the time June rolls around or what they've always thought about your subject or how they feel about being in second grade.

For the older kids, emphasize that they're not *allowed* to turn in more than three paragraphs. Obviously, from the truly inspired, you may get some scandalously run-on paragraphs, but with a twinkle in your eye, cap the assignment. They're all used to teachers setting acceptable minimums, so start the year on a different footing. Be a little playful with them. Set a maximum.

And some of them may actually start the year being a little reflective.

Keep what they turn in.

Maybe on some unsuspecting day in February, when the exercise was long forgotten, show them what they had written. Or maybe hand it back to them on the next-to-last day of school, and make the final homework assignment, "So what was the year really like?"

Finally, be sure to set aside enough time to conclude the day with how you will start the next. Before they leave, make sure each of them has the routine down cold. Go around the room ping-pinging each student in turn to relate the first four things they have to do each day when they arrive, what they need to bring from home, what they need to have with them, and where the homework goes.

* * *

The first day of each year will never come again. Make sure that it is spent feeding their impressionability, shaping their expectations, and defining the routines you insist that they follow. Students will arrive that first morning with their own uncertainties, and if you are strong and organized and confident in your vision for the year, they will leave with a reassuring sense that you may in fact be a worthy leader for the journey you are to share.

Chapter 26

DAILY PLANNING: OVERVIEW

Icarus considered himself equal to the Greek gods he idolized—in both ambition and worthiness. He made himself wings bound and sealed with wax and proceeded to fly to the sun. The heat of the sun melted the wax. He crashed to Earth.

The same fate—an initial liftoff, a sense of gratified relief, and a sudden hair-raising plunge to earth—likely awaits any of us who similarly tries to *wing* it in our classroom. Though the very term "lesson plan" may seem almost confiningly old-fashioned, successful teaching is utterly dependent on preplanning each stage of a lesson and every bridge between those stages.

In the chapters to follow, we will explore in greater depth the power of a cool and passion-based provocation. We will detail a wide variety of teaching possibilities and underscore the value of variety itself. We will openly advocate the daily use of a posted agenda, the vitalizing power of urgency, the leverage to be gained by punctuality, and the dynamic, focusing effect of an opening and closing routine.

What is vital as an overview and as a touchstone in our daily planning is the yearly syllabus we mapped out late in August. We should remain vigilant—even as we embark on a thrilling new laboratory project using the creek behind the school—that we are continuing to honor and respect the intermediate deadlines we have meted out over the course of the year.

As long as we are comfortably within the range of planned progress, the opportunity exists for us to engage in matching the most effective vehicle in our teaching repertoire with the needs and possibilities of each lesson.

Before we begin each lesson plan and just before we consider it complete, it can exponentially increase our effectiveness if we truly address each of the following questions:

- What skills do the students already have? (So many teachers simply and negligently focus just on topics when the underlying skills are at least as important.)
- What skills do we want to reinforce?
- Are there new skills we may need to introduce?
- What materials will we need?
- Is the time frame realistic?
- Have we addressed the variety of learning styles within our class?
- Have we made sure that we have listed every possible needed instruction before we turn the students loose in group or individual work (because it's woefully more difficult to recenter them with an "Oh, by the way," once they are loosed upon a decentralized exploration about the room)?
- Have we created meaningful segues between the phases of each lesson?
- Have we internalized those transitions so that we don't have to interrupt the flow by constantly consulting our notes?
- Have we invoked and reinforced the structure of an opening and closing routine to each class period?
- Have we created homework valuable both as a reflection of the day's work and as a possible preview of the following day's activities?
- Are there skills or details that the students will only discover they don't have when they get home and try to begin the work on their own? What can we anticipate now in order to address these issues proactively while we are still together?

- Have we remembered both to speak and to post the homework so that the auditory and the visual students each have the opportunity to process the assignment details through their preferred modality?
- And finally, have we allowed ourselves a moment at the end of class to annotate our own lesson plan for impressions, innovations, and proposed improvements before we wheel the identical lesson plan out the following year?

THE SUBTLE, FUNDAMENTAL POWER OF PLANNING

Lesson planning may be the quietest, least visible aspect of our teaching, but in the creation of a beautifully designed lesson lies the secret breakthrough of an architect sketching out a design from conception to blueprint or a composer guiding an as-yet-unheard symphony from theme and concept through the delineation of movements, harmonies, and coda.

This quiet planning phase may not represent the most energizing aspect of teaching, but it is surely in the calm of our office or den where the possibilities for contact and connection are forged, as our imagination interfaces with our proven repertoire to create a lesson that will succeed, matter, and endure.

Chapter 27

IN THE BEGINNING: BEFORE EVEN STARTING A LESSON PLAN

Before the first student even arrives, before the morning of the class even dawns, before we even set pen to paper in the log of our lesson plans, we face our greatest chance to create a *great* classroom experience. We have to develop a lesson plan that truly comes to matter, intrigue, and challenge.

We must commit to finding the energetic *cool* in each lesson's wildly beating heart.

We must develop a rigorous ritual that seeks to prevent us from even thinking about entering the classroom door until we have centered the plan on that cool conception.

We must shape it with a conviction that students will also excitedly begin to sense the emergent light and the warm energy of possibility.

We must begin to reveal its power in the controlled, almost daring way in which we thrust the provocation before them.

We must sense it as we begin to move from behind our desk.

And for that brief interlude, whether we are enlivened by the power of perspective in the history of art or the excitement of having our children begin to read long vowels ("When two vowels go walking, the first one—"), it doesn't matter.

What matters first and foremost in the lesson, just as in the class experience itself, isn't as much the content as the energy.

This is how a class must first be designed—that is, by a steadfast willingness to imagine, for when we ask students about the characteristics of their most effective teachers, they cite it. When we ask adults, young and old, to name the traits of those teachers who made the greatest difference in their lives, they name it. By simply stepping across the threshold of a classroom that has come warmly to life, one can feel it.

It is passion.

Passion not only inspires and informs the shape of the lesson but also galvanizes the message of urgency. There is so much to cover, so much to explore, so much to debate and discover. It is passion that stirs the dynamic teacher, that lifts the teacher from the chair, and that unleashes him or her out upon the landscape of the classroom.

Can you see the teacher striding, animated by his or her own sense of excitement? The teacher kneels in front of one of the students that he or she most wants to understand the lesson and most wants to invite along for the trek.

> *"What would Huckleberry Finn be today? What would he look like? What kind of music would he listen to? Would he be a skateboarder? Would he be just as lonely? What if he was a new kid who just walked into this class for the first time? How would we react? Would we all just add to his loneliness? Would he have no choice but to raft down the Mississippi in search of the territory ahead?"*

The difference between this big, creative invitation to dialogue and the ho-hum option of "Open your books to page eighty-six" can determine the course not only of a simple class period but of the value of reading the book itself. And this difference is *not* something that occurs during the class. It arises and comes to life in the planning beforehand.

The one most telling difference between a lesson that thrives, that awakens, that excites and the lesson that is just another in a long gray series of rainy classroom experiences exists in that telltale moment before the pen even touches the paper in our planner. What is cool, what is energizing, what is uplifting about the topic for today?

Suspend the disbelief that allowed so many of our own teachers to humdrum their way through a listless litany of lessons. Become aware that everything we learn *can* be empowering. When and if we come to embrace the possibility, everything else—those pages and problems and all that is to follow—has the incipient power to take on a life of its own.

The moment of conception must be a provocation, a challenge (for the students to imagine, to figure out, to puzzle through, to get on top of, inside of, all around) that opens the door to a genuinely memorable classroom experience. What we have seen in classroom after classroom is that teachers who remain determined to keep in touch with their own passions have an unprecedented opportunity to awaken paired passions in their own students.

Let them feel the kinetic energy of your own excitement. Make it urgent. Make it blockbusting news. Make it something we've just got to share with them.

Stride about the classroom. Pull up short in a dramatic wheeling about that says without words, "Do you *get* how cool this all is?" Summon our own height, as if we'd seen the distant future beckon with radiant promise. This is knowledge we're talking about. This is putting young minds in touch with some of the greatest ideas in the history of life itself.

Each of us can be a great teacher. In the hands of those who push themselves to stay in touch with the passion at the heart of human learning, education can inspire, transform, and ignite the energetic excitement of children.

The precise sequencing of the lesson, the careful selection of the questions we will assign as homework may be what some mavens see as the most we can do to create a successful lesson.

Forgive us, but we say humbug to that. What matters first and foremost—furlongs and furlongs ahead of the crippled nag that is the conventional lesson plan—is the pure potent thoroughbred might of **the energy within the idea.**

The child will sense the quickening appetite for engagement, the wakening thirst for knowledge, the deepening surge of electrical energy igniting his or her own sense of the possible—what is actually possible in this classroom, what is possible from this teacher, and what is possible for him- or herself as a student engaging with the life of the mind.

Chapter 28

ENSURING VARIETY IN A LESSON PLAN

Variety is key, not only because variety is itself enlivening. Having a rich range of options with which to design a lesson allows us to optimize the match between content and delivery, between the chosen objective and the best choice of vehicles, between those vehicles and the students we hope to engage.

That said, herewith is a very partial list for your consideration. Hopefully, even as you begin to explore these, you will begin to sense that this is truly nothing more than a starting point for your own imagination:

- A good old-fashioned lecture
- Small group projects
- Role-playing
- Journaling
- Fishbowl discussions—an inner ring of chairs for those allowed to discuss a topic and an outer ring of chairs for those who must listen, igniting new possibilities when the roles are reversed
- Skits and improvisations
- Partner discussions
- Debates

- High-speed, playful, student-to-student drills and practices of number facts, of vocabulary words, of foreign verb endings
- "Puzzling" or presenting students with a fact or observation or conundrum and asking them to puzzle out possible explanations ("If Louis Pasteur had been experimenting with his molds in the winter instead of summer, thousands of people would surely have died over the next few years. Why do you suppose that is?")
- Outlandish provocations ("Atticus Finch was a glory-seeking control freak. What do you think of that?")
- Lab work
- Open-ended questions and hypothesis building ("How *did* George Washington keep those unpaid, ragtag colonists who'd lost just about every battle they'd fought, sleeping mostly in tents in the snow, all through that long winter at Valley Forge?")
- Students as discussion leaders
- Independent research
- Visiting professors—inviting in experts in the field from the local community college or a student a few grades older to offer sage advice about his or her favorite strategies for success
- Art projects, such as student-created posters, political cartoons, or dioramas on a history topic or book that they've read
- Oral presentations
- Example-building ("This half of the class must work together to come up with as many examples of *i* before *e* except after *c* as possible. This other half must work together to come up with as many examples as possible where *e* just won't wait its turn.")
- Team competitions
- Preparing students to teach the subject to a younger grade
- Curiosity-building ("In the story we're going to read today, Jeremy has taken something that doesn't belong to him, but he's going to end up the hero of the story. How could that be?")
- Constructivist discovery activities ("Today, for the first time, I'm going to

put a pair of equations on the board, with two different variables, and I'm going to break you up into groups of two or three and allow you to try to figure out in forty-five minutes what took some of the world's greatest mathematicians years to crack."

- Interviews and press conferences with students in role
- Open classroom work stations
- Information scavenger hunts—in a textbook, in the library, or on the Internet ("Using only the resources in this room, I challenge each of you to find the name of the largest landlocked country in Asia. You have four minutes.")
- Game show formats
- Popcorn discussions—each student who speaks is required to call on the next speaker
- Writing a children's book to explain the concept to younger students

THE RICHNESS OF VARIETY

We highlight two principal points.

The first is that any teacher with a growing repertoire of effective teaching techniques is at a distinct advantage, because he or she is able to match a concept with the best activity.

And the second point is that variety itself is riveting. Variety is compelling. Variety is tension-breaking and boredom-relieving. Needless to say, in a time when ADD seems more an epidemic than a simple genetic hand-me-down, there is no greater means of engaging the distractible child than with variety.

In choosing a particular dynamic for the introduction of a particular concept, why stop with one? Cob Powlen, one of the finest teachers I've ever seen, packed as many as four or five different dynamics into a single, forty-minute French class—a collective discussion to go over the homework, swiftly segueing into a taped *dictée*, which in turn led into student-to-student discussions in French about their plans for the weekend, followed by the rat-a-tat-tat drill of gender recognition of nouns, ending with a humorous worksheet so that students could put the correct *le* or *la* articles before the nouns they had just identified.   .

Was anyone bored with this approach? You know the answer.

Did Cob have to be a precision planner and an accomplished classroom manager to shift dynamics on a dime? You betcha.

But what a glorious, energizing thing it was to be in his class. There wasn't just variety but a variety of variety. There was something for every taste, something for every learning style, and a pace to keep his students on their toes.

In the end, variety serves many functions in the classroom, not the least of which is to challenge us to remain creatively engaged. It also provides enlivening shifts of focus and modality for each and every student. Finally, and at least as importantly, it enables every student (regardless of the nature of their specific learning differences) to experience periods of enhanced success in each class.

Chapter 29

THE SUCCESSFUL BEGINNING OF CLASS: CHECKLIST

This chapter is intended to be a brief checklist of the various and essential considerations for getting a class off to an excellent start. While some of the issues have been raised at great length in adjoining chapters, this annotated checklist represents an at-a-glance opportunity to review key elements for that most pivotal time in any class period. Particularly if you have felt that the opening of a period (or a day, in the case of a self-contained class) has been a little disorganized, and you are eager for a crisper, smarter start, at least a few notations below can make a telling difference in how the class begins.

Just as we have pointed out that there is no day more important to the school year than the first, so have we come to believe in the research and observation that underscores the proposition that the most vital, tone-setting aspect of each class is contained in the crispness of its first few minutes.

Be punctual.

Make the classroom your space. Make a math classroom "Mathland." Make a history classroom rich with the feel and focus of history. Make a first grade classroom engaging with the opening routines of a successful group of young learners.

Particularly if you are someone who has to teach consecutive periods in far-flung classrooms, it is essential to plan ahead in order to get to each class on time. Do your photocopying before the school day has begun. If possible, make your pit stops when you have longer stretches between classes. And if a supervisor or a student stops you, be prepared to avoid caving in to a four-minute conversation that will make you late by rolling out a prearranged response, such as, "I'm on my way to my next class, and it's important for me to be there on time. I would love to talk with you more about this at 3:00 (or at 11:45 during a free period)."

Post an agenda.

A carefully crafted agenda serves as an important structuring tool that supports smooth transitions between activities for both teachers and students. It can serve as a reminder of "What's next?" and help participants anticipate how individual activities fit into the broader lesson. Agendas can serve to provide:

- Reminders of the daily routine. (Although to save time and space, this may be posted permanently on a bulletin board.)
- What materials each student should have out and at the ready.
- A "to-do" problem of the day (Journal for four minutes on the impact of the Industrial Revolution on the family. Practice adding *s* or *es* to this set of verbs that end in *y*.) or a provocative, opening question for discussion. (How did gender roles likely change as a farming family became a factory family? Can you come up with a rule as to when you should add *es* to a verb ending in *y*?)
- A brief outline of the day's topics, so that students who like the "big picture" can follow along.

The agenda should end with a written, detailed description of the coming night's homework.

For those using multiple classrooms or simply sharing a classroom, we recommend having an agenda already written out on a piece of sticky poster paper. These are an irrationally expensive but wonderfully portable means of getting things moving swiftly and effectively at the very beginning of class.

Take a moment to welcome individual students.

Your tone should be soft, quiet, and confidential. After all, you want most of the students to focus swiftly on the agenda, on getting out necessary materials, and on beginning the day's to-do problem. If you want them to focus quietly on the work at hand, it will prove self-defeating if you engage in boisterous, joshing welcomes with individual students.

Use the time when students enter the room to welcome back one who has been away, to follow up with a student who didn't have yesterday's homework, to (quietly) ask a chronically procrastinating student about progress on a long-term project, and to praise a normally quiet student for really taking on some leadership in yesterday's discussion. This latter point may be spoken a little more audibly so that students will have the chance to witness your praise and to observe what you value and notice.

Ensure that the routines you set up at the beginning of the year remain crisp.

In general, we strongly recommend that students not be allowed to enter the room before you arrive. It's true that if your punctuality is unreliable, this decision may lead to some occasional crowding in the hallway. On the other hand, it ensures that students will focus on you as the ever-present leader of the class and enter the room ready to leave their hallway life behind.

If students have brought in homework assignments, they should know just what to do with them, without being reminded. They should know to have them out on their desks so that you may circle and notate their work in your grade book while they are working on the to-do assignment or to exchange them with other students or to have them out for the "homework helper" to collect or to place them in a designated inbox.

Even if you have successfully made failing to turn in an assigned homework anathema, there will undoubtedly be times when a student doesn't have an assignment. If you are in the habit of taking the homework and correcting it yourself, it will save you considerable time (Now where *is* Rasputin's homework? Did I lose it? Did I skip over it?) if you have come up with some method for having students notate the fact that they don't have an assignment (e.g., filling out an orange slip and placing it in the inbox so that you will be able to see at a glance who doesn't have the homework).

Everyone gets out the materials listed on the agenda. Alternatively, some students may have rotating responsibility for distributing textbooks, whiteboards, protractors, or linear accelerators.

No more hallway conversation. Focus immediately and completely on the to-do assignment. Take attendance, making sure that it is swift and silent. This may be best as a rotating student responsibility.

Close the door at the moment the period is scheduled to begin. This mutes the ruckus of passers-by in the hall. It emphasizes the need for promptness. Late students will consequently draw attention to themselves. It signals a readiness to begin and maximize your time together.

Develop a simple routine by which you notate any students who *are* late. A stern look is essential. Interrupting everyone's to-do exercise by asking Ferdinand Filibuster why he's late today is counterproductive for everyone. We recommend having a small pad, a grade book ledger entry, or a corner of the blackboard on which you routinely note anyone late for class.

If tardiness has become a serious issue, we recommend that, after a final warning, you begin to administer unannounced, unpredictable four-question oral quizzes that begin the moment the door closes and that allow for no repeated questions. A student arriving even one question into the quiz is therefore limited to at most a 75 percent. This is a rather immediate way of convincing the chronically late that there is a downside to lingering conversations in the hall.

Once the homework is collected, begin swiftly and crisply.

Begin with a sense of urgency. "We've got a lot to do today," may be something you have uttered for 114 consecutive school days. If you treat time as limited and critically valuable, this opening statement won't seem like fluff. It will point to the fact that each minute and each student counts.

As you begin the class, make sure that your opening topic does indeed follow that which is listed on your posted agenda.

The checklist noted above should not be something cited as an abstraction, embodied only rarely. As much as possible, this sequence—*your* sequence—should feel integrated into each day's structure. Whatever type of lesson you have planned, be sure that there is a strong beginning to each class period. The sections that follow move beyond these critical, tone-setting, opening moments and into the heart of the lesson itself. The first focuses on a dynamic that is more teacher-directed, the next one more student-driven.

Chapter 30

LEADING THE CENTRALIZED DYNAMIC

This section focuses on establishing strong and effective leadership of a dynamic that we will call, for simplicity's sake, a classroom discussion. The following chapter delves more deeply into the opportunities for more decentralized, small-group work.

MEASURES OF EFFECTIVE CLASSROOM DISCUSSIONS

One of the finest French teachers I know led classroom discussions that were wonderfully energetic for most of the kids, but she hadn't really developed her sensitivity to inclusion and seemed quite unaware that perhaps 20 percent of the class wasn't thrilled, wasn't engaged, wasn't even participating in what must have felt like a very satisfying class to her.

A first grade teacher I observed continually interrupted her own reading of a story to call different students back to attention. Because she rarely left her classroom, she never observed and internalized the countless possibilities for drawing her students back to the book without interrupting the reading itself.

There are five key components to the effective leadership of a classroom discussion. When we look thoughtfully and dispassionately at our own teaching style and identify those aspects we may not have addressed as fully, we create the opportunity to optimize and revitalize the discussion dynamic in our classrooms.

1. Energy

The energy we bring into class is certainly one of the most fundamental predictors of our chance for success in any particular lesson. The key to engaging our students is our ability to tap into our own excitement, our own sense of anticipation, and our own passions and playfulness.

2. Flow

Flow is a measure of our ability to guide an activity, keep it on course, and allow for a fresh sense of spontaneity and new discoveries without swamping the original intention. Notably, it is also a measure of the ability to sense when it is appropriate to allow for a change in direction, because it may just be that time, because an activity may not be working, or because greater gold may have been discovered in an unexpected new vein.

3. Pace

Pace is a measure of our ability to keep an activity moving. It isn't (and mustn't be) a measure of how many quick answers we get. (We have all been in classes in which it almost feels like the teacher is playing a fast, exclusive game of pedagogical ping-pong with the front row kids.) Pace must be adaptable enough to include the reticent and truly thoughtful, but pace *must* remain tight and controlled throughout the class if we want to keep the quality of focus taut and the level of engagement high.

4. Inclusion

Inclusion is a measure of how many and which of our students are actively involved in the day's activity. It is a commonly overlooked issue even among those who have been in the classroom for decades.

5. Control

Control is a measure of a teacher's ability to lead despite the distractions of inattention, benign chatter, whispered rumors, passing carnivals, or the outright confrontation of a cluster of sullen ne'er-do-wells in the corner.

Before you move on, take a moment to gauge which of the five preceding qualities are probably real strengths of yours. If you are willing and able—and it can pay great dividends in developing our classroom management skill set—try to identify the one area that is probably the least developed. Sometimes it just *feels* that we're missing out on something in leading a lesson or discussion. More often, that weaker element will surface through student behaviors—disconnection, disinterest, or tomfoolery from at least a part of the class.

A central tenet of this section of the book is the fact is that misbehavior from students can often be *prevented* with a bit of advance planning, even though many teachers feel they have to directly address these student behavior. Too often, we see these recurrent behaviors as inevitable, given the nature of the students involved—and sometimes that is the case. The good news is that we can minimize or even eliminate some of these issues through the development of a sensitive set of discussion leadership techniques. Negative student behaviors can frequently be reshaped by the simple expedient of changing the way we lead a discussion. Teachers who can look with true, compassionate objectivity at their own style and find even a single step or two on which to work may find that the classroom dynamic improves dramatically along with them.

Let's look at twelve best practices that can bring these skills to life and the particular components that they affect most directly.

1. Begin every discussion with a fundamentally cool idea.

When we allow ourselves simply to plot out a lesson plan, focusing on the curriculum we have to cover instead of the kids we have to teach, we miss the opportunity to fathom what is *cool*—yes, as in neat, nifty, awesome, and energizing—about that particular lesson.

We would argue—and our experience over decades as teachers and as observers in classrooms reinforces this—that the most compelling key to a successful classroom discussion is a teacher's energy and sense of excitement about the topic at hand. Ideally, a lesson plan shouldn't be considered finished—or even started—until one has pushed oneself to find the deeply energizing force at the heart of the matter.

Is it really possible to get excited about every topic? What about something as mundane as doubling the consonant before adding *ing*? The teacher who simply notates this as the topic for the day and enters class without pushing him- or herself to see what is cool about it is tacitly indicating to the students that the topic *isn't* going to be as engaging as whispering, giggling, and clowning around. The teacher who goes that extra step—who, for example, imagines the prehistoric hunters and gatherers grunting to each other and the gradual development of oral and written language and becomes simply fascinated by *how and when* we as a species transitioned to knowing that hopping was different from hoping—has likely captured some educational cosmic energy that will motivate the classroom leadership and galvanize the focus and imaginations of the students he or she is leading.

2. Get up—and move.

No matter how energetic and passionate we might feel about our lesson plan, any chance for genuine engagement with the class is going to be left at the starting gate if we remain seated at our desks.

The fact is that we can probably all remember math teachers who never left the board, history teachers who seemed fly-papered to some favorite map, and science teachers who hovered behind the lab demonstration table, as if it had been specially built as a kind of podium or fortress.

The transformation brought about by a teacher who moves is so dramatic that the reason so many experienced teachers move so little remains deeply puzzling.

What is the importance of moving?

- It instills and embodies and *projects our own energy outward*.
- It provides us with new perspectives on the classroom. How many teachers have taught even five minutes from the revolutionary perspective of the

back of the room? Try it—and see if it doesn't realign the electromagnetic patterns of attention and involvement.

- It exerts a genuine, mobile "zone of control" over the constituencies of a class. Anyone who has had a teacher come stand directly behind him or her knows the suddenly focusing effect that action can have.

- It extends our viewpoint out beyond the thicket of the front row hand-wavers to those otherwise more hidden from view.

- Finally, it shifts us out of the almost universal tendency to develop "cold" and "hot" zones that can seriously reinforce old, unconscious patterns of behavior and prevent us from really reaching those students who have pitched their little tents in the outlands.

Relative stillness in a teacher, no matter how ambitious the discussion or how inspiring the lecture, inevitably limits the flow of energy in a class. Move and keep moving in order to exert your authority, to give your passion full expression, and to actively usher back into the game the kids who otherwise find themselves on the bench.

3. Approach the tuned-out or disruptive.

This is a correlate and a special use of movement that doesn't have to disrupt the flow at all.

Many young teachers keep telling a cluster of kids in the class to be quiet, lecturing them at length about the problems of talking and warning them about the educational downsides of protracted inattention. In so doing, in wasting that time and sidetracking the conversation, they all but kill off the dialogue's inherent flow, consign the students to the quiet shame of "the scolded ones," and concede real control of the classroom dynamic.

By contrast, it is possible to bring foundering parts of the room effortlessly back on board. Don't address their inattention at all. Instead, as you lead the discussion, maneuver your way over and stand close beside them. Just as the image of a police car in a rearview mirror may suddenly affect our attitude to our driving, the looming presence of a teacher can have a surprisingly powerful effect on those who choose to chatter.

4. Make it a bedrock expectation that everyone speaks every period.

This may be the one area that is most neglected by classroom teachers. Students who come to class and say nothing for the entire period present no disciplinary problems. They create no disruption. As teachers beleaguered by ruffians and inspired by the enthusiastic, we have too often allowed ourselves to let sleeping dogs lie.

Alternatively, some of us may feel that encouraging the shy to speak is a threatening stance to take. After all, aren't some people just shy by nature? Why risk mortifying them?

Speaking is a critical skill in our lives, and the skill only gets better with practice. Some of these kids may go through entire days without actively practicing or even getting the opportunity to practice.

Beyond that, do we allow students who are uncomfortable writing not to turn in papers? Do we allow students who feel uncomfortable with their math abilities not to turn in tests? Is it really any different to allow those who feel uncomfortable speaking not to share their ideas, not to gradually build their verbal skills and their confidence?

I happen to know that Shyette is filled with good ideas, but she is so morbidly entwined with her own apprehensions ("That'll sound so stupid.") that she forever holds back. The class is thereby deprived of hearing what she has to say, and she will never take the risk that is so often the prelude to eventual confidence and mastery.

I suspect we all know what an intense, even perspective-altering experience it will be for her when she finally awakens to the possibility of speaking and to her classmates' acceptance of her ideas. Drawing young Shyette out may have little to do with the subject you teach. Math is math is math. The French class will be fine without her. Drawing her out and showing her that she can survive this thing called classroom discussion, however, can become one of our more subtly powerful accomplishments in the course of the year.

How do you set a tone in our classroom so that everyone is gradually welcomed into the discussion? In part, of course, this issue can and should be addressed proactively on the first day by establishing the simple and absolute expectation that everyone participates every day.

It can be reinforced by simply calling on everyone, softly, encouragingly. As teachers, we have the power not only to acknowledge an idea from the reticent but to praise it, to highlight how powerful a perception it was, and to engage in quick, affirming, smiling eye contact.

If it continues to be a problem, if Shyette is really just given to a mortified blush and a barely audible "I don't know," it's important not to give up. You should address the issue gently and privately.

One of the great, underutilized tricks of the teaching trade is to time our parting from a class perfectly to coincide with the leave-taking of a student with whom we'd like to speak alone.

One day as you're gathering your books, you notice that Shyette is just about to leave and that no one else is in close proximity, so accidentally on purpose, you happen to leave as she does.

"Hey, Shyette?"

She looks at you wide-eyed, wanting to flee, hoping she misunderstood.

"Can I talk to you about something for a minute?"

Her seas roil with discomfort, but your voice is gentle enough to soothe the waves.

"I notice that you don't seem to speak in class very much."

She shakes her head, looking down.

"Well, Shyette, I want you to understand that I meant what I said about participation. I really am going to call on you at least once every day. I'd rather not have to call on you when you don't really have an answer. It's not my goal to embarrass you. My goal is to hear what you're thinking. So can we try something? When you think you're ready to answer, please put up your hand, and you may find that getting it out of the way, answering something early in the class, will let you relax and really listen to what's going on without feeling that I'm suddenly going to spring a question on you. How does that sound?"

And who among us can imagine anything but a soft, I-guess-that'd-be-okay smile of nervous relief in response?

In time, once she sees that the ridicule she had imagined for so long doesn't really surface, once she senses the positive updraft of your response to her answers, once her voice comfortably becomes part of the greater dialogue, who knows what will begin to happen?

5. Expand the customary wait time.

One of the more shocking statistics we have encountered in our research is the fact that the average interval in an American classroom between the end of a teacher's question and the first student's response is—drumroll—0.9 seconds. Nine-tenths of a second.

Many of us feel pressured by a perceived need to cover a lot of material in fairly short order. Therefore, we opt to crank up the speed of student answers. This apparently natural tendency has some very unintended and very problematic consequences. "A lot of answers" doesn't correlate very highly with "a lot of good answers." Even more tellingly, it doesn't correlate highly with "a lot of engagement." On the contrary, most fast-paced classrooms tend to have a surprisingly limited number of responders.

No wonder the impulsive are so often allowed to dominate our classrooms. No wonder the shy—and the truly thoughtful—are so often inclined to tune out and simply leave the thinking and discussion to others.

So how do you expand wait time?

The obvious initial answer is…to wait. On some level, it's just that easy. We tend to fall into the trap of overactive Q&A in the same way that we might suddenly realize we're hyperventilating. Take a breath. Pause. Remarkably, like stop-action in a garden, more hands are raised, more flowers bloom.

Coax a few more hands. "I'm going to wait. I want to hear from people I haven't heard from yet."

Challenge a few more hands. "Some of you haven't spoken. If you don't choose when to speak, I'm going to go ahead and call on you, even if your hands aren't up."

But then, too, there are warm ways of inviting the hesitant player who needs to be *sure* an answer won't sound too dumb to the discussion. First of all, when giving a homework assignment, tell your students what you're going to be talking about in class tomorrow. ("I want you to read the next scene and be prepared to talk about how Mark Antony got away with such a challenging speech.") Alternatively, when they arrive in class, create an opportunity for them to practice what you want them to share. Tell them the key question in the discussion you're about to lead, and give them four minutes to journal about the topic. Have them turn to the person next to them and rehearse what they may then say to the class.

It isn't only that you'll hear more voices. It isn't only that the process will be more inclusive, nor even that the process will be richer. You may actually touch young lives and turn the hesitant into the increasingly comfortable and confident.

6. Insist on hands up or some creative alternative.

Clearly, calling out is a widespread phenomenon that needs to be brought under control, but one of the most exciting aspects of watching teachers in action is that we never cease to see new ideas. We never cease to learn.

Just recently, I visited a middle school Spanish class that was filled with more than its customary share of hyperkinetic kids. It was clear to the experienced teacher that these students were going to have a hard time sitting still and waiting to be called on.

Instead of having them raise their hands when they wanted to speak, Imani had them stand up at their desks to be recognized. I had seen the class before and after this brainstorm, and the difference in focus and quiet was astonishing. Not only were these restless and impulsive students allowed to get up and down and up and down, but they seemed to have no doubt that they were now visible. The amount of shouting out dropped dramatically. The need for waving one's hand frantically in the air with a gurgling "Oh! Oh! Oh!" disappeared.

Kids were standing in good order, waiting to be called on. No muss. No fuss. Simple. Brilliant. Effective.

Try whatever works to enable students to gain attention silently, and keep on trying.

7. Forbid calling out—and refuse to accept such answers.

In almost any energetic class, there comes a point in the discussion when little Dickie Farnsworth, born and bred in the heart of enthusiasm, can't hold back from uttering some *pièce de résistance*, some splendid thought he is sure will delight the old professor.

Despite the fact that the old professor has repeatedly cautioned him and others that calling out is not allowed, who can blame the professor for grinning, nay, gleaming with delight at the utterances of this imperturbable young scholar? Who but a stuffy old scoundrel would fail to recognize that sometimes brilliance just *must* have its say?

An effective teacher—that's who.

How to stop calling out? Let's say little Dickie has just summarized the entire meaning of Einstein's Special Theory of Relativity in six succinct sentences that would leave the scientific world atremble. The old professor cocks his head, looks about, and says, "I believe I just heard something, but it certainly wasn't from someone I called on. Did anyone hear anything?"

There is a scatter of amusement.

Little Betsy Bumbershoot raises a wily hand. She gets it, even if Dickie doesn't...yet.

"Betsy?"

Betsy dutifully repeats—verbatim—what young Master Farnsworth just espoused.

"Brilliant, Betsy! However did you think of that?"

Betsy glows. Both she and the teacher cast a twinkling gaze at little Dickie.

"Betsy, your work is just outstanding this quarter. Good ideas *and* you wait your turn! What a great combination!"

Little Dickie squirms in his seat. Lesson learned—perhaps until the next time.

Don't honor call-outs. No exceptions, regardless of their brilliance. Brilliance, like stupidity, can surely wait its turn.

8. Make the process of calling on students utterly unpredictable.

This one is simple and yet constantly undercut.

Keeping the process of calling on students unpredictable keeps every student on his or her toes. While there is value in using raised hands as an indication of readiness to speak, *don't* fall into the trap of only calling on those with their hands raised. Otherwise, you have unintentionally—but very clearly—given everyone instructions in how to safely tune out: simply keep your hand down.

To make it fair and clear from the beginning, make sure that you spell it out on that first day in September. **Anyone can be called on at any time**, so stay focused and be prepared whether or not you've raised your hand.

Just as alarming and self-defeating is the pattern so many of us experienced as students ourselves. Think of those teachers who try to ensure inclusion by calling on everyone in a prearranged order, such as left to right or A to Z. This process has its heart in the right place, for it tries to ensure that everyone speaks every period.

But who among us can forget how it felt to be at the far left or right of a class or to have the last name Aardvark or Zzyzzinksi when the teacher was working his way through the middle of the room or the alphabet? What greater invitation is there to tune out than to know that you won't be called on for some considerable length of time?

Inclusion may have been maximized—but at the expense of engagement.

9. Insert their names into the discourse.

"Now, when we are trying to balance a chemical equation, Edwina, it is vital that we have the same number of each atom on both sides of the equation."

Edwina may have been somewhere out along the asteroid belt, twisting her braid into a small tea cozy, paying no attention to what was going on, but I suspect we all know that one word in the English language most guaranteed to get our attention—our own name.

The chemistry teacher, recognizing the fact that Edwina was out of radio contact, didn't ignore the situation, didn't scold her ("Edwina, how many times blah blah blah!"), didn't make her a goat for his comedy ("Earth to Edwina!"), and didn't break the flow at all. He simply used the one signal word most likely to engage Edwina and bring her back into the flow.

Edwina may look up with surprise. The tea cozy may unravel through her fingers. Still without interrupting the flow, the teacher might then give her a brief smile and a knowing look. In a minute or two, when Edwina's space-craft seems to have successfully landed back in the classroom, the teacher might even do well to reinforce her presence by asking Edwina a question.

Radio contact has been restored without a moment being lost.

10. Respond inclusively to every utterance, even if it's only with a musing nod.

Some teachers aren't even aware of the fact that they only speak in response to a student's answer if it is wrong, if they disagree, or if the answer is incomplete. That subtly creates an environment in which the only reinforcement is *negative* reinforcement.

Because so much of the emphasis of this book has been on staying united with the class, setting high expectations, and building a positive reputation for its students, this pattern (whose equivalent can be *seen* in a paper scratched with nothing but errors highlighted in red) creates unintentional distance and disaffection. Positive reinforcement is as easy to establish as it is easy to overlook. Highlight their success:

- *"Good."*
- Grin.
- "I *like* that idea."
- "I'm not sure you're all the way there, but I like where you're heading."
- "Oh, come on, you're really good at this. Is Louisville *really* the capital of Kentucky?"
- "Perfect!"
- "Did you all hear what Blarney just said?"
- "Magnificent!"
- "Wow! I hadn't even thought of that possibility!"

- Or just a sagacious, eye-twinkling nod.

Sometimes teachers wonder why kids appear tuned out in their class. All too often those very same teachers haven't once considered the possibility that the only reinforcement students ever get for speaking up is correction and criticism. **Welcome each and every student into the flow of the discussion by making them feel good about what they have to contribute.**

11. Intercede immediately if there are negative interactions in the class.

In almost every class, there are those who want to corner the market on cool. Some will snicker brazenly or ostentatiously sigh and tap their fingers at those who don't get it. Just as poisonous for the culture of the class may be those who roll their eyes or let out throaty guffaws at those who use big words, who know the answers, who actually work and actually care. Being above it all and trying to tear down the very foundations of excellence in the class is part of their game, part of the calloused cool they parade.

If our goal is to lead a class that feels like a team, where risk is rewarding, where we really are all in this together, it is imperative that we pull up short and decisively address the voices of divisiveness. These are the times when an interruption is not only okay but vital. This isn't a case of inattention or an isolated case of innocent chatter. These are the forces in the room that can undermine all that we are trying to achieve in terms of solidarity and shared progress. The culture of the class is at stake.

It must be recognized that victimized students—whether they are the ones who never get it or always do—will almost never respond directly to ridicule, particularly if it is as subtle as a *tsk* or a knowing look. Their most common response is to pretend they didn't hear or pretend it didn't matter.

Victimized students will almost never confront a single detractor or a powerful phalanx of naysayers. After all, these are their peers, the students with whom they must later wend their way through the lunchrooms, hallways, and locker rooms.

Insecure teachers, or those naïve enough to think that ignoring the problem will make it go away, may feel reluctant to acknowledge, let alone confront, the source of the problem.

It is up to us as educators to set the cultural tone in our classes.

Even if the undercutting gesture is so subtle as to be almost ignored, such expressions *are* picked up and *do* have a gradually degenerative influence on the class as a whole. If the dunce-beaters and the anti-intellectuals are allowed to snipe at classmates with impunity, everyone in the room gets the message that victims are on their own, and anyone at any moment might fall prey to the predators in their midst. Very quietly and equally mysteriously—at least to teachers who renounce their roles as the cultural leaders of their classes—the energy will begin to dissipate from the classroom. The eagerness of September will fade into a wary lassitude that the teacher may never successfully defuse or comprehend—unless the behavior is addressed fully and firmly then and there.

How to address it?

A moment of stilled and sober silence. A wheeling blaze of eye contact. A few steps in the ridiculer's direction until you are uncomfortably—not to say threateningly—close. He is within your projected zone of control.

There is a fidget of further silence.

"Mr. Bookburner, do you have a problem with that answer?"

"Mr. Bookburner, I'm speaking to you."

His eyes lift, sullen and speechless.

"There are no put-downs in this class. Every answer is to be taken seriously. Is that understood? Everyone is entitled to a guarantee of respect and safety. Even you, Mr. Bookburner. I will accept nothing less."

Another pause. You are unrelenting. He's got to feel the cool heat of your displeasure. This is one of those telltale moments that shapes the character of a class. Step into it. Relish the opportunity to send such a signal to anyone who's ever been a victim.

"Not ever again. Not once. Is that understood?"

And this time, you wait for him finally to glance furiously up at you and answer.

And perhaps, if it is possible, if time permits and he is not so remorselessly negative a figure, you can ask him an easy, interesting question maybe ten minutes later. You don't have to leave the relationship in reverberating opposition. You can begin to honor *his* answers. Begin to draw him back into the very sense of unity he had just threatened to divide. Your relationship with him, however, is secondary. First, stay united with the class.

The need for vigilance in this regard is critical and ongoing. Some teachers pick up on an undercurrent of ridicule with amazing swiftness. Others seem almost unaware that anything has taken place.

It is vital that every one of us attune the sweep of our eyes and the radar of our attention to the prickly possibility that students are subtly and persistently being victimized. Be on the lookout, because whenever a single student is being victimized, something larger, more cultural, and more pervasive is being undermined as well.

Often, one powerful, public intervention can turn the tide in a class, but note that ensuring the openness and safety within the class culture is not a one-moment, one-class exercise. It must be part of an ongoing, long-term campaign.

12. Encourage the students to respond, not simply to you but also to each other.

This is a behavior pattern that college and high school students may have learned more than elementary school kids. In middle school and even many high school classrooms, a high percentage of traditional discussion is a kind of teacher-student-teacher-student ping-pong. Such a process not only degrades into monotony but also limits the real power and potential of classroom dialogues. When students respond to more than just the teacher's question, when they are responsible for listening to *everything that happens in class,* when they learn to listen and respond to each other as well, they greatly enrich the energy of discussions and the quality of their own thinking. In so doing, students move from passive to active engagement as they create and shape the classroom discourse.

It is a subtle but powerful opportunity. Each of us has the chance to encourage this wide-ranging dialogue by actively promoting it as a way of thinking about classroom discussion. By challenging students to interact actively with each other, those who have their hands up won't simply be waiting for their turn, and those who are idle at their seats won't simply be tuning into the teacher's half of each Q&A session.

Shifting students' attention to each other's responses and the possibilities of more multidimensional dialogue will likely be a gradual process, but over time, students will learn to listen, not just to us, but to each other. They will also learn to speak up, not just to us, but to each other. This subtle change in the classroom dynamic can greatly enrich the sense of spirited interactivity in the classroom as well as our own sense that we have empowered them as students and learners.

Chapter 31

SMALL GROUP WORK

The cooperative learning model that has enriched our classrooms for the past several decades has a powerful, student-centered dynamic at its heart. It is guided by a belief that students gain empowerment and greater personal investment in their learning when they are more actively engaged in classroom activities. Many teachers who have shifted a portion, sometimes a significant portion, of their lesson plans from direct instruction to cooperative learning activities find that the students often take greater ownership of their learning.

However, as with any model, there are optimum structures and conditions. We have frankly seen classrooms in which inadequately designed decentralized methodologies have led to instances when the activity is vague or unstimulating, students are at sea, airtime is poorly shared, the reticent keep quiet, the indolent sit back and wait while the responsible do all of the work.

Successful cooperative learning doesn't just mean turning kids loose on their own. Just as with outstanding centralizing models, effective leadership of this strategy is a matter of practice, reflection, and constant improvement. It is important to note that there are a number of excellent books out there entirely devoted to the topic of cooperative learning.

What follows is a series of guidelines that suggest the best practices for enhancing the classroom dynamic:

Make the objective of the cooperative learning time clear and explicit.

This certainly doesn't mean that you have to tell students what they will discover, but we have perhaps all seen classes in which the students assemble into small groups and, after some disagreement and discussion, someone raises her hand and says, "Wait, now what are we supposed to be doing?"

Be as explicit as possible about both the procedure and the ending point.

Choose a cooperative learning model not just for variety but for the best model that will achieve what you want students to learn.

There are clearly times in which direct instruction or individual work might be more advantageous. If you are going to use small group interactions to advance learning objectives, make sure that this is the best design to reach your goals. In general, cooperative learning is terrific for many things—shared discovery, group review, group preparation for some upcoming activity, and so on. Before you embark on an exercise in cooperative learning (or any other format, including teacher-led instruction and discussion), you should be sure that you have chosen it because this model is superior to other forms of learning for this particular goal.

Establish clear group work norms.

Students need to know the following:

- Where to find materials and how they should be distributed
- What amount of noise is acceptable
- How to get our attention to answer questions
- Any restrictions on getting out of seats and moving around the room

- How to settle disputes within the group
- How to collect materials and where to store ongoing projects
- What to do if they finish early

Deliver all instructions orally and in writing.

Nothing bogs down group work more completely than incomplete directions. Anticipate whatever questions or concerns might come up. Imagine students working and finding forks in the road. Clarify before you turn them loose how they are to respond to such choices. Also anticipate that some students will be inclined to think outside the box, and clarify in advance in what situations this is to be encouraged. Establish the materials. Establish the objective. Establish the nonnegotiables, and be sure—even if you have said it all clearly, with all of them presumably listening—to have the materials, the steps, the objective, and any other requisites written on the board, on a poster, or on handouts before you turn them loose. Have each and every step—and answers to anticipated questions—documented in advance so that time isn't lost either having to field extensive questions or having to interrupt the activity and regain everyone's attention to add something you should have anticipated from the beginning.

Having the steps in checklist form can help reduce questions and keep the groups moving independently. Little is more likely to delay and derail an engaging activity than having to interrupt it and recenter everyone's attention simply to add some further clarification. As much as possible, anticipate everything you need to say and everything they might ask before you turn them loose.

Establish clear time deadlines—and stick to them.

I learned from Heidi Hayes Jacobs that fifteen minutes means "about fifteen minutes," whereas fourteen minutes implicitly means fourteen minutes. By the same token, "until quarter after two" means until *about* a quarter after two. "Until 2:14" is a far more specific time frame.

It should be noted that there may well be situations and sufficient latitude in time during which you aren't sure how long some activity will take or how engaged the kids will be, during which a looser sense of time can prevail. Even so, it is important to give students a sense of whether they have ten or thirty minutes in which to work, and if you decided, for example, to give everyone an extra five minutes, announce this. Don't let your deadlines just blur and recede, or they won't believe you when you need them to have a clear deadline.

Noting that it often takes an extra minute or two to bring decentralized student groups back to full attention, it is important to anticipate deadlines for each class in your lesson plan for reporting back, returning to their seats, returning materials, and such so that the class doesn't run late. Deadlines, like most limits, are essentially reassuring and can provide a positive sense of urgency and purpose.

Think about optimum group size.

There are times when paired partners work most effectively. There are times when a larger group is called for. The maximum effective size of most student groups is four, although there may be occasions when a class is divided in half to prepare for a debate. In such circumstances, subdividing the group further is often helpful (with groups assigned to the opening statement, rebuttal, closing statement, etc.). But where larger groups are called for, it is vital to be explicit about the need for everyone to be engaged—and for everyone's voice to be heard.

Assign students to each group.

For the isolated student, there may be no more haunting moment in school than that moment after which a teacher has told the class to find a partner or divide into groups. Almost everyone feels a tremor of uncertainty, sensing the possibility that groups may form and that they may be left out.

Beyond that, we all know that students don't necessarily make the best choices in learning partners. Denise Distractible almost always has a fascination for the antics of Eddie ADHD, and Eddie is often stimulated by Denise's mulish hee-haw. Use wisdom in separating them.

While it may not be fair always to partner Damon Dutiful III with Emily Hopelessly Disorganized, it can be helpful to everyone if the teacher is conscientious about establishing partnerships that don't leave one group with a concentration of the least focused, least able students in the class.

It is so advantageous as to be considered essential that the teacher determines the class partners in group work. Just as it is with the need to assign seating in a class, so, yes, we are actively deciding to usurp student power in this specific case. Students don't make the best choices. They don't think about which students bring out the best in them. They tend to think about who's fun, who's whacky, who's a hoot. And more quietly and lonesomely than that, there are students who will always be the last one picked, so there may too often end up being a team of outcasts.

Partnerships shouldn't depend on popularity, which they almost always do, when left to the students themselves. Partnerships should be forged on the basis of the wise and thoughtful linkage of students who might bring out the best in each other or, conversely, based on a clear sense of avoiding partnerships of students that would likely bring out the worst in each child.

Assign roles.

The teachers who see the best results from cooperative learning have established clear roles from the beginning of the year so that time isn't taken up during each activity clarifying individual responsibility or letting the most brassy and impulsive simply take charge. While different proponents suggest a wide variety of roles to be assigned, some of the more useful are the following:

- The leader: The student who is ultimately responsible for keeping partners on track and for clarifying when they are off topic. It should be underscored to students when introducing this role that it is one of facilitation and oversight, not a free ticket to do all the talking or bossing around.
- The time-keeper: The student who is assigned responsibility for completing a task by the deadline. "We've got four minutes left."
- The encourager: The student who is responsible for making sure that everyone is participating and supporting the quieter student in their involvement. "Wait, we've all had a chance to talk. Let's hear from Casper." Depending on the culture of the class, this can be a very

important role. As you circulate, take special pains to notice and to praise effective encouragement.

- The recorder/reporter: The student in charge of taking notes and, if necessary, speaking on behalf of the group. It is important that the recorder be expected to include all voices in his or her report.
- The scrounger: The student in charge of collecting necessary materials and ensuring that they are all returned neatly at the end of the activity.

It is almost always better if the teacher assigns roles—intentionally or randomly. The advantage of doing so is that the same student doesn't always assume leadership or isn't always left to take whatever is seen as the least attractive alternative. It sets the students directly to work and doesn't launch the exercise with quibbling and hurt feelings about who got to do what. One system that seems to work effectively—in randomly assuring that everyone will eventually get all roles and in eliminating the time and emotions wasted in assigning roles—is to have a series of cards handed face-down to each group, with roles clearly labeled on each.

Allow the groups to spread out—but not all over the school.

Some elbow room is a nice feature of cooperative learning, as is a group's ability to stake its claim to a favorite corner in the hall. Your willingness to allow them to stake out their own turf needs to be balanced by your ability to maintain effective oversight. The group who expresses a strong preference for meeting in the deepest recesses of the boiler room may have other motives for choosing this location. Even if not, it may be more than a little irksome to have to seek them out to inform them that the sun has now set and the deadline has passed.

Allow them to scatter but not so far as to be out of earshot or easy eyeshot so that you can complete your circuit of oversight and support.

Closely monitor each group during the activity.

We have seen—on too many occasions—classrooms in which cooperative learning seems almost like a free period for the teacher. "Hey, I've come up

with a great activity, and the important thing is to let them operate independently. They'll call me if they need me."

Humbug.

At no other time in classroom activities is there more likelihood for disagree-
ments, slights, snickers, or examples of exclusion. Students also unsurprisingly
tend to rise to the occasion and to want to shine more completely, focused and on
best behavior when they know that the teacher has a thoughtful eye upon them.

Circulate among the groups, listening, making suggestions when appropriate, and answering questions. Despite the inevitable imbalance in the needs
of varying groups, try to avoid getting bogged down by any one group, because
the others may feel as if you might as well be reading that newspaper. By the
time you surface from a conversation with the team over by the cow shed, the
cluster on the fire escape may well have fled for the day.

Remind them when time is almost up.

Even though you may have assigned a time-keeper, a standard "two minutes
left" can be vital and can reinforce rather than undermine the role of the
time-keeper.

Allow time at the conclusion of the activity for a debriefing.

If time permits, it can be valuable to have groups report back on their internal
dynamic. "No names, please, and no personal blame. But how did you feel
you operated together as a group?" Even though this might run the risk of
surfacing some internal dissension, it also encourages a sense of reflection. As
cooperative learning is intended, the gains of the day are not only measured
according to the fulfillment of the objective but also according to how those
ends were accomplished.

In addition, hearing the results of each group's work can enlighten and
enrich the dialogue, because others may have come up with very different
perspectives or approaches.

End by providing feedback to them on both their ability to meet the objectives and to function effectively together.

"I loved the fact that so many of you accomplished this in the limited time—that's terrific." "I was concerned that I saw several groups in which a few people did almost all of the talking." Critiquing is important. Leaving them feeling good about the experience and highlighting, if possible, a specific, successful outreach for inclusion by an encourager or the swift and successful return of all of the equipment will not only conclude the activity on an upbeat note but will also continue to empower each of the students in their assigned roles.

As we have noted and as many of us have observed, student-based learning offers a rich model for class work organization; however, too many teachers have allowed this structure to remain far too unstructured, with the result that students' focus, efficiency, and even morale suffer. By turning students loose on independent projects with clear roles, structures, and expectations in place, it is possible to create an atmosphere that is both energizing and engaging.

Chapter 32

THE FINAL THREE MINUTES

We have seen countless teachers get it all right—a brilliantly original lesson plan, a tight, focused beginning, a compelling and well-orchestrated lesson—who then look up at the clock and, as if surprised by the fact that time actually *passes*, let the seamless procession of the class completely unravel at its conclusion.

While it is clear that sound opening routines and beautifully designed lessons are critical, what often goes unrecognized is the power of an effective finale. A successful lesson has been, in part, squandered if the period is forced to end abruptly.

A thoughtful conclusion not only serves as a fitting bookend for the opening ritual but also has the power to accomplish the following:

- Review the day's work
- Create unique opportunities for thoughtful and spontaneous feedback
- Define the homework that students are expected to do on their own
- Offer a meaningful preview of the next day's lesson

The fact is that teachers too often dismiss a class with an unplanned suddenness, as if the exact moment when a period ends is as unpredictable as a fire drill. Day after day, they are unknowingly letting slip one of the briefest and most potentially valuable parts of any class period—the final three minutes.

The habit of running late is a problem for many teachers. I confess that it was a problem for me for a long time. I would get caught up in the energy of a class discussion and be reluctant to let it wind down. The result was a hectic packing up by the students, an artless flurry of farewells, quiet resentment from their next period teachers, and a failure to take advantage of this prime time at the conclusion of each class.

The routine for the end of a class is in some ways harder to invoke and harder to enforce, because there is already such momentum and because the clock on the wall is down-ticking the seconds to dismissal. It is vital to get a clear sense of how much time an orderly, effective closing routine will take. It is just as vital to be strictly disciplined in stopping with that much time to spare.

It is not only that critical information needs to be covered and shared. It is not only that running late can inconvenience colleagues and students alike and leave them irritated with you for what too many of us simply shrug off as a harmless eccentricity. The most lasting impression of any class, by defi-nition, comes from the feeling imparted in those final moments. A class that was beautifully conceived, artfully choreographed, and skillfully performed may be a lost impression if its concluding moments were ragged and hectic.

Map out the final routine on your lesson plan, on the agenda, and in your own reflexive awareness of time. A class that was well planned and well achieved deserves to be well concluded. Everyone involved in a successful enterprise—students and teacher alike—deserves to leave the class feeling a kind of unhurried, reflective satisfaction over what was just achieved.

What follows is an end-of-period checklist that you should use:

1. Keep an eye on the clock.

Plan to stop the lesson three minutes early, no matter what. If you are someone who likes to set his watch ahead or never quite get yourself to stop as quickly as you want, aim for four minutes before the period ends. Even, if necessary, until it becomes ingrained into your own rituals, get in the habit of making yourself a small index card with the stop-time duly noted.

2. Make the conclusion a set, prescribed ritual for yourself and for the students.

Don't let them start packing up. No notebooks away. Be explicit that this is one of the most important moments of the day and that you expect full attention. (And then, of course, be sure that the students *do* have time to pack up and put their notebooks away.)

3. Ask for a summary of the day.

What was learned? What were the key points? What one thing struck you most about today's class? Did anything surprise you? What did you—or should you—highlight in your notes? Or as you bow to their persistent concern about the topic, ask them what they expect from today's experience will be "on the test." Consider giving them a moment to scan their notes, highlight the day's key points, and consolidate their thinking. After all, as much as you are teaching them the content, you are also (ideally) teaching them study skills. You are allowing them time and tactics for developing the art of reviewing for saliency.

It is in this final three minutes of each period during which such skills can be most fully developed. In this way, what you are teaching has the capacity to transcend your subject area and transfer effectively across the disciplines and across the years.

4. End on an upbeat note.

Just as you began the lesson with a note of urgency ("We've got a lot to do today"), it is helpful in building a class-wide reputation to end on a positive note ("We covered a lot. You made some great points. Your focus was strong. I'm impressed.").

5. Give them time to copy the homework from the board.

We have probably all seen (or perhaps had) teachers who announced the homework into the mayhem of the end-of-class scramble and then are scolding and baffled the next day when some of the students have done the wrong assignment. Make the moment of going over the homework assignment one of peace and focus. Because not everyone is an auditory learner, don't just tell them the assignment. Write it on the board. Insist that they copy it down somewhere reliable, not on a shirt cuff or a sweaty palm. If appropriate, require them to transcribe the homework into an assignment book or atop the day's notes.

Before you move on, ask them if the homework assignment is clear. Include, if necessary, a listing of any materials they will need for the next day, and remember to remind them of any concurrent long-term projects.

6. Share with them the key focus of the next day's class experience.

This doesn't only provide a neat, predictable segue into the next day's activity. Tomorrow when they arrive, they will already be orienting themselves to what lies ahead. More than that, it may help focus their attention in their homework assignment.

For example, if you have assigned reading in history and they know that tomorrow's discussion will focus primarily on the agrarian economy of the South, sharing key points for tomorrow will sharpen their reading for issues, quotes, statistics, and such in anticipation of that discussion. Finally, for those students who perpetually hang back from class discussions, endlessly rehearsing answers, it may well provide them the opportunity to come into class already having prepared for a conversation.

7. If necessary, as you head for the door, take the time to have the one-on-ones with students who have been badly out of step with the rest of the class.

If you have told a misbehaving student that he needs to see you after class, *don't* forget or fail to follow through under any circumstances. If there is someone who needs a private face-to-face about a snicker at someone else's expense, about calling out without being called on, about an ongoing ADHD issue of focus, take the student aside and have the conversation in private. Rather than focusing on what went wrong today, focus on a more positive future.

"I don't want you ever again to laugh at another student in here, particularly when they're wrong and already feeling embarrassed. You're too good for that. Is that clear?"

8. If possible, this is also the time to have one-on-ones with students who deserve special attention.

These parting conversations don't have to be negative or warning in tone. In fact, as we emphasized by positioning "positive tone" at the gateway to this book, positive recognition is vastly underutilized and richly beneficial. Therefore, take a moment to scan the class as you gather up your books. Look them over for someone who could use a good word—the shy student who has finally spoken up, the student who struggles to provide even one good answer, the student who hasn't been getting his or her homework in regularly but who did so today, the student who simply referenced another student's work in a positive way. Looking out for the student who is working above his or her usual performance takes some attention during class.

Catch him doing it, and stop him briefly at the end of class. Let him feel a momentary unease at the realization that you want to speak to him, and then mingle the relief with the radiance he will feel that you've noticed, you've taken the time, you've put into words something that he may not have even noticed.

"I really liked the fact that when you started speaking earlier, you started by saying you thought Frieda had made a good point. I noticed how Frieda looked when you said that. I'm sure that just seemed like a small thing to you, but it made her feel good. That's the kind of thing I've come to expect of you." You can be sure that this will not only make him feel good but will make it more likely that he will repeat those behaviors that earned recognition and praise. That final moment before everyone is gone is a golden one for continuing the ongoing work of reinforcing those behaviors and characteristics you most want to see replicated in your class.

9. And finally—something few of us take or make the time to do: make notes on your lesson plan about what worked and what didn't.

Make each year's class better than the one before. Even as you teach, focus on what questions fell flat, what experiments took unexpectedly long to set up, what elements of the lesson you wished you'd thought of in advance.

$$\star \; \star \; \star$$

There is so much focus—in this book and in education itself—on the lesson plan, on opening days and opening minutes, that we too often lose sight of the fact that the second most important time in each class is the very end. How we wrap up, how much time and focus we devote to it can have a dramatic impact on how we and the students feel about the overall success of the class.

PART 4

Optimizing Assessment
and Feedback

Chapter 33

ASSESSMENT AND FEEDBACK: OVERVIEW

Previous units in this book have focused on some of the big, make-or-break issues in the profession of education. What kind of tone we set in our classroom—whether or not we can face and pass the inevitable testing and how we can manage the dynamic of an unfolding classroom discussion—are concerns close to our soul and satisfaction as educators.

The issue of assessment may seem, by comparison, something of a quiet backwater, and while we would be inclined to agree that it is probably the rare teacher who has gone home fretting more about a student's failure to pass the test than their own failure to pass a very different kind of test, effective assessment is key to *our* understanding of *student* understanding. If we are to make a difference as the intellectual shepherds of the children in our flock, the issue of assessment is central to our mission.

Teachers have been setting positive tones, establishing discipline, and creating effective classroom dynamics for generations, but how many have been making equally effective use of student assessment? Where grades are given at all, how often are they simply notated in a grade book, averaged at the term's end, and recorded on a grade card?

In the section that follows, we will examine the question of grades—not as to whether or not grades themselves are abhorrent or beneficial. We will approach the issue of grades, assuming they are given in your own school environment, from a perspective of *how* they can be derived and used to maximize student learning, motivation, and self-esteem. The point is not to indulge in the widespread practice of inflating grades but to begin consciously to shift the balance between the disproportionately long time the traditional educators spend on assessment and the remarkably little time those same educators typically devote to making effective use of such assessments.

We will also focus on testing as well as underutilized alternatives to such testing (because the same types of students tend to get about the same grades on the same kinds of tests). We will focus on homework—a subject of widespread controversy in some quarters, exactly at the time we bemoan our country's poor academic standing in the family of nations. Finally, in this section, we will discuss varieties of feedback given to students and parents, including a section on written comments and parent conferences.

EMERGING OPPORTUNITIES FOR ASSESSMENT

A small revolution is underway in the field of assessment—one that we would emphatically like to encourage. This revolution has its foundation in the following revelation:

- Standard assessment tools are too often dull, blunt instruments.
- Even as an increasing number of visionary educators embrace variety in their teaching techniques, they are encouraged to rely upon outmoded assessment methodology.
- Instead of simply recording grades and moving on, the purpose of assessment should be to redirect our teaching energies to address the gaps in student learning revealed by those assessments.

In short, the purpose of assessment can and should be actively forward-looking, not passive reflection of what has already been covered.

This unit is devoted to learning about each child's progress and communicating that information to the child and the parent. This is necessarily some of the most important work we do in the course of a year. Mishandling this sensitive information can block progress or even lead to serious tension between a teacher, a child, and the child's family. The sensitive assessment of a child's progress—and the equally sensitive communication about that assessment—can allow a child to feel seen, understood, and part of an ongoing dialogue. No matter how difficult a child's situation, a positive belief in the partnership with a child's family can go a long way toward ensuring effective communication on behalf of the child's ongoing growth.

Chapter 34

TESTS

It is a math class. It is a Friday, and in classrooms across the country, just as surely as the heavens wheel above us, it is "test day."

Students file into the classroom, uneasily muttering to each other or to themselves. The teacher, with an almost religious solemnity, distributes photocopied tests to each student. Silence reigns while the teacher from her perch at the front of the room scouts the hunched-over masses for signs of crib sheets, whispered answers, or straying eyes.

The class ends as solemnly as—and perhaps even a little more forlornly than—it began. In the hallway, some students experience an almost routine sense of satisfaction, and some students grab others' elbows with quick outcries of "What did you get for number sixteen?" Others shuffle away with a sense of grim resolution or defeat.

The teacher quietly gathers the papers and retreats to her office to correct them. When the last has been corrected, she painstakingly enters the allotted grades in her grade book. At the end of the term, she will balance and weigh the scores along with the accumulated others and produce a final grade.

REGULAR TESTING HAS BENEFITS...

What is right with this picture? Actually, quite a bit.

The teacher is assessing what students have learned. She has not simply taught and taught and taught without regard to actual progress.

The students have been given a sense of the time frame. Instead of simply experiencing an unbroken linear sequence of endless new topics, they have been presented with a reasonable span in which to master a reasonable amount of material. What we know about human memory reinforces the belief that we should engage in regular exercises of memorization and consolidation.

Further, a test deadline itself fosters a crescendo of focus and attention for most motivated students. The beleaguering question "Will this be on the test?" underscores the extent to which students prioritize what matters in a class. Even the inclination for high school students to underline in a text or for younger students to ask for their mom's or dad's help the night before is sharpened by the imminence of a test.

Beyond that, each student has been asked to record precisely what each has learned. Unlike a class-wide discussion on the same topic, during which one student may speak while twenty-three others are silent, the test represents an on-the-spot moment that requires students to reveal the depth of their knowledge or misunderstanding.

Because such moments happen recurrently during the term, any one topic, any one bout of flu, or anxious aftermath of a bad family fight doesn't depress the average as much as it might should any individual grade be required to stand on its own.

If we never tested, our impression of student success would likely remain... *impressionistic*. Almost everyone who has given a test has experienced moments of surprised rejoicing and despondent headshaking. (Why *didn't* I take that job painting stripes down the center of roads?) At the very least, testing gives us one kind of objective reading from students about what they have learned at a given moment in time.

BUT TESTING CAN BECOME MONSTROUS...

So what's *wrong* with this picture?

One of the simplest changes that we can make—without changing the biweekly pattern of "chapter tests"—is to create a variety of question types in what testing we do use. Math test questions, for example, are almost invariably the same, and yet what might we unleash if we were to roll out essay questions in a math test?

Instead of old fashioned tests, there are alternative forms of assessment that require students to demonstrate their cumulative knowledge in richly diverse formats:

- Students can do individual presentations that further inform members of the class.
- They can engage in debates on a critical topic that bring them to class energized with anticipation (rather than dulled with the dread a test often fosters).
- They can engage in improvisational role-play as characters from *Ant and Bee* or as members of the U.S. Supreme Court (or as delegates to the delectably named Diet of Worms).
- They can truly delve into a particular topic that interests (and might even come to fascinate) them by preparing a major project or "science fair" exhibit. It is even possible that such a project or exhibit might become, on your caring, enthusiastic watch, a tradition, one of the anticipated, remembered hallmarks of that particular school year.
- Additionally, one might encourage the creation of student portfolios, collections (often digitized) of student work from throughout the term or year, and the immediate, self-evident difference between these collections of student learning from the deficit orientation of most testing is as different as a hallelujah is from a ho-hum. In such portfolios—think of them as scrapbooks of student achievement and productivity—there is abundant opportunity to celebrate what has been mastered and what been produced.

Some of these forms of assessment are particularly timely if assigned just before major busy points in a teacher's year. For example, assigning a clever role-play in the week leading up to the end of the marking period enables the teacher to leave class each day *already* having graded and created rich notes in anticipation of preparing progress reports.

Beyond that, however, is the indisputable fact that recurrent, redundant test patterns challenge—and inevitably defeat—the same students in the same way. There are students who might suddenly come to look forward to a particular class if they understand that it isn't just going to represent an endless, dulling landscape of the same old same old. In fact, some of their unrecognized talents might have the chance to come into play. They might have the chance to succeed or even excel.

Tara was a student who loved history, prided herself on her capacity as an emergent historian, and thrived in classroom discussions, but because a learning difference precluded her from writing effectively, she floundered repeatedly in testing situations and, of course, on those long-term papers that comprised the other major component of her quarterly grade. She was likely on the brink of losing heart and giving up on seeing herself as a history student when she came upon Mr. Darlington, who peppered the year-long assignments with requests for historical maps, political cartoons, debates, and oral presentations. For once, Tara had a history teacher who understood the multidimensional growth of student cognition, who drew on talents and forms of expression other than writing, and who measured student growth that more fully accorded with understanding, passion, and a simple awareness that multiple intelligences exist.

...AND TESTING CAN DO SO MUCH MORE

What else is wrong with the testing picture?

Look at the tension and anxiety filling the room. It is common for teachers of young children to wonder where the wonder went. Somehow, over the years, the thrill of learning for learning's sake, the pride of mastery that comes to the young is supplanted by a dreaded fixation on grades. In the end, it doesn't matter how well we *think* we understood a chapter. If we've gotten a grade significantly lower—or significantly higher—than we expected, that's all that counts. It is foolish to blame all of it on testing, though it would be naïve to suggest that tests had no impact.

Consider the percentage of the year consumed in biweekly tests. In a course that typically meets five times per week, with a test every other Friday, we are actually sacrificing 10 percent of our available teaching time. Is such testing worth 10 percent of the school year?

Rather than even entertaining the question, let's consider a shift in the question: *how* can we make the assessment process worth the time invested? That opens up a far more enriching and creative spectrum of thought.

What can we do, therefore, to make the results of testing far more positive for our students?

On the first day of his mathematics class, Shiro Matsui spoke to the students and affirmed that the most important thing he hoped they would learn that year had nothing to do with mathematics. It would be how to learn from each other. He tried to help his students develop a sense of error analysis and understanding what a classmate didn't get. He required them to exchange phone numbers. He had them put difficult problems on the board while he stood to the side. They would point things out to each other and offer alternative ways of arriving at a solution.

When he presented them with their first simultaneous equations—two equations, each with two variables—instead of showing them the four ways that the book showed for solving them, he turned them loose in teams to see if they could find any of the solutions on their own. Invariably, thus charged and pridefully challenged to anticipate what they would have to learn, the students came up not only with the full four but with a fifth that the book hadn't even touched on. The experience was heady for them.

Matsui encouraged them to create the equivalent of a law school study group. Sometimes a cluster would even stay after school, cracking open the book and solving homework problems together in a kind of creative, social, laughing, and utterly focused manner. Instead of simply going along for the ride, they were able to hear each other's errors and missteps and even sense each other's thought processes and solution strategies. They didn't learn less from working together. They learned fabulously more from the experience.

What Matsui said that first day was true. The most important thing they learned was how to learn from each other and how to teach each other, but what he hadn't said that first day was equally true—that expanding the universe of possible teachers from him to the entirety of the class brought in a rich array of new explanations and understandings. And we all know—but often fail to fully utilize—the old saw that one of the surest ways to deepen our understanding of a concept is to teach it ourselves.

All of this is to underscore the potential unleashing power of a beautifully conceived and *precisely designed* (for there is almost nothing more common than a casually designed group project) collaborative assignment. If the process is designed and modeled for them early on, students can become extraordinary resources for each other in the classroom.

At heart, though, the real issue that renders current approaches to testing obsolete is the inexplicable imbalance between the abundance of time spent assessing student understanding and the equally inexplicable paucity of time actually making use of that information. At the end of even the most mundane form of assessment, a student presents his teacher with a kind of cognitive X-ray of his knowledge. After scanning the X-ray, the teacher typically tells the student—in bloody red pen—how many informational broken bones he has. There is almost never a follow-up—it's always time to move on to the next chapter. Those very teachers who have required the devotion of untold hours to capturing precise data on the state of each child's informational skeleton have, in almost every case, done so without the slightest intention of splinting or casting them or notating in their own grade books precisely which bones had minor cracks and which might have represented the intellectual equivalent of compound, through-the-skin shattered spiral fractures.

IN CONCLUSION

We are deeply hopeful—and hesitatingly confident—that the future of education will be transformed by the compelling power of individual assessment.

Assessments won't simply be designed to score how many things a student didn't understand. Assessments will be designed not only to elicit how many things a student didn't understand but to identify the nature of that misunderstanding. Teaching won't be about blithely going on to the next chapter but will focus, student by student, on analyzing and remediating those errors.

In the meantime, we live with schools where testing still looks backward, where errors are counted as percents wrong, and where teaching proceeds as if documented, incomplete understanding didn't compromise the very next lessons to come.

We do not need to abide by the limitations of the present.

We can notate individual misunderstandings and respond to them.

We can conduct swift follow-up even before we move on.

We can deal responsibly with the information that we ourselves have elicited and that each individual student has supplied.

Rather than simply number-crunching each student's detailed expression of what they understand and what they do not, we can make our classrooms laboratories for learning. Quiz more often, more briefly, more quickly. Respond more swiftly and urgently. Notate not the percentage wrong but the concepts wrong. And circle back around to ensure that students have a chance to learn before they compound the difficulty by knowingly layering misunderstanding upon misunderstanding.

There is a revolution on the educational horizon, one that will transform the use of assessment and vastly accelerate the speed and effectiveness of learning. We encourage you to become part of that revolution. Use assessments, not to learn about the past, but to chart a dramatically more effective course into the future.

Chapter 35

GRADES, FEEDBACK, AND COMMENT WRITING

We confess that this is one of the more miscellaneous chapters in the book, but so many issues arise from the process of correcting, grading, and providing feedback about each student that we felt none of these matters could reasonably be left out. That said, let's take a look at each.

GRADES

For some educators, the use of grades is a point of sharp controversy. For others, it is as routine as attendance. The purpose of this book is not to engage in the hoary debate about whether or not grades belong in schools. The issue we will address is how to give grades in a way that is most meaningful to our students.

If we are in a circumstance in which no grades are given, either because we teach young children or because we are in a school environment that doesn't use them, there are still issues about whether or not individual assignments—spelling tests, for example—should record the percent correct. In almost every case, there is a prevailing practice within the school or grade level. It is vitally important that all teachers new to the school familiarize themselves with school culture in this regard.

In a school setting without quarterly grades, it is almost invariable that written comments are a critical part of the communication with parents. While a teacher is perhaps liberated from the preoccupation with quantified scores (that previously mentioned 82 percent both conveys and fails to convey a great deal), there will almost inevitably be a requirement and expectation for dramatically greater communication.

For those of us not expected to give the equivalent of an 82 percent shorthand for the student's work in a given term, we must be prepared to speak more completely about the children and the nature of their progress—what they have accomplished and what they have begun to work on mastering. Keeping a log throughout the term, one with notations of high points, amusing moments, recurring difficulties, and specifics about projects and progress, will make our narrative comments dramatically easier to complete in the high-speed blur that accompanies the writing process at term's end.

Based on two lifetimes in education and countless observations of classrooms in action, the issue as to *whether or not* we grade is far less fundamental than *how* we grade. Yet the former seems to attract the controversy. Once a school embraces or accepts the necessity of giving grades, at least for students above a certain age, the debate tends to die. And truth be told, we tend to give and use grades much as our forebears did.

The conventional focus is to mark down from 100 percent—thus focusing students' attention on what they have missed. The opportunity to focus on what they have mastered, subtle as it may be, shifts the perspective from deficit to achievement.

The student who receives the aforementioned 82 percent is generally presented with a situation in which the 18 percent missed is given greater prominence than the 82 percent actually learned. After we have spent an entire period determining the precise nature of the student's weakness, we notate it as an 82 percent in a grade book and go blithely on to the next chapter, leaving the 18 percent in the student's cognitive wake.

How much better would it be if, instead of starting at 100 percent and counting down, we started and zero and counted *up*, marking *c*'s instead of *x*'s, highlighting concepts mastered rather than those misunderstood? How much better might it be for student learning if, as some farsighted educators do, we required some form of follow-through on those areas they have not yet mastered?

It seems like a highly questionable practice to take the time to elicit the precise misunderstandings of each student and then to do nothing with that information. At the very least, students should be required, as a subsequent assignment, to correct every problem missed until each one is, in fact, correct. In some cases, of course, this will result in the easy remediation of what are too often carelessly referred to as "careless errors"—a questionable designation, because most students *do* care and the use of that catch-all generic term shuts down our curiosity about what exactly led to each error. Dramatically important is the opportunity provided for the student to reconsult a text or to come to us for assistance in order to determine what caused the error. What would it feel like to lead a classroom in which students were regularly required to take the initiative to seek us out about those specific issues they hadn't yet mastered? Or to seek to understand their work and study habits more completely? Isn't that by definition an optimized learning environment?

The process of requiring such self-correction can emphatically build confidence. It is a process that finally makes sense of the fact that we conventionally spend so much time determining individual student misunderstanding and so little time addressing it.

Annotating Student Errors

Beyond the issue of what to do with errors, we humbly encourage educators to abandon the red pen. In this culture, at least, red is the color of danger, of stopping, of warning, of disaster, of emergency. Endless studies have demonstrated that human beings really do react differently to different colors.

Mightn't there be some subtly more positive—or at least less negative—optic/biological response if, instead of using the traditional hue "wrong red," we marked on papers and tests with, say, "peacock blue" or some shade of "victorious violet"?

INCENTIVES TO EXCEL

Depending on the culture prevailing at one's school, we seriously advocate providing bonus problems on tests. For those successful, aspiring students in each class, there is a sense, a possibility, an aspiration of actually exceeding the hundred-point ceiling. Alternatively, there is an opportunity to offset a dunderheaded error with an ingenious solution.

Bonus problems should be just what we imagine them to be—extra, complex applications of what we have focused on in class, implications of the more factual matters we have discussed, a chance to roll out a full, challenging sentence in Spanish that draws together not only the verbs from the latest chapter but the vocabulary and structure from the full scope of the year, some exponential form we mentioned one afternoon in passing as an elegant extrapolation, a challenge to the best and the brightest to make connections and *really* see the big picture of the work we have been doing together.

Bonus problems, if missed, should ideally not be counted wrong. They represent a kind of extra credit. We wouldn't hold a student's imperfect extra credit against him or her. Tackling a bonus problem may not yield successful results; however, it shouldn't be held against the student for trying.

WHEN GRADES ARE ALL THEY SEEM TO NOTICE

During the time that I taught high school English, I experienced the frustration common to many English and history teachers. I may have spent fifteen or twenty minutes carefully annotating, correcting, reinforcing, and suggesting improvements in each student's writing, yet when I handed the papers back, I watched in mute horror as the students flipped *past* my comments to the last page, where the grade was noted.

Consequently, I stopped putting the grades on their papers. They went in my grade book. The first time I did this, I was met with confounded outcries. I told them that if they really read the comments and reflected on their own effort and understanding, they would likely be able to determine their grade, but they were also each free to come to my office and find out what the grades were.

Probably 70 percent of the class came by that first time. There were a few wrinkled brows or raised eyebrows, but no one seemed genuinely taken aback. By the time I passed back the next paper, only 20 percent came by. After that, it was rare to see anyone in my office asking for his or her grade. They mostly knew exactly how they'd done.

And they no longer flipped past my written comments. They read them.

TURNING ISOLATED FEEDBACK INTO AN ONGOING DIALOGUE

It is particularly valuable—unless one has an almost photographic memory—to make brief notes in our grade books that transcend the mere B- notation. If we have tried to remind a student about the difference between *affect* and *effect*, if we have encouraged the use of more sensory adjectives, if we have scolded the student for failing to use any expected quotations from the book, it is vital that we notate this in our grade books and deftly refer to it as we look at subsequent assignments.

One teacher we know required student to hand in their work in a folder. Summary comments from each assignment were recorded directly in the folder, providing a clear reference for future use.

The student who has finally learned how to *affect* your perception of his or her work should expect to see the *effect* of this learning. The student who has provided particularly blistering adjectival detail in his or her next assignment should be congratulated for the follow-through. On the other hand, the student who has again failed to cite quotations should be addressed differently from the one who has failed to do so for the first time—perhaps even with a private conversation.

When students come to understand that we remember what we have written, they will undoubtedly respond more emphatically to our comments. They will likely come to believe that they are genuinely involved in an individualized dialogue with us about the growth of their writing.

ESTABLISHING WHAT MATTERS MOST

Whenever I marked a spelling error on a social studies assignment, my third graders almost invariably thought I had "cheated." This wasn't *spelling*. It was *social studies*. At their age, they were accustomed to see each subject as its own separate domain, but while much of their confusion might have been something they would eventually outgrow, the fact was that their frustration also reflected a small failure on my part.

If you are assigning a major opus—a project, a term paper, a presentation—it is important to define in advance how we will judge their success. How important is the quality of research? Will artwork truly matter or be seen simply as a sort of frivolous extra? Will it help a student's grade to use something like a PowerPoint presentation? Does neatness count? Does spelling?

Beyond the simple, apparent fairness of advance notice, such a proactive policy can dramatically channel student energies into those skill areas that we truly care about developing. If the quality of research is what we really hope to enhance, letting them know far in advance that 60 percent of their score will be based on this will cause a demonstrable shift in focus for the student who might otherwise have spent many an evening leading up to the deadline creating gilded graphics or glow-in-the-dark holograms of the actual moment when Marie Curie discovered the X-ray.

GRADING COOPERATIVE PROJECTS

One of most tender and controversial aspects of group projects is whether to give a single grade to each member of the team or to reward the child who really perseveres and honestly evaluate the student who follows passively in everyone else's slipstream.

We forewarn against the difficulties of assigning major group projects to be done at home. There are children who are occupied evenings and weekends. There are parents with many other offspring or jobs who simply don't have the time or ability to transport them. There are children who live far from the school neighborhood for whom transportation is a serious concern. There are children who deliberately make themselves unavailable in order to have the rest of the team carry their load.

As teachers in the classroom, we unfortunately have no real ability to distinguish one case from another. We have no ability to mediate such disputes, notably because other members of the team may honestly not know whether this little hiccup is just sloughing responsibility or whether his family's only car is (embarrassingly) inoperative.

Beyond this, we have given up perhaps the one most valuable thing we can bring to such projects—the ability to shape collaborative work. Children, particularly those who have been accustomed to solo schoolwork, can profit immensely from learning how to assign and accept roles, balance responsibilities, and resolve conflicts. In fact, one of the most compelling memories students have of group work, usually far more vivid than the subject of the project itself, is whether or not they got along. It is important for us to realize that what we have asked for is not only intellectual but richly, deeply social.

As to the decision to give everyone on a team the same grade ("It's your responsibility to get everyone to participate equally"), we think this is well-intentioned and wrong-headed. As teachers, we aren't even able to get everyone to participate equally. It is beyond the power and purview of any cluster of students to finally get La-Z-Boy to work as hard as they do.

How do we resolve this?

As one of the rubrics for success in the achievement of the project, have a clear category labeled "cooperation" or your own version thereof. We can thereby give a group grade for the finished project, while we differentiate between those who pursued the task with impressive energy and those who approached it with the enthusiasm of an elderly slug with a head cold.

MAKING COMMENT WRITING EASIER

It would be ideal if every teacher had the opportunity—and took full advantage of that opportunity—to write at greater length about the nature of the student's interaction with the learning process.

For each of us who considers a child's growth, the opportunity provided by comment writing—to encourage, to congratulate, and to set clear goals for the coming term—is one way we have to recruit the parents as allies and partners into the educational process.

If we are to work toward the reduction of stress during report writing season, one of the best things that we can do is to make our grade books more than a string of sequential grades. Providing oneself a little more room—even a separate grade book for each class section in cases where we teach multiple classes—can allow us to notate the fact that the student's "hero project" focused on Peter Pan, that the child had finally mastered his wayward tendencies as a "line leader," or that the child was *still* ignoring one's requests to show units with his work in geometry.

Even though it requires some investment of time throughout the term, such time tends to be less stressful than the last days before the deadline. Having such facts at hand can make the transcription of a student report vastly more efficient and informative.

In conclusion, the way we construct feedback creates an opportunity for dialogue with each student. Not withstanding the fact that we do have enormous amounts of material to grade each year, making small but well-reasoned changes in the way we provide student feedback can pay leveraged dividends in the value of the feedback, the chances for student follow-through, and our own sense of connection with these students.

Chapter 36

HOMEWORK: OVERVIEW

There are minefields; and then there are *minefields*.

The great debate over homework centers on whether or not homework is simply one more element in developing overstressed children in a culture that is already gasping from a chronic overdose of adrenaline. There is certainly good reason to monitor our children's stress level. At the same time, we would note that the very parents who complain about the amount of homework and blame the school for not allowing their children time to be kids are at least *sometimes* those same parents who have simultaneously enrolled little Pat in horse breeding, weight training, telepathy, conga, tango, and bongo lessons.

On the other side of this debate, it is difficult to see how teachers, particularly in the upper grades, can make any real progress in their coursework if students are not expected to read texts and novels or write papers and practice newly acquired skills anywhere but in the classroom. Those who recognize the relatively anemic academic standing of American schools in the family of nations might well ask if it furthers our country's long-term interests to cut back on what time students do spend on homework, specifically considering that few schools are in session even half of the number of days in the year.

Research has shown that one of the great strengths we can give our children is the gradual development of a compelling "work capacity" so that no student ever gets to high school or college or adulthood with an outcry of "Whoa! I wasn't ready for *this*!"

While it is not our intention to take sides, we acknowledge that there is value in such a debate; however, clarifying what is a reasonable amount of homework for a student of any particular age is likely going to be a hopelessly unsatisfying battle. That said, clear expectations are vital among students, among teachers, and among the parents.

Few of us are free to set our own standards and expectations regarding homework. **Anyone new to a school must explore—in considerable detail—the precise range of prescribed expectations within the school culture:**

- Is homework expected at my grade level?
- How much homework is expected each night?
- Is homework assigned over weekends?
- Is homework assigned over holidays and vacations?
- Is homework graded, and does it *count* toward term grades?
- Is there a prescribed policy for late homework or homework missing because the dog ate it, the computer froze, or the nursemaid sold it to Venusians?

We strongly (and earnestly) encourage you to clarify expectations in writing on that first day of school on the "expectations sheet." If you have in fact violated some long-standing covenant, it is better to know from the very beginning. Otherwise, it is vital that you establish your own covenants in writing, ideally with the knowledge of parents from that same very beginning (i.e., have the students bring the "expectations sheets" back the second day, signed by the parent).

Below are some fine points of assigning homework that we encourage you to take to heart. You may be the Elvis Presley of classroom management, the Oprah Winfrey of student empowerment, and the Liberace of candelabra'd bulletin boards, but the one aspect of your teaching that is most visible to parents is your assignment of homework. Give too much, give it too unclearly, give it without enough notice, give it without enough information, and the child's late-night panic attack may well be deservedly laid at your doorstep the next morning. And the Presley/Winfrey/Liberace persona that you are heralded for in the hallways will avail you little if you are seen on the homework front as the ruthless reincarnation of Attila the Hun.

ANNOUNCING HOMEWORK

This is a simple one, but the number of teachers who don't get this one is discouraging.

Don't just announce it. **Post it in writing *and* announce it.**

If you want the visual and the auditory students all to turn in homework, use both modalities. If you want the child who is insecure or simply conscientious to be able to come back to check before going home, write it down in the same inerasable corner of the board each day so that students can come back to double-check before they leave. In the case of students who might come in the next day claiming that you had only assigned pages 56 and 57, it can be an immediately effective argument-snapper to have it cleanly and clearly posted—right there, same place, next day—that you had, in fact, assigned *volumes* 56 and 57.

SUPPORTING HOMEWORK

Remember that homework is meant to be accomplished independently by the student. Be sure your instructions are clear and complete for each and every one of your students, hours after they have left your class for the day. Take time to go over it. Take time to answer questions.

Even better, at the beginning of the year share a written set of expectations with students and with their folks at Parents' Night. Take time to go over them all.

It isn't only that you'll likely get the kind of homework handed in that you want and expect, and it isn't only that you'll probably relieve student anxiety. It's that our responsibilities as teachers extend to teaching them *how* to do the homework we assign. Provide specific information and/or models of what we expect them to accomplish. Simply telling them that each child is expected to create an anatomically correct puff adder out of Cheez Doodles—or even something more recklessly ordinary, like crafting a sonnet with a prescribed rhyme scheme—by Thursday morning is likely not only to unleash a baritone outcry from the ranks of the sculpturally or poetically challenged. It is likely to enrage that parent who thrives on rage like a great white does on hapless Australian surfers.

Additionally, short-cutting homework instruction is tantamount to short-changing our own responsibilities as a teacher. Even as we assign such projects, we should hand out a chart with the physiology of a puff adder. We should model how to build one together. We should know which particular mucilage bonds best with tasty orange comestibles.

In the case of the poetry assignment, we should perhaps try to write one together. We should be sure that students understand rhyme schemes, and we should *certainly* be sure that they really go home understanding a sonnet structure.

In clarifying each assignment, however briefly, we can appease their insecurity, make sure that they understand the nature of the assignment, and improve the odds of their succeeding.

Be particularly careful to monitor the progress of longer-term projects with clearly defined checkpoints along the way.

Depending on the age of the students, be sure that the parents are aware of these intermediate deadlines, as well.

It is so common as to be almost a cliché that the child given two weeks to make fourteen recordings of the exact time the sun set will instead write down the time the sun set on the last day fourteen times or that little Hapless Harriet will begin burbling that she's just got to go to the library for the project at 10:15 on the night before the entire assignment was due. **So don't just bemoan human nature. Anticipate it. Accommodate it.**

Break *any* long-term assignment into discrete checkpoints. Do a careful task analysis of all the steps necessary to complete the assignment. Don't allow a student to get fourteen days behind. Have each one of them present their resources and their bibliography two days into the assignment, their note cards five days in, an outline of the paper after seven days, and a first draft after ten.

In further regard to long-term assignments, we have seen more than a few teachers who, while they apparently are giving the class fourteen generous days to complete an inventory of the family's drawer of shame, they are simultaneously continuing to give regular nightly homework throughout the period. While teachers might later claim that the students had fourteen plenty-of-time days during which to complete the assignment, everyone involved knows perfectly well that it's a classic case of educational double-booking.

Finally—and this is an area that is the subject of many a long debate—determine, publicize, and enforce whatever you intend to do about late homework assignments. (As before, first check to see if there is a school-wide, grade-level, or departmental policy that will take away your right to choose and relieve you of the need to stick your neck out on this most insufferable of educational debates.)

If you have some latitude in the decision, we would encourage you to consider the following: Depending on the assignment, the work may be of less value if it is less timely. In such cases, it is arguable to deduct one letter grade (or some variation) for each day late. Notably, this is not simply an issue between the teacher and Tiffany Tardy. If the rest of the students who *do* get the assignment in on time receive no relative benefit for having done so, the urgency of your deadlines, however much you may sermonize about them, will almost certainly begin to recede.

Significantly, if we are trying to build a work ethic that truly adheres to deadlines, there is a downside in even building in "late" options. The moment we declare a late policy like the one mentioned previously, we are tacitly *allowing* late assignments.

While it is up to each teacher, the policies that we have seen to be most effective have been those that impose a serious penalty for lateness (even a whole letter grade per day) but that still require the completion of the assignment. In the end, as one begins to mature as a classroom manager, the real consequence for Nematode's turning in a late assignment (in addition to any quantifiable penalty) should be the disconcerting, uncomfortable fact that she has let both the teacher and herself down. This kind of consequential unease will almost certainly require a dedicated moment when the student experiences your personal surprise and disappointment that someone of such potential and talent has let herself down.

Depending on the age of your students and the culture of your particular school, homework may well be an integral part of the learning process. Far too many teachers take a passive approach to homework when, in fact, a fundamental part of our roles as teacher is teaching students to *learn how to learn*. Setting up clear guidelines, deadlines, and structures for at-home assignments can vastly reduce student anxiety, as well as parental second-guessing.

Chapter 37

HOMEWORK: COLLECTING IT

Regardless of the age of your students, it is important to have a standard procedure for handing in homework at the beginning of each class. Why?

- Routines that open a class period have a focusing effect that is beneficial. Let students leave their gossip, their flirtations, and their rivalries in the hall. From the moment they enter your classroom—even if you are late or busy talking to an individual student—they should know what is expected.

- Procedures that are automatic consume much less time than those that must be improvised on a daily basis.

- Students who know that they must have the homework out at the beginning of class may even pack materials differently the night before and thus cut out the distracting disemboweling of their backpacks when everyone else is trying to focus.

It is even beneficial to make use of the moments when students are turning in homework to ask them questions: How did it go? How long did it take? How hard did they find it? If students were particularly frustrated by how long the homework took or how impossible they found it, it is important to allow them an opportunity to express this frustration. If a number were truly stymied by a particular assignment, it will be advantageous—if not necessary—to open the period differently, with a reiteration of the lessons underlying the homework.

WHAT KIND OF PROCEDURE IS RECOMMENDED FOR COLLECTING HOMEWORK?

The process of collecting homework depends on the process for correcting the homework. If you expect to grade it yourself, having a bin or basket for each section you teach can be helpful and handy. Notably, if you have difficulty with a student "forgetting" to do the assignment or insisting that he's sure he handed last Thursday's assignment in, it's better to do a quick roll call. "Annabelle." Annabelle rises and puts her paper in the bin. "Antony." Antony does the same. Quickly. Efficiently. Anyone without a homework has to explain why on the spot.

If you want students to grade their own homework, you should emphasize that as part of the swift and invariable opening routine, they are absolutely to have it glistening on their desk at the beginning of class. I have a rule in my class that students are forbidden to talk until they have their homework out from the moment they enter the room.

Some teachers want to *see* a particular assignment and are content to give it a quick once-over. To do this, they generally give students an issue to write about in their journal or a few problems to solve at the beginning of class. While students are working on these, the teacher walks methodically about the room with the grade book open. The teacher swiftly reviews each student's homework, makes any comments or points out any significant errors (or highlights anything worthy of commendations), and makes a brief check, check-plus, check-minus (or zero) notation.

Some teachers prefer to have students check their own homework assignments. This can be problematic if students are inclined to "cheat" or ignore their own errors, but if you are able to set up—ideally from the first day of school—a regimen that underscores the importance of *learning* (and the practical inevitability of tests), students will be encouraged to grade their work honestly and will be motivated to question why answers were wrong or how a correct answer was derived.

To accomplish this process, teachers can either read out the right answers or, better yet, have the answers immediately visible with the use of an overhead, a projected computer screen, or a piece of poster paper with the answers written in felt marker.

Some teachers have students correct each other's work. While this can be the most sensitive means of correcting homework, it is actually the one I prefer, depending on the age of the students and the culture of the school. I prefer it because correcting homework at the very beginning of class provides all of us with immediate feedback on how well they understood the previous night's homework. If everyone assumed that they understood it—and they didn't—then I'm prevented from compounding the difficulty by teaching blithely onward. I can stop and review and course-correct *before* I start on the introduction of the day's new challenge.

I also believe that students are more likely to be accurate and objective in grading each other's homework than they would be grading their own. The papers are scored and handed back to the student. As I read quickly through the roll book, the students tell me their scores.

But you may ask the following: Aren't kids embarrassed or humiliated when they do poorly? Sometimes, yes. When this procedure is established on the very first day of school, however, I underscore—in no uncertain terms—that we play together as a team, that there is *never* to be cruelty or mockery of another student, and that any student who has a question about a homework grade or is simply shy about announcing their score can come up at the end of class and tell me privately. Such a process is certainly not the only possible solution. It does take some genuine control. It does take some well-established mutual respect within the culture of the class. It does take a willingness to keep an eye out for even the slightest snicker. But it is quick, efficient, and objective, and it truly can prevent all of us from moving to the division of fractions if we discover at the very beginning of class that they completely bollixed the multiplication of fractions.

Like so many classroom procedures, making them transparent and routine from the very first day can create an environment in which expectations are clear and time spent on "housekeeping" details is at a minimum. The collection of homework should certainly be at the forefront of such procedures.

Chapter 38

HOMEWORK: CORRECTING IT

The teacher who has gone into education because of the prospect of correcting homework is probably a rarity. Sitting before a pile of math quizzes, Latin tests, or narratives on the development of the fur trade in early French Canada may not be the most inspiring moment in our teaching years. And yet, if we look upon the task as part of the teaching process, as another stage in an evolving dialogue with our students—and if we are savvy about how to avoid wasting our own time and energy—it will prove to be far less of a burden than it might otherwise have been.

The fact is that some teachers spend far too long correcting homework, and the fact is, too, that the longer it takes to return homework to the student, the less meaningful any feedback will be. In this chapter, we focus on the turnaround of homework that has been handed in, with an emphasis on the **speed**, **relevance**, and **effectiveness** of feedback delivered to the student.

Skim each homework page to get an overview.

If it's a paper, a workbook sheet, or a math assignment, give it a three-second once-over before you begin to plow into the details. Take a moment to reflect on its appearance and the student who turned it in. How are they doing? How does this homework appear to compare to those in the past? Regardless of the specific grade you will eventually give this specific assignment, have they started slipping? Have they begun to try harder? Take a moment to reflect on the larger picture of this student's progress and incorporate it into whatever you will scrawl on the paper or say to the child privately the next day in class.

Limit your time.

Be conscious of the need—and your right—to limit the amount of time you spend correcting each homework assignment.

While we emphatically don't want to see English teachers dismissing and undercutting the vital role they can play in improving each student's writing skills, we also recognize that there are times when we might view the stack of freshly minted papers with a certain dyspepsia. Such dyspepsia can lead to avoidance, procrastination, or only the most cursory and inconsistent reading of homework assignments. It is vital to find a way to approach the correcting of assignments that is efficient and effective. In fact, it can be much more positive to think of yourself as "responding to" students' work than as simply "correcting" students' work. It puts a very different, less negative spin on it. Finally, as a further practical tip, teachers who teach several different courses tend to find the pace and workload most manageable if they intentionally stagger the assignments.

Don't mark everything you notice.

Our audacious, almost treasonous inclination is to tell you not to mark everything you notice. If it's a history paper, avoid marking every spelling error. If it's French homework, we suggest that you not correct every *accent grave*. Avoid the buckshot approach, and in so doing, choose the particular issue that is most critical or chronic. Focusing on everything can overwhelm student learning. The real point in checking over an assignment is to guide that learning. Stay focused on the central point of any lesson for the sake of sharpening student self-correction *and* for the sake of your own time.

You might think, *Then how are they going to learn? Aren't we advocating a kind of educational laziness?* In response, we would ask the following: How many of us have watched students look at an assignment as it is handed back? How much time do they spend going over it? If they spend *far* less time reviewing it than we spent grading it, then something is clearly out of balance. Either students should be expected to make corrections—and thereby really have to understand and address what they missed—or we should be narrowing our focus as we grade.

Certainly, it makes sense to respond to major errors, but by focusing primarily on one particular aspect—the agreement of subject and verb, the vitality of adjectives, the ability to effectively compare and contrast—we are able to throw into effective relief what the student should be most focused on to make real progress. Documenting five completely different types of errors likely will yield a less energetic, less focused response than pointing out several examples of the same type of error.

We are not, after all, correcting papers for some end-of-the-world perfection contest. We are correcting papers to provide students with **meaningful feedback for improvement.** And we suggest that limiting the scope of one's feedback and really focusing strongly on one major skill area in an assignment will provide greater likelihood that the student will notice and internalize the point.

We also note that if you correct everyone's assignment with an eye to the same issue, as you hand them back, you have a perfect opportunity to review the key concept in a mini-lesson while students look over their work. This is a particularly valuable way to emphasize the importance of a skill and to reinforce its technique.

Try to find one thing to praise in each assignment.

Note a terrific turn of phrase, a rhyme or rhythm that works particularly well, a whole translated sentence without a mistake, or a particularly neatly presented solution.

"Fabulous phrase!"

"Whoa! Persuasively presented!"

"I love your word choices, Bartholomew!"

Like all praise, this creates a positive tone.

If at *all* possible, give them something to look forward to. Students who expect only to see errors marked on a paper are inclined to give only cursory attention to the corrections.

Most importantly, praise highlights success and provides the student with a self-made model of their work at its best.

For too many teachers, correcting homework becomes a one-dimensional taste of drudgery. Effectively and efficiently responding to homework can have a profound impact on our time and private lives. Beyond that, it can create a vitalizing dialogue with our students that can subtly transform that drudgery into the human connections that underlie successful and meaningful relationships within the class and within our lives as teachers.

Chapter 39

WRITING NARRATIVE COMMENTS: SIX CRITICAL RECOMMENDATIONS

Perhaps we are simply duty-bound Pollyannas, but we are of the view that writing comments can afford each of us an unprecedented opportunity to sense the progress of each child. Those of us who routinely teach 156 students in the course of a week are unlikely to experience 156 sky-clearing revelations, but if we are determined and conscientious in our approach to this responsibility, we will undoubtedly come to see a number of our students in a new light. There will be those who have traversed the preceding marking period with quietly deteriorating grades—whose decline we may not have noticed until this summative moment. By the same token, there are very likely students who have put together a string of successes—or at least significant improvements—that just as keenly warrant our attention.

This can be a time to expand our awareness of certain unnoticed students in our class. This can be a time to create a set of internal resolutions. ("Congratulate Tommy personally on the turnaround." "Follow through with little Mayhem on why his homework is always missing on Thursday mornings." "Speak to Marla immediately about the pattern of late long-term assignments so that she and I can track her progress more carefully on the history of the universe paper due next Tuesday.")

Finally, this can be a time for sharing information and building partnerships with parents. While it is clear there are parents—particularly those of our most discouraged students—who seem to be detached from their child's progress in school, it is vital to undertake the writing of each and every comment with the same conviction. Speaking as parents ourselves, we can aver what is true for the overwhelming majority of parents—that **comments individually written by the teacher about their child likely constitute the most important mail they receive all year long.**

That said, there are clear recommendations that can ensure that these comments have the intended impact and produce the positive results that justify the time and thought invested in them:

1. Begin with something positive.

At the very least, even if the child is rarely in class, even if the child has been placed in Mandarin IV without ever having taken any other Mandarin courses before, and even if it has been clinically confirmed that the child's IQ really *is* negative, we dare to suggest that it is still possible to begin your comments with a positive. Only through such positives are we likely to engage any lingering hope on the part of the child and parent.

- "While Odysseus has rarely shown up for class this year, we do continue to believe that he has considerable potential in this course."
- "While Clytemnestra is too often engaged in distracting conversation with her good friend Aegisthus, I am hoping that the new seating arrange-ment—with their thrones now across the room from each other—will result in our seeing the kind of dedicated progress of which we know her to be capable."
- "It is clear that Siren has a lovely, almost irresistibly beautiful voice. It is my hope that in the next term in choral music, she will focus her attentions less on an imagined audience of wayward sailors and more on the tempo and tonality prescribed by the choral director."

Beginning with a positive may seem obvious, but often we forget. No matter how difficult the marking period that is just ending, at least one can point across the gap between production and potential, highlighting the perpetually positive possibility, however mythical it might at times appear. It is a means of creating hope and dialogue rather than simply delivering what may otherwise be experienced as an alienating condemnation.

2. Do not draw conclusions.

Instead, spell out the details actually observed.

Powerfully negative judgments are best left off of any student report. As we have noted elsewhere, it is potentially damaging to attribute an unseen cause to an observed outcome.

For example, many well-meaning teachers would urge a student who seems to understand the material but who consistently underperforms on tests to simply "study harder." It is far better to describe the phenomenon observed ("Her test scores—64, 81, 68, 72, and 56—appear to reflect little of the natural historian we see so fully and insightfully engaged in our classroom discussions.") Let the parent muse on possible causes, and if it is a serious enough situation, once the parent has been alerted, communicate and see if together it is possible to put together a hypothesis and a set of shared solution steps.

3. Comment on everything, not just academics.

Particularly if you are a lower school teacher or someone who is the child's primary teacher, provide yourself with a thoughtful checklist of all of the domains of a child's interactions during the day, not only the academic but the social, behavioral, personal, creative, and extracurricular.

Parents of children are often hungry to know whether the child's woeful complaint that they don't have any friends is really true. They want to know if you, as a presumed expert on child development, really see any of the child's inherent artistic or altruistic qualities. It can provide balance in a report concerned with academic progress to begin with an example of the richness of the child's thoughtfulness, generosity, or imagination.

No, you don't need to be a trained psychologist to share anecdotes and reflections on these more personal aspects of a child's development—no more than one needs a degree in psychology to be a warm and supportive adviser. We are the primary representatives of the outside world, and even in our first year, because we can be objective and we have a normative group within which to see the child, we are relative experts in the field of education. This is not to argue for psychoanalyzing a student or pontificating to a parent. It is to suggest that most parents are hungry to hear about how their child is doing, and you will earn great, genuine credit toward any prospective partnership if you identify some particular positive about the child.

4. Be specific.

Instead of "disappointing record on homework assignments," list each of the scores, or at least document the average. Describe precisely how many out of how many were turned in late. When numbers are available, don't replace them with adjectives. Where there are statistics available, use them.

Guide parental support and supervision by **being specific** in describing successes and deficiencies. "She earned a 71 percent on the April project. I hope she does better on the next one." This statement is likely to elicit nothing more than a concerned, confused frown from a parent. What if you said this instead? "Because she turned in the project on serotonin reuptake inhibitors two weeks late and because she appeared to have done none of the required experiments on the depressed meal worm she had been given, Raquel earned only a 71 percent on her recent project. In anticipation of her upcoming oral report on hysterical laryngitis, I will be sending home a step-by-step set of deadlines and expectations. I hope together we can create a partnership that is successfully supportive for her. She clearly has considerable gifts in the field of molecular pharmacology for someone still in second grade."

Be *just* as specific about raves. "Did a great job on" may feel good, but it is almost impossible to reproduce. Instead, by focusing on the specifics of what was successful, that success is dramatically more likely to be reproduced and even expanded upon. Instead try these: "His attention to sensory description made me feel like I was really there in the helicopter along with him." "Jean-Claude's recent decision to use graph paper for his math tests has enabled him to align his columns of addition so well that he showed measurable improvement on the final exam." "Her ability to yodel while suspended from the rafters of the theater caused everyone else in the drama class involuntarily to echo her cries."

5. Say how to improve.

Focus just as much on the specifics of *how to improve* as on the specifics of what needs improvement. Saying that "Cheryl's painstakingly crafted catamaran went down during a hurricane in the South Atlantic because she had fashioned the hull out of toilet tissue, which was not on the approved list of materials" is significantly detailed and provides guidance as to what went wrong. Adding "For the upcoming Warp Drive Galaxy Cruiser Project, I will require her to bring in her design along with samples of the materials she intends to use in order for the vehicle to exceed light speed" can reassure the parents that you are on the case, can confirm that you are not giving up on their child, and can alert them to undertake their own inquiry about acceptable materials.

The most effective partnership we can make on behalf of a child is most often with the parents. There may be no more effective way of achieving that partnership than through the construction of thoughtful and responsive communication channels with the home.

6. Never surprise a parent with a comment.

Finally, we underscore what needs to become an enduring vigilance: Unless something major has genuinely occurred within hours of the comment writing deadline, **parents should never hear about a major concern for the first time in a written comment.**

No matter how difficult the student, no matter how intractable the problem, no matter how demonstrably disengaged the parent, we owe it to that parent, we owe it to the student, we owe it to ourselves to provide "fair warning" to parents of any significant decline in a student's performance.

For the overwhelming majority of parents, what we have to say is some of the most significant information they receive all year long, yet we owe even the most apparently disengaged parent timely information, because no matter how unresponsive they may appear, we must always assume that what we say matters.

We owe it to the student, because if we begin to give up on the children in our charge, we no longer belong in the classroom.

And we owe it to ourselves to provide "fair warning," because otherwise if parents first learn of a significant decline four weeks after it began, we have prevented the parents from doing what they could to turn the situation around. By failing to give fair warning, we sell the parents short, and we leave ourselves open to responsibility for insufficient communication and even for the depth and duration of the child's decline to some extent.

Give fair warning, and set yourself an ironclad rule: Even if it requires you to make a sudden call halfway through writing the comment, never hide crucial information about a downturn, and never let that information first be delivered via a written comment.

Written comments about a child can be a deeply personal means of communicating with the family and with the child. They can be used both to assess progress to date and to establish goals for the coming term. As such, they have enormous potential power—to fault or to congratulate past performances, to set out priorities for the days ahead, and to establish deep and meaningful connections with the child and his or her family.

Chapter 40

EFFECTIVELY MANAGING PARENT CONFERENCE DAY

Each school will have its own routines for handling parent-teacher conferences. Some are carefully orchestrated and beautifully documented. We have also visited schools in which parents rush up and down stairwells to beat each other to sign-up sheets. We have seen schools in which each family is provided with a full half-hour of private time with an individual teacher. We have seen schools in which there is a photocopied sign on the door stating "Kindly confine your conference to three minutes"—and the discussion is held with the next families sitting right there, able to listen and ready to clear their throats and pounce the moment the three minutes *are* up.

Parent conferences offer the greatest, planned opportunity in the course of a school year to get to know a family and to communicate with them about their child. The importance of that communication can lead to tension and enduring mistrust, especially when a delicate situation is mishandled; but when that communication, however difficult, is handled with professionalism, care, and expertise, new frontiers can open for a previously deadlocked child.

Creating a successful parent conference day requires that we go far beyond gathering up a grade book and having the schedule of meetings ready. It encompasses everything from a genuine awareness of the sensitivity of parents to the advantages of speaking with teachers from the students' past. It necessitates that we have something positive to open with about each and every child, that we have done our homework about possible testing, tutoring, and therapy (so that we don't open our mouths only to put our foot squarely inside it), and that we have identified the principal themes we hope to address in the course of a brief and vital interchange.

Those who underestimate the power of these conferences will likely get far less from them than those who invest time and thought into each meeting. Beyond that, those who underestimate their importance may be setting themselves up for a day that is both unproductive and potentially problematic.

No day likely has higher stakes for your self-esteem, and no day likely has more potential to build partnerships with the families of each child in your class. Enter the room and open each meeting with a conviction that today will make a positive difference in the lives of many of the children you teach. Begin with a smile. Open with genuine, deserved praise. Touch on the issues that matter. Listen warmly and closely for what is said and for what lingers in the undercurrents of subtext. Conclude with a handshake and a smile and, if recommended or required, follow through.

You are building and deepening a partnership on behalf of each child that you teach. Almost nothing in your professional life is more important than that.

BEFORE CONFERENCE DAY

- Recognize that conference day can be one of the more emotionally grueling experiences in any school year. While most conferences end with a relatively neutral or upbeat sense of partnership, those few that go badly can prove exhausting. Husband your energy and equanimity as much as possible in anticipation of the day.
- Be prepared. Have your grade book there at hand (although not so visible that a parent can see that *neither* of the Clodhopper twins has ever gotten a grade above a 58 percent).
- Be prepared, particularly for the hard cases you may have to encounter.

Have an index card with points to make, ready to pull out when those particular parents arrive.

- Be prepared. If possible, have samples of the child's work—either in a portfolio format as a saved assignment or as part of a bulletin board display. Specifics and examples are dramatically more effective in bringing a point home than trying to find just the right adjective.
- Be prepared. Some teachers who teach five fairly crowded sections will have 165 potential conferences, each family arriving whenever it happens to arrive. Others will have an orderly, scheduled set of twenty-two. While the process of preparation will be different, it is important to have papers and examples of student work well organized in advance. If you have a small number of conferences, it may be possible to have a folder of each student's work samples. If you have unseen hordes of parents waiting for you, having sample assignments in an alphabetized folder will allow you to find each child's folder quickly.

ON CONFERENCE DAY

- Have your materials at the ready. Be certain that no parent can see the grades or notes regarding any other student or family.
- Review any instances in which you had promised to get back to a family with follow-up information on the progress of a particular student.
- Plan (and preserve) break time. It is not uncommon for the terminally generous or the terminally disorganized teacher to talk clear through whatever break time might have initially been available. Worn nerves and distended bladders are not ideal anatomical precedents for the *next* battery of conferences.

AT THE BEGINNING OF EACH CONFERENCE

- Begin on time. This will require that you are strict and scrupulous about *ending* each conference on time. Be conscious that getting off from work to attend a conference is a deeply important ritual for many parents, but they may feel pressured to get back to work in a timely fashion. Having them wait even ten minutes fretting about their boss (or child care) before starting the conference can cause the conference to get off to an unnecessarily brittle start.

- Stand briefly and shake hands, using warm and welcoming eye contact. Parents recognize that you are seeing many different families on this day. Let your initial body language say that each child and each family deserves (and gets) your undivided attention.

- Begin with something positive. Make it genuine, make it warm, and provide a specific example. "He is such a nice boy" will feel nice and is undoubtedly a better entry point than "He is a scoundrel vilified by anyone who cares about the future of humanity," but "He is such a nice boy. He was the only one who suggested we have a New Orleans–style funeral procession in honor of the late, lamented Class Guppy" is significantly more telling, more repeatable to the child afterward, and more likely to induce tender tears of parental pride.

- If there are difficulties that must be addressed, then begin with the simple, serviceable, "I need your help." This is respectful. It provides a token of fair warning that something less positive is going to be broached. At the same time, it asks for a kind of partnership, a kind of shared solution. "I need your help. Over the course of the past week, Fred keeps getting up from his chair and doing the 'Curly Shuffle' whenever I say the word 'Antarctica.' Much as I adore the *Three Stooges*—how can anyone fault a trio that finds such rich social commentary in a food fight?—because we're going to be studying that marvelous, frozen, almost tourist-free continent where it's so cold even bacteria can't live (thus making the common cold all but unheard of) for quite a while, I'd like to see if together we might find some way of restraining his enthusiasm for the 'greatest entertainer of our time' until, say, recess."

DURING EACH CONFERENCE

- Be conscious of time.
- Don't dawdle before getting to the "hard" issues, if there are any. They will certainly take some time to work through for most families.

- Share specific examples of work or of behavior.
- Smile. True, it may seem incongruous to smile while you tell the parents about a sequence of crimes and misdemeanors (In such cases, simply warming the eye contact can be sufficient.) In all other cases, however, smile. Research demonstrates again and again that smiling *does*, like sugar, help the medicine go down, and smiling even jump-starts our own serotonin levels.

TOWARD THE END OF EACH CONFERENCE

- When the conference is just about to conclude, have a fairly standard wrap-up line. "Thank you for coming in." Stand up. "Let's keep in close touch. I really care about making this a great year for her."
- Shake hands. Give a warm smile.
- If follow-up steps were promised, note them in scarlet letters somewhere on your calendar. Chances are this will be a day with an unprecedented number of distractions and things to remember. Keep track of each as they come up.
- If the conference ended badly, be quick and cool about informing your supervisor. As we will discuss later in the book about dealing with a difficult parent, there is good reason that you be the one to inform your supervisor even when you most ardently hope he or she will never hear about the trouble. Leaving a supervisor to be blindsided by a parent is a disservice not soon forgotten. For almost all of us, the more practical angle is that the first version we hear of a tale provides the framework for that tale. The second version merely gets to edit the first. Go directly to your supervisor—no hemming, no hawing. Report it as coolly as possible. "I just thought you should know. The Pancreas family conference didn't go very well, and I didn't want you to be caught unprepared if the parents come in to see you." Go into whatever detail is necessary. Try to learn from the experience, and when sufficient time has passed to allow for a fresh perspective, replay the incident and find out what you might have done differently.

AT THE END OF CONFERENCE DAY

- Shake your own hand. Give yourself a groggy, goofy grin in the mirror. You made it. You probably even did some good for some kids. Go home.
- If there *was* anyone who came in and really laid you low, *don't* go home to an empty house. You have been through a long and trying day. Your resiliency is probably at some low ebb. Unless you are the sort who can go home and truly leave work behind, find someone to talk to about whatever you are feeling. Over the years, we have come to the inescapable conclusion that isolation is the most fertile growth medium for anxiety, regret, and paranoia. Find a confidante—even if it is only your perpetually bewildered dog. You deserve to feel okay about the day and good about the year.

As with narrative comments, parent conferences provide a rich and fertile opportunity to communicate your concerns, your recommendations, and your caring. Because of the extremely personal nature of the exchange, there are necessarily potential pitfalls and cautionary warnings one must heed, but having heeded them, one can look forward to parent conference day as one of the most positive and productive exchanges of the year.

PART 5

Beyond the Classroom

Chapter 41

YOUR TIME, YOUR LIFE

In Ernest Hemingway's *The Old Man and the Sea*, an aging fisherman catches a huge fish far out at sea—perhaps the trophy of his life. He marvels at its size and even allows himself to marvel at what a gift this great thing is.

All the way home, riding in the boat alone with the great fish strapped alongside, he is forced to fight off the countless predators, the smaller carnivorous fish who come to take pieces of his prize for their own consumption. His battle is noble and heartfelt and futile.

By the time he reaches shore, there is little left of the great fish that was so recently the prize of his life.

In our lives, we are given the gift—or so it would seem—of time, of afternoons, of days, of seasons and years, in bumper-crop abundance. There are periods when there almost seems to be too much time, and we are bored, listless in the lolling, directionless craft of our lives.

There is a reason that the hero in the Hemingway tale is old. He has the perspective needed to recognize that time is finite. This single, brilliant narrative reveals the fate of each of us. What once seemed like the gift of life itself—time—is eaten away, is consumed, is helplessly lost as we look on. By the time each of us reaches that final shore of our own lives, we may begin to realize how much has been lost along the way.

Why are we waxing philosophical in the course of a book on classroom leadership?

Because we deeply believe—and we passionately care—that those of us who devote ourselves to the young make the most of our own lives. The great teacher is one whose life can become interwoven with his or her work and students ever after.

To the committed teacher, reflections on the day and resolutions for the morrow can linger, as if he or she were part of some perpetually unfolding drama in which the characters are real and the lives they lead are susceptible to private pain and personal triumph.

All of us who have come to care about our students and our colleagues and even our schools know that there is quicksand potential in our commitment to our jobs. Until three o'clock, we are giving ourselves to our students, to the photocopy machine, to conferences about the child with the cancer-stricken father, and after three o'clock—often long after—we are still similarly occupied, grading papers, writing tests, drafting lesson plans.

We can come to feel the stress of an overstretched life. We can lose touch with the potential to honor, to inspire, to recognize. We can doubt that the marginal salary we earn is worth the toll taken. Perhaps it would be better if our jobs had less meaning, and ended at quitting time.

If we lose hold of the one best thing we have to offer our students—our own best energy—it will be easy and almost inevitable to question where we are going or what happened to our own needs, dreams, and desires.

Because teaching can be immensely time-consuming, those who leave religiously at three o'clock, without work to take home, are almost certainly reducing the potential of education to little more than a job, and those who too often finally finish correcting papers and planning the next day well into the darkness are almost certainly doing so at the cost of their own depleted energies.

The focus of this chapter goes beyond the issue of teaching in the classroom. There have been times in my own life when I found myself working until the wee hours on lesson plans and the like, when I suddenly looked up and realized that I had gotten into the habit of investing so much time in my career that I had lost track of my interest in painting, of my most important friends, of the larger meaning of my life. I was spending excessive, exacting time in the minutia of teaching while my own more personal life was passing me by.

I don't say this to encourage educators to reduce their calling and their career to the containable, humdrum status of a *job*. I say this because we are at our best in the classroom, we are at our most open and supportive with our students when our own lives feel rich. It is hard—at least for me—to feel the generosity of energy and spirit that can guide great teaching when we are feeling impoverished ourselves.

It is too easy for almost all of us to slide on the slippery surface of the day-after-day, unable to find purchase, to establish a foothold, to experience our own passing lives and to stake out a fresh sense of direction and purpose. When we reach out to sow those personal fields left too long fallow, we may come to realize a harvest whose bounty is not at the *expense* of education. Instead, through our own, enhanced satisfaction, through this sense of rediscovered richness, we can attune ourselves to the creative, life-size energies that almost certainly represent ourselves at our very best.

One of the great, vestigial gifts of the teaching profession (at least in most parts of the country) is that its roots arise from deep in the soils of an agrarian society—a society that required the children to stay home to help with the tilling and the reaping of those amber waves of grain. Because of that tradition, even though it has become little more than quaintly coincidental in the vast majority of urban and suburban settings, we continue to have a large chunk of our summers off.

For a time, I worked in publishing. Of all the perquisites available to us as teachers, the one that I missed most deeply and personally wasn't the prospect of long and recurrent vacations but the fact that in most professions like publishing, there never really is such a thing as the beginning of a new year.

There is no time set aside when the entire organization stands down, regenerates, and is challenged to dream anew with genuine determination and fresh imagination. For those of us who work in most American schools, the summer stands as a time for genuinely making new year's resolutions.

The lawyers and bankers and hedge fund managers who pull down astronomical salaries undoubtedly may have a massive financial advantage over the rest of us, but we all have the same amount of time.

We have, through the generous fluke of our agricultural past, moved into a profession that can inspire us to dream and to live with our jobs—and maybe beyond our jobs. That said, the richer we find our outside lives, the more energized our teaching will be.

In this high-demand, fast-paced culture, what is important seems always to play a sleepy, unnoticed second fiddle to the mad and riveting violin of what is urgent. It is imperative that we begin to listen to what is important more than to what is urgent, for therein lies the richness of our lives and the health and wealth of our energies as a professional.

We have a gift. In fact, we have two gifts: the time we have to live, and the time with which to reflect, to imagine new possibilities and priorities, and to plan what we do with the time we are given.

Because this—right now—is the time of our lives.

Chapter 42

HOW TO ESTABLISH A GOOD RELATIONSHIP WITH YOUR SUPERVISOR

Of all the aspects of life related to our role as teachers, perhaps little has more to do with our self-esteem and sense of identity than our relationship with those who supervise us.

Sometimes, a story can remind you of the way it never should be.

I was halfway through the very first morning of my very first year as a teacher. I was teaching third grade in New York City, and I had followed the sage advice of my lower school principal, which was to vastly overplan that first day so that I wouldn't come upon a dead space with forty minutes to go.

In fact, until that point, the morning had gone remarkably well. I had welcomed a somewhat anxious group of young roustabouts, many of them a little wide-eyed at the prospect of their first male teacher. We had talked and gotten to know each other. I had laid down the law, although not with the structured expectations I would come to use as a foundation of every first day in the years to follow.

The school offered its students a midmorning snack in each classroom—orange juice and graham crackers—and I was contentedly sipping at my little paper cup, looking out over my charges with a certain wonder and bemusement. With a suddenness and violence that left us all a little bug-eyed, the windowed door into the classroom was flung open so vigorously that it smashed into the wall behind it. In strode the school's assistant principal. Without so much as a glance in my direction, he crossed the length of the classroom in five strides infused with fisted righteous indignation. He flung up the desktop of anxious, little Tommy Trembles, thin as a twig and buck-toothed as a gopher, and from within the depths of that desk, he victoriously brandished the graham cracker found inside.

"They'll do this, you know," he snarled to me with a look of menacing warning.

With just as little ceremony, he strode across the room, flung the graham cracker into the wastebasket, and slammed the door behind him.

Now, first of all, it should be noted that I had never met the man before. I would also note that even after I had eventually come to spend six years at the school, I knew of no rule that prevented a little nine-year-old student from squirreling away a graham cracker for when he came down with a case of the midafternoon munchies. Beyond that, this assistant principal certainly knew that I was a new teacher and that I was probably working to create a certain atmosphere within this, my first class. Nonetheless, he chose to launch an overt (not to say somewhat bizarre) invasion of territory that the students and I were somewhat nervously trying to establish as our own.

Whatever mood I had succeeded in creating, whatever warm bonds I had tried to instill in these impressionable young students had, for no supportable reason, been shattered. The students gnawed nervously at their graham crackers like badly frightened gerbils, and crackerless little Tommy Trembles looked as if he had just taken a round of buckshot in the hind quarters and would never be the same.

It is unfortunately true that what we all suspect is actually true. There are some achingly poor supervisors out there. In response, we are inclined to share a simple "Get used to it, and get over it." We're also inclined to say that it may be wise to think of moving on at some point.

There are also outstanding leaders out there. There are supervisors who can mentor, console, inspire, and support you as you learn and grow throughout your career.

Walter Birge was the principal (*not* the assistant principal) of that first school in New York where I had taught my cracker-munching little third graders. In the course of my time at the school, he consistently found moments to share with me good things he had noticed and gentle times to share observations and recommendations. After I had been in a tough dispute with a colleague, he even called me at home to see how I was feeling.

He seemed to watch over the entire faculty with a sense of pastoral guidance, sensing just where each of us was in the unfolding seasons of our career. He could identify the first grade teacher who was still energized by the richness of a partnership with a new co-teacher, the physics maven who was perhaps just beginning to be overtaken by a droning inertia (and needed oversight and administrative imagination), and the physical education teacher who had proven herself and was ready at last to take on a fresh challenge. Often that same physical education teacher had no idea that she was ready or that anyone else had noticed. (By the way, that same PE teacher is now the head of a leading boarding school in the Northeast.)

This ability to sense each teacher's engagement was a world-class strength of his, and as a young teacher, I always felt his watchful support. Sometimes, to my dismay, he demonstrated even greater belief in my readiness for a challenge than I was ready to believe.

At age twenty-four, while I was still perhaps his youngest faculty member, he placed me in charge of the school's sprawling summer program. I would never have presumed to apply for the position; however, I discovered I was ready, and I found that colleagues took my leadership seriously. I began to learn things about leadership and about myself that might have waited a decade to unfold in other circumstances.

There aren't many Walter Birges out there, truth be told. Even so, you do have the right to a good, supportive supervisor. You have the right to support in your teaching. You have the right to thoughtful mentoring. You have the right to job satisfaction.

If you are inclined in that direction, you have the right to opportunities for personal challenge and career advancement.

COMPLEXES...AND COMPLEXITIES...

The relationship with a supervisor is one of the most complex relationships you will ever have to negotiate. The culture of each school is naturally distinct, if not unique. Just as naturally, the style of each supervisor will be highly individual and will likely take some getting used to.

The simple fact is that every supervisor potentially has a thumb on your financial IV, with its attendant ability to stop not only the flow of income but of self-esteem, self-definition, and personal satisfaction, too. No matter how long you have worked together, this will remain at least a subliminal part of the relationship. He or she has the capacity to hold your contract in jeopardy, and even if that is something you eventually move far beyond contemplating, he or she alone has the power and the right to call you into the office for a potentially unsettling conversation. No matter how close one might eventually feel to a supervisor, there will always remain an essential imbalance that will shape the relationship and likely forever limit the parity that underlies true friendship.

There may be something in a relationship with a supervisor that inevitably brings back subconscious associations we have concerning our relationship with our parents. There are those teachers who seem forever stuck in a kind of adolescent rancor, chronically outraged at the latest insensitivity perpetrated by the ever-imperfect "administration." There are others—and this was certainly true of an early supervisory relationship of mine—who may adopt a kind of perfectionistic eagerness to please, as if they are forever seeking some elusive adult approval. There are certainly those who seem to have outgrown all such associations or who would deny any such lingering parental afterimages exist (although some of us might honestly admit that the school *does* feel ever so slightly different on days when the supervisor is away at a conference). Others might still be willing to reflect on the following question with a small perplexity: If our supervisor were of the opposite gender, would that make a difference in the relationship?

There is no strategy to recommend here. It is simply an additional lens through which to see and reflect on the complexities inherent in the powerful dynamic of the employee-employer relationship.

SEEING THEM FOR WHO THEY ARE

In actively working to develop a positive relationship with supervisors, it is vital to be open to seeing them as they are. Supervisors deal with enormous time pressures. Problems can arise from anywhere in their domain. They are susceptible to an outbreak of parental protest. A teacher might quit midyear. A board member might be riding them about the need to add Mandarin to the school's curriculum. The parents of a student accused of plagiarism might threaten action in the courts. Their personal life might be in crisis. Their own children might be struggling.

Those higher up the academic hierarchy face ever-broadening constituencies. Principals may face school boards, superintendents, parent committees, boards of trustees, and even the potential for press coverage and letters addressed to their own bosses. While it can no doubt be problematic to have a complex relationship with one's own immediate supervisor, most heads of school have a whole collective of supervisors. They can never be sure of the support of all those to whom they report. They can never be sure that there aren't phone calls and emails circulating a whisper of dissatisfaction. Because they may report to multiple constituencies, they can never have the easy assurance that one supervisor's approval will be enough to protect their jobs, their incomes, and their reputations.

I speak as a veteran teacher and a veteran supervisor. Consider all of the aforementioned constituencies—board members, administrators from neighboring (even competitive) schools, union leaders, superintendents, other administrators within the school, difficult students, parents of all stripes, and then the array of teachers within the school.

As a teacher new to this domain, chances are that you may have attracted some special notice, and for as long as you are new to their world, your supervisors probably feel a special watchfulness about how well you are performing.

In light of all of those competing constituencies, how much attention do you really get? If a school principal's time and focus are broken out into a full 360 degrees, how large is the arc attentive to your needs and success? Look just at the faculty, people with dissatisfaction, great new initiatives, professional development, eager promotions, and a respected teacher's spouse known to be weathering a brutal battle against cancer. Add all of the other political players, and you may expect to get the equivalent of two, maybe three degrees of the 360-degree sweep of their attention.

For supervisors, big conclusions are built upon small amounts of information, probably necessarily.

Your supervisor will likely be trying to fathom whether or not you are a good fit for the school and the position, and that assessment will almost certainly be based on insufficient information.

Is that unfair? Probably. Is it inevitable? Most likely. Is there anything one can do about it? To some very real extent—yes.

How do you create a positive impression without lolling back, polishing one's nails, and indulging in a suspender-snapping bout of outright bragging?

Engage your supervisors with regular, short communication—face to face and eye to eye. Leave small notes. Send email responses. Slip them a copy of the class newspaper, *The Sumerian Tattler*, which you and your fifth graders have created. And if you and your class are doing something even moderately cool, perhaps playing *Name the Tyrant Jeopardy* ("I'll take 'Infernal Colonels' for $400, Alex"), portraying a second grade send-up of *Finnegans Wake*, or a presentation of dioramas of diseases of the digestive tract, then invite your supervisors in. It's partly just a youthful show of your own enthusiasm. It honors the work of your students (and may, assuming the kids know it in advance, raise the stakes and improve the product). It also presents your very busy supervisor, who, like most supervisors, genuinely feels he or she doesn't get out of the office enough, with a great, public, and ceremonial occasion to enjoy the life of the school.

Don't expect them to stay for the entire unwinding of the fortnight-long Joyce production. Consider that they might, like a candidate on the hustings (whatever *that* means), drop in and wave and then move on. Don't expect thanks or praise or a nice note in the morning. Instead, thank them for coming. "I know how busy you are. It means a lot to the kids."

Make brief, upbeat, regular contact. Make it about the teaching. Make it about the kids, and it will quietly, effectively come to be about you.

Recognize how little they will actually come to know about you, and control that information flow as much as you can.

GET TO KNOW WHO THEY REALLY ARE

Understand that some of the clichés about leadership and power actually have some basis in reality.

School supervisors actually are susceptible to loneliness or a form of professional isolation that teachers don't experience or even sometimes understand. The camaraderie in the faculty lounge or the ease with which one teacher might invite another over to dinner or out for drinks most often doesn't extend to supervisors.

While there are clearly some schools where such extracurricular activities may be discouraged, this wasn't the case in the school where I worked way back when. Years ago, I took the entire group of teachers new to the school out for drinks on the first Friday afternoon of the school year. I invited veterans along too. The meeting was, as you can imagine, spirited and convivial. The relief of having made it through the first week, the bonds fostered by parallel anxiety, and the inevitable connections forged over glasses of draught beer raised on high made a palpable difference to the spirit and culture of these young teachers. The Friday afternoon trek to the pub became something of an institution.

Four years passed.

The ritual of spending Friday afternoons at the local dive has now become a tradition. Clusters of teachers crowd tables; however, I have since stopped going. I no longer feel entirely welcome. Perhaps it is some shortsightedness on my part, but I truly don't think it's because of *me*. None of the administrators goes. It's become a time and place in which teachers can let off steam. I have come to sense that my presence would crowd them. If they want to grouse about me or about one of my administrative colleagues, my presence would just make it harder, more awkward, or impossible.

Thus, it happened that a tradition I was somewhat responsible for starting outgrew me or moved in a different direction. The assumption became so powerful that teachers with whom I get along well will make plans to head over after work right in front of me, without a thought that I might love a beer and some of the camaraderie on a weary Friday afternoon.

The point is not this particular episode. The point is that teachers often assume an ease of finding someone to ask out for a cup of coffee or to go to the movies. They can ask random teachers over for a put-together evening of potluck offerings without the suspicion of favoritism. The administrator who asks a few teachers over puts him- or herself in a slightly precarious position— why them and not me?

Simple, human outreach can be relatively simple for a classroom teacher. For administrators, it can become a loaded issue with overtones of favoritism that, if heeded, can leave professional administrators with a serious sense of personal isolation.

It was a late afternoon in November, and a smoky light suffused the western sky outside the window. The head of school and I had settled what business we had. The conversation had become quieter and more personal.

I asked him what it had been like to move to New York by himself. He was, it should be noted, a principal who was widely liked and admired. After a time, I was startled to see that there were tears in his eyes.

"Other than members of the board," he said, "no one asked me out to dinner for the first two years."

The easy collegiality that so many of us take for granted as part of the teaching corps of any school diminishes sharply as individuals move up through the ranks of administration. There may be some out there whose attitude toward their supervisors is simply "tough luck," but to those who truly want to establish a good relationship with their supervisors, understanding who they are and where they are coming from can be powerful.

I would also add a third point to the changes that are wrought when someone moves from the ranks of teachers into school administration.

If one is a sound and thoughtful administrator who seeks to recognize and motivate one's faculty, there will be thanks and compliments for jobs well done doled out among the participants. Someone who invites a supervisor in to see a class play likely expects to hear some deserved praise. Someone who has taken on leadership of a committee at the behest of a supervisor likely expects to hear some deserved thanks.

For whatever reason, we expect praise and thanks to trickle down from on high, from department heads and division leaders and principals. It is, if I may return to that perspective, something that children expect from their parents; however, children beyond a certain age rarely return the favor, and it is relatively rare for a supervisor to receive thanks for support, for a meeting well run, for being there to honor a teacher. It is just as rare for a supervisor to be praised for vision, for making tough decisions, for speaking well.

All of us carry with us a hunger to be honored, to be recognized, to be thanked. One secret then for establishing a good relationship with a supervisor shouldn't be very much of a secret at this point.

See them as individuals no less hungry than yourself—and perhaps a little more starved for the kind of praise and support many of us take for granted from good administrators. Don't focus, as so many teachers do, on whatever weaknesses may be apparent, for weaknesses will be apparent in the extended, on-stage life of any administrator. Focus instead on what many take for granted—whatever strengths they may have.

- Do they run meetings well?
- Do they delegate effectively?
- Are they simply hardworking?
- Do they tackle tough issues?
- Do they support teachers?
- Do they speak well?
- Do they hire effectively?
- Do they care about the kids?
- Do they care about the teachers?
- Are they cheerleaders?

Find what they do well. Notice it, and thank or compliment them.

You may get an "it's all in a day's work" nonchalance in return, but I suspect you are wise enough to know what it must feel like inside. Just as insults and battles can continue to burn long after their infliction, compliments can glow like stowed treasure. Getting off to a positive start with a supervisor may well begin by seeing them for who they are and by recognizing and addressing certain unfulfilled hungers in their lives.

IN THE TIGHT SPOTS, REACH OUT

Beyond such sporadic and ceremonial efforts to remain in decent, positive contact with your supervisor, know that there may well come a time when you need his or her advice. This may arise from the most natural and positive situation ("I'm having the Parthenogenesis family in for a conference, and I wondered if you've had any experience dealing with them.") to the somewhat difficult or embarrassing.

The former case is an obvious opportunity to reach out, to be proactive, and to gain potentially worthwhile information. The former case may require nothing more than a little confidence and experience. The latter may require some more serious settling in.

Let's assume that you're in something of a spot. You handled a situation in class a little poorly. Or maybe you handled it well, but the family doesn't seem to think so. You had a parent conference that you know probably shouldn't have ended in mutual death threats. Your third period class is so out of control they're holding your grandmother hostage, and you know in your heart of hearts that if you were more experienced, more balanced, more fleet of foot, none of these things would have come to pass.

Perhaps your greatest fear is that your supervisor will find out. What to do? Horror of horrors: You tell your supervisor.

Why?

1. If it's serious, they're almost certain to know or to find out soon enough.
2. It's far better—and this is one of those powerful little life lessons that the timid are slow to learn—to be the first one in to frame a situation. Better that you sit your supervisor down with your own explanation of the trouble than someone else get there first and frame the situation before

you. In my experience, the first explanation lays the groundwork. The second explanation only gets to edit it.

3. It clearly takes a little courage, and that alone can be impressive.

4. You can own up to having made a mistake. "I make dozens of decisions every day in how I handle situations. I'm not always right, but I want to learn from my mistakes. Looking back on it, I should have spoken to him privately rather than embarrass him in front of his friends."

5. Begin with the standard opening invitation that has made a vast difference in my own life: "I need your help." This simple sentence should probably have its own small bestselling volume in the self-help, business, and psychology sections, but you should take it as a standard. Whenever you are afraid, angry, inclined to pout, or at a loss for words, "I need your help" can be a powerful opening line. It establishes rapport. It establishes hope. It establishes parity and partnership. It suggests a common goal. It doesn't sound afraid or angry or pouty or speechless. It appeals to the other person, and it is, quite simply, appealing. It even suggests expertise, and it can serve to enlist your supervisor's more thoughtful and mentoring side.

6. Don't be defensive.

7. Learn openly.

8. Seek to grow.

Note on points six, seven, and eight: In my experience, the one greatest difference in longevity and satisfaction of young and struggling teachers is their willingness to be undefensively open to their own growth, to be grown-up enough to know that they don't know it all, to be confident enough to acknowledge errors.

It is the rare supervisor who actually looks forward to the prospect of having to sit a young teacher down and raise a loaded issue. Therefore, to have the young teacher actually come forward with the problem and take the initiative by asking for help creates a warmly different dynamic for the supervisor. Such a dynamic suggests openness, humility, and willingness to partner and to learn.

1. Take notes on what the supervisor suggests.

2. Summarize what you've learned and what you intend to do.

3. Smile.
4. Say "Thank you for taking the time. This matters a lot to me."
5. Follow up.
6. Try, as much as possible, to internalize the lesson of the day.

In conclusion, being proactive and taking the initiative in matters that trouble you can have a lasting, if not transformative, effect on the resolution of the problem and on your relationship with your supervisor.

SEEING YOUR SUPERVISOR AS AN ALLY

There may be schools or settings where the very idea of a supervisor as an ally seems laughably far-fetched, but you should return to the opening anthem of this chapter: You have the right to a good, supportive supervisor. You have the right to support in your teaching. You have the right to thoughtful mentoring. You have the right to job satisfaction. If you are inclined in that direction, you have the right to opportunities for personal challenge and career advancement.

When you begin to grow comfortable and more familiar with your supervisor and when it begins to feel natural to engage in longer conversations, you will probably know it. As much as this small section is about advancing your own ideas and objectives, remember who your supervisors are. They are always hearing about others' problems, grievances, absences, intestinal maladies, and mandibles that keep getting stuck in the on position in midyawn.

Share the positive with them. Ask about them. Try to picture the day, the week, or the year from their perspective. An empathic perspective can close vast distances.

When it feels comfortable, share a little of your long-term perspective. "I really love my classes this year, *and* I've begun to develop a greater interest and curiosity about committee work."

The emphasized "and" in that sentence would have often come up a "but" in common conversation, as if a growing political interest in school life had to be at the expense of life in the classroom. Picture, if this is a sample of what you're feeling as you are growing as an educator, that they are mutually supportive.

"I need your help."

Pause. Smile. "I've been here now three years, and I love my job. The kids are great. I love working with Colleen. You've been very supportive. In the next year, I'd like to try my wings at playing more of a role outside the classroom, too."

Let them know what you're looking for. Don't say too much. Don't push too hard. Just awaken their imagination a little. Put a brightly colored Post-it next to your name in their internal Rolodex. Engage their thinking.

Make the conversation brief and reflective. Ask them, if it feels right, for any ideas they might have. Keep it soft and pressure-free, but try to make it at least partly a dialogue. Engage them. And yes, of course, thank them. We all live lives that lack thanks, and few do so more than supervisors.

It sounds so simple, but it is something that eludes even many fairly sophisticated educators, because it's considered routine to grumble publicly about one's boss. If you want them to become an ally to you, first become an ally to them.

WHEN IT ISN'T GOING WELL

The old bestseller, *The Peter Principle*, suggested a starkly negative view of the workplace. As long as a young up-and-comer proved him- or herself worthy at a particular level in the hierarchy, the employee was considered a good prospect for advancement. It might take time, but as long as the employee was proving him- or herself to be competent, he or she was destined for promotion.

That much seems fairly straightforward. What then was the negative view contained in *The Peter Principle*? Well, if those who prove themselves competent are always moving up the chain of command, what does that say about those who have stabilized? The book is witty, incisive, and a little scandalizing. It suggests that, as a culture, we will each rise to that point in the hierarchy in which our incompetence becomes apparent or even dominant. Why else would we stop being promoted?

Clearly, the book is targeted toward the honeycombed hierarchies of the business world more than the field of education, and obviously, the book is as much a daring exploration as it is a scientific tome.

It is not only that administrators may deserve the same human empathy as a struggling teacher but also that those administrators who feel less sure of themselves may be that much hungrier for an outstretched hand, for a compliment and recognition for those times when they *have* done something well. When you look back from some better future, do you want to feel that you bested or showed up some struggling supervisor or that you were wise and patient and sensitive enough to be able to establish a decent working relationship with them?

Some supervisors used to be better teachers than they would eventually prove to be administrators. Sometimes it does feel as if we've landed a lemon for a supervisor, and no law yet devised allows us to return them to the manufacturer for a replacement and a refund for the time we toiled under their mismanagement.

As long as such a situation exists, it must be dealt with patiently, honorably, and effectively. Ultimately, it may be wise to consider moving on (although candidates for positions who come to our door with numerous short stints rarely make it past the waiting room). Beware of antagonizing a supervisor, regardless of what it does for your mental health, regardless of how much you may appear to be the populist James Dean renegade among your faculty friends.

If there truly is a seemingly intractable difficulty between you and a supervisor, try to picture a decent but limited time frame to remain on the job. Three years, unless the circumstances are truly dire, seems a plausible minimum to remain at any one teaching assignment. That may seem an unacceptable eternity, and perhaps it would be best to move along more expeditiously; however, simply having a sense that there will be an end point and that the suffering won't last a lifetime can bring the extent of that suffering into a more reasoned perspective.

Why three years? A shorter time than that may raise questions in the course of interviews further down the line. When you are thinking about your own future, recognize the unalterable power of that supervisor's position vis-à-vis your own reference and recommendation. If it is possible—and it very often is, even if it takes a running leap of faith—work through the relationship to the point where there can actually be positive support for your growth and development, for there is value in that.

It may be important to recognize that there is a genuine upside to the fact that teachers work in such isolation. Even if we have landed the Wicked Witch of the West as our cackling, broom-surfing supervisor, she's got a lot of other munchkins among her constituents to supervise. In the course of a week, how much time do we actually have to be in her presence?

There is one additional perspective I would note here. Whether your supervisor is good, bad, or indifferent, it is always wise to step outside yourself and see them as a case study in leadership. Watch how—or if—they can establish an overriding vision.

- How do they go about setting goals?
- How collaborative are they, and how do they establish (or fail to establish) team spirit and a sense of unified direction?
- How are they at setting up and leading meetings, and if the answer is "awful," then what would you do differently if you were in charge?
- It is too easy and a waste of a valuable professional learning experience to dismiss a supervisor's approach out of hand. What specifically could they and should they have done differently?

If you have the good fortune of working alongside an effective leader, push yourself to recognize the specifics of what makes them effective, and if you are working alongside a fumbling, grumbling stumblebum, you are missing an opportunity if you don't make him or her a silent mentor—learning what not to do.

WHEN YOU ARE AT THE BREAKING POINT

If the relationship is strained, it may be that the supervisor is an unknowing example of the aforementioned Peter Principle in action. From a more forgiving perspective, it may also be that the difficulty arises from a difference in styles.

Just as within a family or any other important relationship, it is best not simply to absorb the pain and retreat to your hovel to whimper alone by the hearth. It is incumbent upon you to work it through. Most of us dread such confrontations. Most of us can look back on times when we handled such a situation with an appalling lack of grace, either because we blew our stack over what later felt like a relatively minor incident or else because we let things accumulate until we suddenly and almost uncontrollably gave vent to the acidic bilgewater of our frustration.

There are positive ways to deal with conflict that are superior to both absorbing wounds in silence and publicly berating a bewildered supervisor.

The following is a list of options to consider at the moment of staggering, pot-boiling outrage. From our own history, we know that when we have been at our worst, it is often because we have lost track of things that we already knew. As with all such lists in this book, many will be obvious, but perhaps at a time of stupefying, even reckless fury, there will be one restraining item that helps and that rings true.

- It is almost axiomatic, but it is vital to remember to allow some distance and some time to elapse before you approach your supervisor about a concern. Sometimes, to our retrospective surprise, the big deal, that emotional Mount Vesuvius that had threatened to blow, expelling vile, deserved lava all over the primitive monkey-beast that is our supervisor turns out to be little more than a discarded match on top of the very proverbial molehill. It may be fun to vent. It may make us feel *alive*. But almost always, even the most fully deserved uproar can cause us to cringe with regret later, primarily because we were not at our best and because this individual does have a kind of absolute power over us after all. Such outbursts rarely have the power to convince a supervisor that we are right and good, and such outbursts are rarely completely forgotten.

- Don't storm into an office. Breathe. Set up an appointment for a meeting in a day or two.

- If the issue doesn't disappear over time, it is important to address it; however, before you address the problem, it is just as important to establish a mind-set that is positive, regardless of the negative impulses that may have accumulated. Think "dialogue," not "confrontation." Visualize, hard as it may be, a positive outcome, a meeting that ends with both of you standing, smiling, and shaking hands.

- Find, if possible, a balanced, veteran, *confidential* ally you can vent to and share with before any meeting. A second, supportive perspective may help shape your own.

- No matter what the circumstances, never take on and never try to show up a supervisor in public. Regardless of how correct the entire heavenly host must know you to be, no one deserves—and no one is likely to forget or forgive—a public showdown when a private dialogue would have been available.

- No matter what the circumstances, *never* take on a difficult subject by email. (The "unsend" option is, for many of us, the computer age's most valuable development.)

- Reference one of the key habits in Stephen Covey's list of seven: "Begin with the end in mind." What do you want to accomplish? If it is just to vent, just to tell her off, then that's likely all that will happen. Expect a very one-sided meeting and some serious repercussions down the road. If you can picture an end that is one of mutually enhanced understanding (even if that seems galling or impossible in your pre-meeting fervor), you will enter the meeting with a very different mind-set. As most of us know from our personal lives, there are "fights" that end up with reconciliation and fresh appreciation of another's perspective. Picture, prep for, and work toward an ending that works for both of you.

- When the meeting begins, use that very familiar saying, "I need your help." "I need your help in understanding why you opened the faculty meeting with that joke about my mother's moral turpitude."

- Acknowledge different perspectives. In your own mind, even before you enter the dialogue, recognize that people can disagree without either of them being wrong, stupid, or hatched from the vile eggs of Satan.

- Follow another wonderful "habit" outlined by Stephen Covey: "Seek first to understand and then to be understood." Don't start by doing all the talking. Don't spend all the time the other person is speaking coming up with your rebuttals and rejoinders. Listen. Seek first to understand.

- Use "I" statements. Speak for yourself. Don't say what others think, and don't talk about them or about platitudes. Speak personally and vulnerably about how you felt. Probably not: "You're a hurtful, insensitive moron, and everybody knows it." Better: "When you referred to me as 'the village idiot' in front of my students, I felt a little nauseous."

- Commit yourself to brevity. Ask your question, make your point, and then listen.

- Be comfortable with silence. If you have raised a sensitive issue, avoid the temptation to let your nervousness lead you on an interminable yak-a-thon. Expect a response. Be comfortable with your own silence. Give your supervisor some time to reflect. You knew what the meeting was about in advance. Chances are that he or she didn't. Know that you deserve a response, but be patient.

- When your supervisor has finished speaking, try paraphrasing what you think you have heard. Give her or him a chance to correct or amplify upon any point. Make it clear that you have been listening.

- In the end, make sure that the meeting is working toward a better future, one enhanced with new perspectives or approaches. In effect, it's also important to *end* with the end in mind. At some point early in the meeting, begin to move beyond the past. Instead of tangling in a crack-brained, downward-spiraling debate about whether or not something happened precisely the way you remember it, keep the conversation about the future, the way you'd like to be treated from now on, and the means of establishing better communication.

THE SUPERVISORY RELATIONSHIP: FINAL KEY POINTS TO CONSIDER

In summation, the relationship you develop with your supervisor will prove to be one of the most important, complicated, and potentially valuable relationships you will experience in your professional life. As with any relationship, it is important to see the other person in his or her own world and, as much as possible, from his or her own perspective. Even in the worst relationships, there can be the promise of improved communication and understanding. Even in the best relationships, there will almost inevitably be moments of misunderstanding and points of contention. Open, thoughtful, well-intentioned communication is the key to working through whatever issues arise.

There is incalculable value in the positive support of a supervisor and the chance that a "boss" can eventually become a mentor, even a cheerleader for your own growth and progress. Here are some actions you can take to begin to build this relationship:

- As you move more deeply into the life of a school, begin looking for opportunities to participate.
- Choose your times to speak up—particularly in faculty meetings—wisely and carefully. Remember that you have relatively few opportunities to create an impression in the scheme of life. Supervisors and even colleagues are busy people with countless other constituencies on their radars. Don't preen or speak to make an impression. Be yourself. Speak from the heart, but be aware that you *are* making an impression.
- Be *organized*. Disorganization is one of the most readily apparent flaws in a new employee. A messy desk, a forgotten meeting, and a missed deadline are all too apparent and carry a disproportionate weight in forming an early impression.
- Share the positive with your supervisor. Don't brag, but don't only speak to him or her when you're upset. Invite your supervisor in your classroom, or simply grin about the cool new thing you tried and how well the kids responded to it.
- Become part of the team.
- Build bonds with other new teachers.
- Grow outward into the community when you have achieved a level of comfort within. Coach. Tutor. Join a committee. There are countless opportunities within any school community to take on responsibility. Look for an opportunity to do something that's not already being done. Start a club. Start a lunchtime study hall for kids to drop in and get work done. Start a Friday-afternoon-at-the-pub outing with a few cronies. Notably, it may well be advisable not to coach in the first year at a new school. (It

may also be advisable to beware your overcommitment in the fresh energies of September, because come February, your energies may be largely exhausted.) Taking on new challenges is not only a way to grow but also a way of keeping your professional life fresh and constantly renewed. Finally, albeit indirectly, it is important to recognize that through these new ventures, you will come in contact with other individuals and other aspects of school life, and you may well be seen by your supervisor in a new light, perhaps as an initiator, as a contributor, as someone to keep an eye on.

Supervisors play a critical role in our growth as professionals. There is a great deal we can do to build the kind of trusting, mutually supportive relationship that will lead to our own greater growth and satisfaction.

Chapter 43

KEY PEOPLE WITH WHOM TO ESTABLISH GOOD RELATIONS

It is no secret that the most important individual in the school with whom to establish good relations is your supervisor, but there are also countless, relatively obvious people with whom you teach—co-teachers, department members, and other colleagues—upon whom you will likely come to depend for support, feedback, and camaraderie.

This section suggests some less obvious relationships within the school and individuals with whom you may have only the most passing acquaintance. Building genuinely respectful, appreciative connections with the people who take care of us simply makes good sense. When the time comes that the chips are down, the toast has popped, and push comes to shove, having already established a warm and friendly relationship with any one of these players may pay considerable dividends.

THE PRINCIPAL'S ADMINISTRATIVE ASSISTANT

Probably not a lot of explanation needed here. If you have taken an interest in the photograph of the Labrador retriever, the Lamborghini, or the loving llama perched like a shrine beside her paperclip dispenser, chances are when you really need access to the big boss, you may find the elusive appointment to be a little less elusive. Sure, we are having a bit of fun with those examples, but the fact is that genuine warmth and outreach is not only of practical value, for having a sense of warm connection throughout the building naturally leads to an enhanced professional experience.

THE CUSTODIAN OR MAINTENANCE SUPERVISOR

The position goes by a thousand different titles, but it's the individual who locks up, knows the boiler, has access to secret closets, and handles deliveries. Often he gets little attention, little recognition, little in the way of thanks. Mostly people just notice him when something's gone wrong, and such people are likely to get slower service than those who, when there is no crisis brewing, happen to notice the shiny floors, the repaired drinking fountain, or that his favorite team is on a winning streak.

THE SCHOOL COUNSELOR OR PSYCHOLOGIST

Take the initiative early on to develop a strong, effective relationship with the school counselor or psychologist. Take your class roster to them. Ask for some inside information early in the year or even before the year has begun. Value what they have learned over the years, and it may be that they will be there to support you when you are dealing with something unpleasant.

THE LEARNING SPECIALIST

There may be no frontier in education developing more swiftly and more significantly than that monitored by the active learning specialist. What we have learned about the brain, about learning differences, and about learning styles has the potential to transform education over the coming decades.

Learning specialists tend to be overworked and undervalued, as if their only expertise were the "slower" population in any school, but they are often at the forefront of a school's understanding of how best to reach students who are hardest to reach. One of the key, positive surprises of this expanding field is that what is good for the student who has auditory processing issues is good for the entire class. The more we learn about how each child learns, the more effective we can become for all of our students. They are good, worthy, well-positioned partners in your own professional development.

THE BUSINESS MANAGER AND THE BUSINESS OFFICE STAFF

There is almost certainly going to come a time when your paycheck is wrong, you need a last-minute check for a class trip, or you are hoping to get reimbursed for something you purchased for your classroom, and if you are an indifferent stranger in the business office, you will likely be helped…all in good time. It is easy to *plan* to get to know key players, but those who establish warm, effective connections throughout the building early on in their time at a school are also, by no coincidence, those who are far more likely to be dealt with appreciatively and responsively.

THE SCHOOL NURSE

She is someone who often has valuable information on your newest and most unconventional students gathered from those frequent nurse visits for mysterious head or stomach aches. While she must necessarily respect the oath of confidentiality that affects everyone in the medical community, she can (and must) speak freely with educators about many of the allergies and other medical needs of the students in the school. On that morning during which you waken with your own unprecedented symptomology, it can be relieving in the extreme to have developed the kind of relationship that allows you to slip into her office before school starts for a little wisdom, expertise, and advice.

IN CONCLUSION

The culture of each school is different. The array of job descriptions varies from place to place. There are almost certainly other individuals who straddle the central arteries of your school. Reach out early on, as if they were long-lost friends, seeking nothing more or less than recognition for the work that they do.

Chapter 44

MAKING USE OF OUTSIDE RESOURCES

It was the day before my career was to begin. I was rushing about my very first classroom, trying to prepare for the next day, straightening the ragged edges, and prettying up the bulletin board. I was in the throes of a serious adrenaline rush. I had a thousand things to do, and there, in the doorway, stood an interruption and her son.

It was Mrs. Riggs, and she wanted nothing more than to make the next twenty-four hours a little easier for Jerry, her firstborn son. They had just moved to the area that summer. Jerry was going to be in my class. He was likely as nervous as I was, and Mrs. Riggs thought it would be helpful for him to come over to school the day before it opened and meet his new teacher.

I did an artful job of turning away from all that I had to do and working to make the mother and son feel welcome, reassured, even a little excited about the year to come. We spoke for quite a while. When at last they left, I felt a certain pleasure that at least one family would likely think I knew what I was doing.

Eight weeks passed, and it was parent-teacher conference day. Mrs. Riggs came in with her ministerial husband and her bullfrog purse. She clapped her hands together enthusiastically. "Jerry is just having the best year ever, and thank you so much for giving him preferential seating because of his deafness." I smiled benignly, sagely nodding, beneficent, magisterial, having *no* idea what she was talking about.

As I look back on it, I realized that in the course of that first afternoon meeting just before school began, she must have said something to me about the fact that Jerry was totally deaf in one ear, and perhaps it was excusable that I simply never took it in—never remembered it, never even remembered that I had forgotten it—seeing as I had so much to do. It was clearly important, but it had left absolutely no impression. I had given him a front row seat by luck.

If we are lucky enough to work in well-organized and conscientious school environments, we will *all* experience information overload at precisely that moment when we are most preoccupied with preparing for the school year to come. We will hear from the principal, from the school nurse, and from the guidance counselor, and we will often hear about students who at that point are nothing but names.

It might well be easy to shrug it off and assume it'll stick when we get to know them better or that we'll make time someday to go visit the school nurse and get the low-down once the year is underway and we're not so overloaded.

But someday rarely comes.

Instead, on a school trip to the Museum of American Pickpockets, a student you are escorting is stung by a bee. And despite the fact that you were fore-warned about the child's hypersensitivity back in those hazy days of August, you have no EpiPen. The child begins to experience anaphylactic shock.

Little Miss Muffet has been adopted by a devoted single father. The exact situation isn't clear and isn't even relevant, but by the time May rolls around, you have long since forgotten this fact, as you observe the child's awkward discomfort when asked to create a lavish Mother's Day piñata.

You are sitting down to a parent conference with the Gander parents when you naturally mention the fact that Goosey seems to be kind of distracted at times. To your sudden discomfort, Mr. Gander looks up and begins to sputter in pate-reddening fury. You were told back in August that the family, after three years of pressure and persuasion from the school, had agreed to have Goosey taken for a complete, phenomenally expensive set of psychoeducational tests. At the time, Mr. Gander had even suggested that the tests wouldn't be worth the cost, and here, just ten months after the school received the comprehensive report, Goosey's teacher doesn't know a thing about it. The teacher is incompetent. The school is incompetent. And your supervisor is certainly going to hear about it before Mr. Gander has left the building.

Dorothy Hutcheson, a former supervisor of mine, once shared a concise summary of a parent's priorities. "Are you a pro, and do you care about my child?" In response to each of these above situations, it might not be too much of a stretch for parents to conclude that you aren't a pro and that you don't even know their children.

Schools—conscientious schools—will overload their teaching faculty with too much information at the beginning of each year. Teachers will be told about psychological backgrounds, physical impairments, illness in the family, learning differences, and life-threatening allergies. There is every reason to throw up one's hands and plead that you were overwhelmed, but that will never be an acceptable excuse. The luck I experienced with the Riggs family isn't something anyone can count on.

And the consequences can be even worse. Colleagues who taught at a nearby school took a high school class for an overnight trip out of town to see a Shakespeare production. One of the students, a tenth grader, was feeling unwell and asked to remain behind. The lead chaperone insisted that someone stay behind in the hotel with the student. The student was equally insistent, but he said that he was just under the weather. He would certainly have been allowed to stay home alone with a similar illness. "Go on. Go on. Enjoy the show and keep the flock together."

The issue of safety was given secondary status. When the class returned from the production, the student was dead in his hotel room.

This issue is that serious. There is nothing anywhere else in the field of education and there is nothing anywhere else in this book as serious as the safety of our students. Being able to teach a compelling lesson in geometry, being able to maintain discipline in an ornery environment, being able to uplift a student with genuine praise—none of that matters at all if a child's well-being and safety is compromised.

If the school where we work is conscientious and plies us with a full battery of information at the beginning of the year, it is vital that we maintain our own confidential records of this information as reference and reminder. One key strategy for keeping a reference for all such information is to have a coded section in your grade book, a section that you keep stapled closed. In this way, it is there to be opened when you need it but is also kept from idle, prying eyes.

If the school isn't so conscientious, if we never do get briefed by those with access to this essential information, it must be up to us to seek it out.

If we do so, we will be far more prepared to teach effectively or to head off an unpleasant situation. In the end, we may be able to come to the aid of a student in a time of crisis.

We need to create open, effective, remembered channels of communication with the resource people in our schools, and as the year progresses, it is equally important that we keep appropriate colleagues and administrators informed of that information we obtain.

If a relative of a student is ill or incarcerated, if a child is being tutored or is now in therapy, if we learn of a medical condition—or recently diagnosed allergy—affecting the student's well-being, we must share this information. In any such cases, it is urgent to notify a supervisor, the school nurse, and the guidance counselor.

As a teacher on the front line of communication with the child and his or her family, we will likely gain access to important information about some of our students during the year. As part of a school working to maintain a current and complete overview of each child's situation—familial, physical, psychological, and cognitive—it is essential that we become active partners in the growing number of resources available to each student, to each family, and, in turn, to our own colleagues.

PART 6

Special Circumstances

Chapter 45

DEALING WITH THE CHILD WHO DRIVES US CRAZY

We can do everything right.

We can become truly masterful teachers.

But there will never be perfection.

There will never be a class without problems, a child without challenges.

The transaction at the heart of education is essentially, inescapably human, and therefore, our relationships with our students and their families are necessarily destined to be arcane and imperfect.

We will not always respond as we should. There will be children who drive us crazy. There will be students whose learning style is so confounding or compromised that we don't know how best to reach them. There will be children whose quiet is almost an invitation to overlook them. There will be classes that make us feel helpless and hopeless. There will be parents who test us as angry adults turned loose in defense of their child.

This final, major unit of this book was written to address these issues most fundamental to the quality of our lives and the education we hope to inspire. We will confess that there is no absolute remedy for pain, no memorizable litany of steps that you can take to guarantee success with any student or parent. There will be difficulties and setbacks in the course of time. Life is like that.

But life is also susceptible to learning, and the quality of that life is improved by that learning. Here, thanks to all of the educators we have learned from over the years, is a unit that addresses each of these major issues in an explicit and practical format.

The following names have been changed to protect the innocent and friendless.

Jimmy Knotwell was a boy with whom I went to grade school. As I look back, I feel there must have been a terrible sadness in his house. Perhaps the parents were alcoholics or hermits. In a small, neighborhood public school in which all of the families seemed to know each other, no one had ever really seen Mr. and Mrs. Knotwell.

Jimmy had dark creases under his eyes, which were accentuated by a stark, bony nose. Frequently throughout the day, he would open the lid to his desk, take out a jar of Vicks Vap-O-Rub and a Q-tip, and in front of us all—even at an age when cool was beginning to be important—would douse the ends of the swab and swirl the Vicks up into each nostril. He walked like a posture-broken old man. He was so lonely and out of it that no one even made fun of him.

Darby Headstrong was obviously a little crazy. He was in my Cub Scout troop. My mother and father were the den parents. Our troop built a bridge across the creek that had annoyingly split the large playing field behind our neighborhood for years. Darby never showed up for the work that we did until his mother brought him by as we were completing the project. His mother, a woman with the kind of sequined spectacles I associate with pink flamingos, explained that they had been out to buy Darby new shoes.

Darby walked out onto the bridge and jumped into the creek in his new shoes. Instead of the what-are-you-thinking dismay one might expect from a mother, Mrs. Headstrong simply turned to us all with a meek, perky aspect, and said, "Darby just loves the water!"

In class, he was no less bizarre. He would excuse himself and go to the drinking fountain by the sink in the back of the classroom and "anoint" himself. That was how he described the increasingly obsessive ritual. A few times kids physically harassed him on the way home from school. I can't imagine what kind of homework he turned in.

Justine Limelight was the quintessential Queen Bee. She seemed to have it all—effortless looks, grades, and classmates who strove to be her friend. She doled out that friendship by parsimonious thimblefuls. And classmates could never tell who would next be her new best friend—and who would be the outcast, subject to ostracizing rejection by the new inner circle. Her influence may have been pernicious—but unlike many of her male contemporaries, her use of power was subtle and often completely unseen.

Steven Swagger was the cool, wanna-be-James-Dean of our seventh grade class. For a time, he held all the cards. He was reckless and ruthless, grimly handsome with steel-cold eyes, aware of sexuality and the power of challenging a teacher. He was someone everyone watched when a teacher suggested a new project. If he bought in, we all knew it was okay to buy in. If he sneered—and his mouth seemed always to be set in a kind of latent sneer—none of us would go along.

I know how deadly it was for a young teacher to have Steven Swagger and his weak, surly posse in a class. I observed, with a strange detachment that was half sympathetic, half curious, as he took apart young Miss Participle.

I know there were teachers who just thought Jimmy Knotwell was an ignorable loser, socially clueless and physically unsettling. Darby Headstrong probably gave the willies to any teacher who was told he would be in his or her class. Justine Limelight seemed able to direct the flow of popularity—and rejection—to such an extent that everyone in the class felt a perpetual insecurity when she was around. And Steven Swagger represented the power that children and young adults can hold and withhold from a teacher who isn't yet sure of him- or herself.

There are many variables in the reasons why a student might drive us crazy. Sometimes, it is simply a passive loneliness that might evoke our distaste. Perhaps there is an element of our own emotional history involved. Sometimes, there is something more deeply wrong—and it is difficult for us to react any differently than the rest of the students do. Sometimes, it is a student who directly challenges our authority, our ideals, our self-image, and best intentions.

Dealing with students who, for whatever reason, evoke a slight, almost biological shudder in us is something that most teachers never really consciously address. The lonely boy with the jar of Vicks is just allowed to drift as a kind of mockery. The boy who is disturbed and has parents who are absolutely clueless will probably remain a serious outcast and may even become dangerous in his own time. The students who are reckless and popular are likely to be left in the position of power broker in the classroom, in the locker room, and in the lunchroom.

We can join the cavalcade of teachers who came before and simply accept the student—and our first, reflexive reactions to that student—as a given, but that, we would argue, is the weak, defensive, unreflective side of ourselves as teachers. That is the perspective of one who has lost track of his or her ideals, because it is in the lives of these very children that the greatest, most healing transformation can be wrought by us.

It will no doubt be an uphill struggle, one that may pay, if we're honest, only incremental rewards, but imagine Jimmy with an even slightly greater sense of inclusion. Imagine Darby as someone who begins to be treated as the class historian, as the expert on insects, as the line leader. Imagine Justine with her power moderated—and the rest of the girls feeling your very real, ever-present support. And imagine Steven, who will probably not concede all of his heady power to any adult, as someone in whom a teacher perceives real poetry, discussion leadership, or a strength in mathematics that he can't help but think might add to his cool.

Because the student who drives us crazy comes in so many different varieties, there can be no single checklist for addressing each and every one.

The suggestions that follow may offer one or two possibilities for liberating a child from the long-held, deep-seated trap of a reputation. On behalf of the lonely, the poorly parented, and the reckless rebels who fritter away their promise and potential, we offer the following advice when you are working with these students.

SUSPEND DISBELIEF

This may be the most difficult task of all. In too many cases, no teacher has ever suspended a disbelief in the abiding "truth" of a child's accumulated reputation.

Jimmy, Darby, Justine, and Steven were simply accepted as the somewhat monolithic, unchanging, and unchangeable persona they presented, but is any one of us ever just one thing? Is reputation not in itself a stultifying straitjacket? Don't children evolve and grow up enough to surprise us and themselves? And isn't it likely that there is some dormant yearning inside them, some better angel of their nature seeking only to take even the most modest of flights?

It is so effortless and so tempting and so easy simply to accept the child and the persona he or she presents as immutable, as changeless, and rock-hard and forever, yet the first essential step in his or her liberation and growth is simply to see the child as he or she might yet be.

In some ways, this step is both obvious and monumental. It may be that other, earlier teachers have tried. It may well be that they have not or that the time was not right. Suspending disbelief isn't a passive process but one of focus and imagination. Take a moment when you are feeling particularly hopeless and dare to believe. Who is the lonely, struggling child within? What has he or she suffered? What good has no one else bothered to notice? What talent? What potential? Dare to imagine at this most disheartened moment that there truly might be a better angel within, damp and vulnerably cocooned within the difficult, obstreperous persona he or she presents as an offensive defense against the pain of life.

CONSIDER WHY

When I would come home from school with some latest can-you-believe-it story about Jimmy and Darby, my mother's face would almost always soften, and she would murmur, "Aw—" Despite the fact that I really *wanted* her to shake her head in shared mockery and disbelief, that "Aw—" almost always had a profound, perspective-shifting effect on me. From that moment, in spite of my own petty propensity to share the world's distaste for the child, I began almost telescopically to see beyond the child to the curtained house, to the hapless parents, to the fact that the child was never included in sports teams or birthday parties.

Think about all the reasons why the child may act the way that he or she does. Are there hapless, clueless parents, so beset by their own issues that they can't really help their child? Is there an illness or a dominating depression in the household? Is there poverty, too many children, a missing parent? Is there a rashly, crushingly competitive parent who is secretly—or overtly—proud of the son's reckless disregard?

Next, we need to evaluate our own perspective on the situation. We need to find out more about him or her from past teachers, from watching the child in other classes, from the family, and from our own imaginations. Who is this child? What better child might be lurking undiscovered within? Why is the child so apt to drive us crazy?

- Does he or she remind us of someone we once knew?
- Someone we once were?
- Is he or she just unappealing?
- Is he or she likely to lead a mob in a round of ringing laughter at the expense of our ideals?

Empathy arises from asking why, and empathy is the one skeleton key to the locked door of the closed-in child. In beginning to support his or her liberation, we also have the opportunity to improve the tenor of our class and the nature of our own sense of mission.

RESIST THE TEMPTATION TO PLAY INTO THE REPUTATION

In the dry heat of the summer sun, wagons follow the courses set when the road was slick with mud. The ruts petrify, and then, even in totally different weather, the ruts simply deepen. Any cart that seeks to track a different path must resist the gravity that draws it back to the lowest common denominator.

Most children who drive us crazy arouse in others an almost automatic set of responses. What teacher wouldn't feel a kind of inner shudder at the vision of that Q-Tip and its viscous ritual? What Cub Scout who had worked in the summer heat building that bridge would have felt anything but further pompous dislike for the boy who didn't help, for the boy who took the "crazy" leap? What teacher wouldn't feel a kind of unsettled fascination with Justine's power? And what teacher wouldn't feel a sense of shame or outrage, watching the ovine willingness of so many classmates to bend to her authority? What teacher, sensing his renegade presence in the room, wouldn't feel his or her own kind of oppositional ferment when Steven Swagger slung into the room and cocked back his chair?

It is not only that such children have certain persona, but that each persona sends out its own shockwave of reaction. The reaction echoes back to the child so that he or she is seen as unlikeable, nuts, or feared. And so the reputation feeds itself. It is not only that the child is what he is. It is that he evokes in us a reaction that reaffirms what he is.

It is our conviction that the greatest resistance to the growth and evolution of a child is not some stillborn, failed mechanism within. The greatest inhibitor of growth is to be found in the fact that those around the child are so uniform in their expectations, perceptions, and beliefs that the reputation becomes a self-fulfilling snare.

If we are to hope for the gradual, incremental, occasionally breakthrough growth of a child, we must first actively come to recognize—and then to actively disbelieve—the nature of that reputation. It is all too easy to play along, to accept, perhaps even to follow our own unconscious inclination to isolate the boy in the harmful and isolated persona he presents. Instead, speak to him privately of your awareness of his potential. Call on him and be ready to find a nugget in the dross. Make him a leader. Defy his own tendencies to hide, to rebel, to undermine. It may take time, for it has no doubt taken years for him to learn to hide behind this difficult exterior, but for all that you are worth and all that he might someday become, don't give up on him.

RESIST GOSSIP

It is also very important that we resist the temptation to share our own "can you believe it?" war stories in the faculty lounge.

A favorite pastime of teachers everywhere—and something we consider as natural as it is unhealthy—is to spend time in the faculty lounge sharing stories of our own frustrations with our students. Once we commit to sharing a story at a child's expense—no matter how irresistible the anecdote—we have distanced ourselves from really experiencing that child as he or she might yet become. We have resorted to creating an image and reinforcing a reputation for others who may also or who may someday teach that child. Even more damagingly, we have internally given a tightening tug to the laces that bind them to an unalterable (and generally unappealing) reputation.

If this seems too harsh, too unreasonable, too "Oh, come on," then imagine the converse. What if you were to come into the room and talk about the success Darby Headstrong had had with the aquarium—how he had even started to get to school early to feed the fish and had taken pride in using the squeegee to keep the glass free of algae. Imagine how different your investment in his ongoing growth might become. Imagine how that might be perceived by teachers who had only heard others critical of him. Imagine how this might gradually begin to lift their own expectations of this sad and downtrodden student. There are vicious cycles all about us in schools. We have the unique potential to turn that momentum around and to quietly transform lives in the process.

BEGIN TO ENVISION A WAY FOR THE CHILD TO BECOME MORE SUCCESSFUL

Think of a bulb planted in the soil. At some point only nature will truly understand, when the weather above is sufficiently warm and hospitable, the roots begin to reach out for moisture and nutrients from the soil. What will become the stem and flower work past pebbles and silt, loam and decaying leaves to make their way through to the sunlight.

It may be beyond our ability as teachers to bring each student to such springlike, breakthrough growth, but it will definitely be beyond our abilities if we never pause to envision it or to sense our roles as prospective suns for that deep and untapped darkness.

I know from the years I shared a class with him that Jimmy Knotwell was an unknown, unrecognized master of history and that he had a quiet, oddball sense of humor that almost never brightened those dark-rimmed eyes. He did his work. He was hygienically unappealing. He never caused any trouble.

I suspect that Darby Headstrong, wherever he is, has a top-of-the-line, even home-brewed sound system. There was something I could sense whenever music stirred the classroom. During these moments, he seemed somehow above his own nesting problem, at one with something good in his life from which he was otherwise so alienated.

Justine was an artist of the first water. Yet it brought her little pride in contrast to the high she seemed to get from playing with the puppet strings of popularity. How might her teachers have rallied to make that artistic prowess closer to the center of identity?

We all knew that Steven Swagger was a sharp mathematician, but in the two different math classes I shared with him, the teachers were far more concerned about his behavior than about his talent. Neither of them seemed to have any idea that the way through his behavior might first have been to address, to honor, and to hone his talents. It might have gone wrong anyhow—Steven was pretty well fused to that role as rebel-in-waiting—but neither of them even tried to see what gently, quietly transformational change there might have been, if only they had begun to treat him as one of the prospective leaders of the class, to suggest that he might just belong on the math team. Even if he refused with a scoff, would he really forever forget the outreach?

We lose our students when we fail to envision them growing beyond where they are now. The parent of the child learning to walk believes that the child will walk and so responds with support, with watchful excitement, with rapturous encouragement as the child first begins to "cruise" from end table to coffee table. The teacher of the first grader believes that the child learning consonant sounds will read and so is steadfast in her repetition of each letter, knowing that the words will come. So often, however, there is almost a collective failure to believe that the child who does not fit, who can't sit still, and who drives us crazy will ever be any different.

Until we can imagine the seemingly lifeless bulb, acknowledge the rigorous course it must force through that packed soil, and somehow find and envision the kind of sunlight potential that will best foster growth, the bud will likely never reach the surface. It is not only that there is real potential for evolutionary change in each child we teach but the fact that if we can truly overcome our initial negativity, *these* are the children, these outsiders and outcasts whose growth may someday bring us the greatest pride and pleasure in the work that we have done.

KEEP THE CORRECTIONS LOW-KEY

There will likely need to be correcting along the way. Darby, for example, needed to suspend his pseudo-religious rituals in the back of the room. But the correction should be private, because his classmates will take their cues from you about how to treat Darby.

You might approach a Darby in this manner: "Darby, you are such a good student and such an interesting boy that I'm not going to let you do any more fooling around back by the sink. Do you know what I mean?" (Insert meaningful, watchful pause.) "From now on, starting right this minute, if you need a drink, you get a drink. Otherwise, if you continue to go to the back of the room for more than that, I simply won't let you up from your seat." It is vital that he understand that this is not simply "classroom management," not simply one more prohibition in a string of such prohibitions, but an attempt to promote a better image, a greater reputation. "I know you understand why I am speaking to you about this." (Insert a pause, with warm eye contact.) "You have so much to give. You are such a bright, good kid." (And then conclude with warm eye contact and a soft, encompassing smile.)

And if he rises again and tests you—as he very likely will—make your voice as cool as the swish of the wind. "Darby. Down. In your seat." And go immediately into the next phase of the lesson. Or move, even as you continue to lead the discussion, to the back of the room, and guide him back to his seat without missing a beat.

MAKE THE PRAISE STRONG AND DOMINANT

"Did you all hear what Jimmy just said about the Marshall Plan? That if there had been a Marshall Plan instead of the Treaty of Versailles, there would never have been a World War II?"

An admiring, warm-eyed look at Jimmy, and a pause then, allowing the class to experience the power of your praise.

"Jimmy, I've really been impressed by some of your thinking in history. Class, you haven't seen all of the homework and papers Jimmy's handed in this year. He's quiet about his skills, but this boy is one of our real historians."

And after class, stop him in the hall for a minute.

"Did what I say surprise you?"

A glance down, a meek smile with bad teeth—but then a glance up of something close to that of a rescued puppy. The boy with those hollow eyes, who may never have heard much praise from his reclusive mom and dad, now looks upon you with unaccustomed curiosity and questions. Do you really notice? Do you really care about *me?* Who can I become in your eyes?

The vast majority of our time as teachers is spent dealing with the required routines and the daily discussions in our classes. Almost unnoticed—and clearly unaddressed—by the great, striving, and overworked educational community are those missed moments when we can touch an individual life. In the course of a year, in the course of a life, Jimmy—and the countless Jimmys out there, male and female—may well forget almost all that transpired in your class, but chances are that even if it does not have the power to change who he is, he will never forget that quiet, shared moment with you.

IN CONCLUSION

When we have refused to accept and reinforce a child's negative reputation, when we have begun to envision a child growing into a yet unrealized future, when we have taken the moment to picture him or her aligned with talents and interests and possibilities beyond the present—these are the moments in which we can begin, however incrementally, to create the kind of deep, abiding, and transformational growth of which each child—and the whole of education—is surely capable.

Chapter 46

SUPPORTING STUDENTS WITH LEARNING DIFFERENCES

The issue of students with learning differences (or, as they are called in somewhat outgrown terminology, learning disabilities) is one that affects every teacher. Not only do these students often baffle us, but there is a high—but far from absolute—correlation between LD students and those who demand disproportionate amounts of our energies as teachers.

Learning differences first began to attract public attention (and creep into public parlance) through specific sets of behavior. The most recognized are those termed dyslexic, who, among other things, often have trouble distinguishing b, d, p, and q and those termed ADD (attention deficit disorder) and ADHD (attention deficit hyperactivity disorder) who have difficulty maintaining focus.

While it is probably clear why such students often require so much of our time and attention—the former are slow to learn to read (and often to learn their math facts) and the latter often prove bewilderingly inconsistent in attention and achievement—we have learned much about the brain in the last thirty years that has revolutionized our understanding of the process of learning.

Taking in and feeding out information is a process whose complexity is far deeper, far more impressive, and far more subtle than most educators and scientists were aware of thirty years ago. Educators once upon a time routinely wrote off those student who exhibited LD behavior as simply (to quote educator Richard LaVoie) "Lazy and Dumb." Countless adults—many of them very successful—can now look back on their own childhood educational experiences and realize that they were left as struggling outcasts when, thirty years later, they might have been understood far more empathetically and taught far more effectively.

In almost every classroom, *at least* 10 percent of the students will have learning channels compromised or idiosyncratic enough that they verge into the category of students with learning differences. It is vital to our students' ongoing growth and our own sense of effectiveness to understand that learning differences—while still clustered as a single, generic term—have remarkably different manifestations.

The quiet girl who sits with a dutiful smile does well enough on a Tuesday quiz and performs as poorly the very next day as if she had been absent for the past month. This inconsistency may be a sign of quiet attention deficit disorder—perhaps even attention deficit hypoactive disorder (meaning unusually low activity levels).

Here are but a few examples:

- The impulsive boy who is irrepressibly fun or exhaustingly tiresome. He can barely sit still. He's up for water, for trips to the bathroom, for meandering journeys to the aquarium to see if the guppies are okay. As a student, he is constantly distracted and distracting. His performance is at best inconsistent. Attention deficit hyperactivity disorder (ADHD) becomes a possibility.

- The child who, while perfectly sighted, simply can't make sense of what he sees. Graphs, maps, and geometric figures convey little meaning.

- The dysgraphic boy who, despite his best efforts, cannot get his hands to do what his mind may envision and whose handwriting is painful to execute and nearly impossible to read. While in past years, his low, laborious writing production might have labeled him as short on ideas ("dumb"), the *only* shortcoming he may be experiencing is a weakness in the neural feed between his mind's intentions and the motor connections with his hands, with which to convey that intention. As in so many other instances of learning differences, a simple compensatory mechanism can revolutionize a student's success, reputation, and self-image. In this case, for example, such students, if allowed to use a computer—even just for taking notes, writing papers, and finishing essay tests in the classroom—often show dramatic improvement in their writing output.

- The child who hears perfectly but whose auditory processing system is so cumbersome that he is still trying to make sense of a question while the other students are fighting over who gets to answer it.

STUDENT LEARNING DEPENDS ON EVERY ASPECT OF THE BRAIN FUNCTIONING EFFECTIVELY

There are as many learning differences as there are conduits in the brain; however, just one learning difference can have a profound effect on a child's ability to learn in school. This is because there are so many complex and various parts involved in what it takes to learn successfully in a school setting. Step back and really consider just a few of the myriad, simultaneous aspects of success in school:

- How well we can focus in on a particular task (while we also focus out the huge infusion of competing stimuli)
- How we learn (through each of our senses, looking at outlines and maps, listening to accents and music, manipulating tools and lab equipment)
- How we internally reckon with all of that inflowing information (active working memory, short-term and long-term memory, along with our capacity to search out missing words and half-remembered facts)
- How we communicate our learning to others (speaking up in a fast-paced classroom, kinesthetically through dance or athleticism, and writing— *writing!*—during which we must grip the pencil effectively, fashion our ideas, break the ideas into words, words into correct letters, correct letters into correct letter formation, all while holding firmly onto our ideas)
- How we manage the organizational demands of materials and ideas

- How we manage the emotional demands of risk-taking in the throes of our own preoccupation and uncertainty

It may strike us as almost miraculous that any of us can survive in school at all. And yet we do—with countless discrete systems functioning with speed, coordination, and accuracy. But a child with a learning difference does not have the same experience.

To the boy in question, a breakdown in a single one of these extraordinary systems doesn't feel that he still has 97 percent of the rest of his brain circuits primed, plugged, and utterly productive and only 3 percent slowing him down. To a child who is measuring himself against his classmates, his siblings, or his parent's unspoken hopes, there is too often awareness only of the gap.

In the end, the most damaging result of a learning difference subject to long-term neglect or misunderstanding is an inexorable erosion of self-esteem. With that, motivation breaks down. Behavior may become reckless (look at anything but my failure) or depressive (I'm not worth looking at).

MAKING A DIFFERENCE TO ONE CHILD AND TO EVERY CHILD

The issue of learning differences is an important piece of your success in helping every child perform at their best in your classroom. Being aware of these issues will benefit you and the students in a number of different ways.

First, gaining even a rudimentary understanding and appreciation of the nature of such differences can help make every one of us in education more empathetic with the silent, often shaming struggles these students experience.

Second, if we can truly begin to understand and reach these students (who are often as perplexed by their own inconsistent performance as we and their parents are), we will have gone a long way to improving some of the most distracting and troublesome behavior we are likely to see in our classes.

Third, by educating ourselves and being attuned to these patterns that lie well outside the norm of student learning and behavior, we can serve such students by providing our schools with a kind of early warning system. If we can raise important questions about the gap between a student's perfor-mance and potential, we may alert others to the importance of the need to provide educational testing and learning specialists who can address the child's issues more effectively.

Fourth, learning more—enough to actually be able to help students compensate for an inherent weakness—can enable us to be dramatically more effective as teachers, to help these students feel actively included in our classrooms, and to liberate them from the shame of learning differences that set them apart— usually far behind—the rest of the class. In so doing, we may also succeed in minimizing their destructive and distracting behavior.

Finally—and this is vital to understand—this awareness will benefit your whole class, not just the LD student. Every educator who learns how to fine-tune her or his teaching to the child whose performance may be affected by learning differences is likely to discover a more sensitive array of teaching styles. For example, a teacher who regularly engages in spoken introduction to new material may learn that he or she can greatly assist the child in the class who has auditory processing issues if he or she includes an outline of major topics on the agenda and makes notes of important topics, transitions, and definitions on the board. What the teacher may not realize is that beyond the student with auditory problems, within every class exist students whose preferred learning style is visual and who will be helped considerably by these outlines and notes. In the same way, allowing students to summarize, asking a class to verbally explain directions given mostly by diagram, and making sure that everyone (even the girl with ADD) is called on will provide specific support for the student who has difficulty comprehending visual information while these actions benefit the whole class at the same time.

Thus, one of the great secrets of supporting the LD student is manifest: *By attuning our practice to the needs of the few, we can actually provide support for every student in the class.*

IN CONCLUSION

This chapter is, of course, just an introduction to the issue of learning differences. We recognize that it would be grossly naïve and performing an active disservice to teachers and their students to try to cover the field of learning differences in a single chapter in this book. The field is so rich with fresh information about brain functions, learning styles, and student behaviors that learning specialists have become the fastest-growing subset of the educational population.

We encourage you to learn more about this important topic. There are countless outstanding resources out there—books, websites, blogs, workshops, and conferences. These resources can enable us to gain an understanding of the diversity of student learning styles. They can sensitize us to the enormous, impressive differences in how students learn, think, and behave. If we are to go beyond this, to really begin work to maximize our effectiveness with these individual, outlying students, we will come to realize that what we have done for the individual has also contributed significantly to our ability to engage the entire class.

Chapter 47

SUPPORTING THE QUIET CHILD

It was an early Monday morning during the weekly collection of teachers and advisers who oversaw the seventh grade students. As the middle school principal, I opened the meeting by handing out index cards. Those gathered in the room had no idea what this was going to be about. When everyone was settled and had a writing utensil out and ready, I announced that they had four minutes to write down the names of as many seventh graders as they could. If they had any lists memorized (of advisees, for example) they were forbidden to simply rattle these off. They were to pick the names and faces as quickly as possible from thin air.

At the end of four minutes, the teachers and advisers handed in the cards. We tallied the number of mentions.

There were students named by virtually every member of the team. Unsurprisingly, these tended to be those students who truly stood out because of academic excellence, because of rat-a-tat-tat participation in almost every classroom discussion, or because of the fact that they were precisely those students who drove every teacher crazy. The names were disproportionately male.

And then there were students whose names showed up on almost no one's list. They tended to be quiet, responsible, and disproportionately female.

After a long discussion about the meaning of the tally, we committed as a faculty to radiate particular warmth and attention toward the three students who had showed up on no one's list. In the course of the following weeks, teachers exchanged regular email messages and updates about the students involved. I stopped each one of them in the hall with particular and specific praise.

Though each seemed, because of a certain personal shyness, to be a little taken aback and even a little uncomfortable hearing something positive, each was being placed in a new position in the attention of the faculty and each was being seen in a new, more focused light.

Do we owe it to our quiet students to try to help them find their voices? Absolutely.

We are all impoverished if some citizens in the classroom fail to speak up, fail to share their individual perspective, fail to make their feelings known. The tendency of some, particularly girls, to "lose their voices" has long been documented.

In case any of us feel that we are intruding on the issue of personality by asking the reticent child to speak up in class, we would point out that we never allow the nervous child to skip a test nor the reluctant writer to skip a paper. Oral presentation—even simply taking part in a class discussion— is a critical skill in the development of confident, well-rounded students and adults, and we can probably all think of classmates we had known and students we may have taught who seemed forever to seek the shadowy silence of classroom invisibility.

We owe it to the class to establish an expectation of universal participation, and we owe it particularly to those who might seek to disappear that they are drawn into the light of conversation. What follows is a set of perspectives and strategies with which to address the issue of the persistently shy child.

THERE IS NO UNIVERSAL PORTRAIT OF THE QUIET CHILD

While most have typically tended to be girls, this does shift with age. Many high school boys have adopted the posture of the mute and sullen slouch.

Quiet children vary in their performance as well. While we can likely all picture the child who is frozen by fear of making another foolish response, we can just as certainly picture the shy girl with straight A's who goes through class hoping no one will notice.

IT IS ESSENTIAL TO MAKE UNIVERSAL PARTICIPATION A CLEAR, ENFORCED EXPECTATION

In too many classes, the teacher is willing, even relieved, to have the quiet remain quiet. There are enough eager beavers in the front row to fill a dozen conversations, and with all of the problems of impatient kids calling out, it's seen as a blessing to have some who just prefer to remain on the sidelines.

If we truly believe in developing our students' skills, then allowing any subset of a class to avoid the daily rigor and oral practice of speaking up is comparable to allowing any other subset to avoid a lab, a paper, a project, a timed quiz. Avoidance of skill development isn't something we as educators typically allow—except in this critical area of oral presentation.

It should be stated expressly on the first day as part of the opening expectations for the class that everyone speaks every day. We must follow up on this by focusing on those students who haven't yet spoken. We should keep ourselves attuned to those who have chosen to remain silent. We should keep a sharp eye out for those who may suddenly, finally raise their hands. In the end, too, we can simply say overtly as the class proceeds, "Who haven't I heard from yet?"

INTEGRATE THE SEATING PLAN

Formal gender studies and our own more informal observations affirm that those classes in which students are allowed to cluster by gender support a stark imbalance in class participation. Boys will typically dominate the seats in a teacher's "hot zone," and girls, with an equally practiced eye toward the subtleties of a teacher's preferences, will favor the "cold zones," typically those seats toward the rear and toward the door, as if escape were somehow an unconscious part of the mapping of a classroom.

Research has demonstrated that integrating the seating plan and providing girl-boy-girl-boy seating throughout the room prevents clustering and cliques. Beyond this, such a seating plan can disperse hot and cold zones, discouraging collective impulsive behavior and encouraging the quiet to find their voices.

MOVE

We have mentioned it before, but it warrants particular attention in this case.

We have found it to be almost impossible for teachers to break the unconscious spell of a classroom seating plan, and we have found again and again and again that students—consciously or not—recognize where they should sit if they want to participate or if they don't.

The most potent way to overcome the patterns of calling on students—in which some areas of the classroom are represented four times as often as others in discussion—is by moving around. Teaching from the side of the room, leading a discussion from the rear of the room, hiking up some center aisle and pausing there while watching the conversation or silent work unfold can lead to subtly but powerfully different perspectives on how we perceive a class of individuals.

UNDERSTAND THE SHY CHILD'S NEED TO REHEARSE

As most of us realize, it isn't that the quiet students are simply tuned out. They are often bright, focused, and *internally* engaged, but something close to stage fright, some hesitancy to appear foolish or wrong—or too smart—holds them back.

Give the shy girl a chance to rehearse, and her odds of participating and the frequency at which she participates will both rise significantly. What are some ways to allow for such rehearsal?

- Announce, as part of the homework, what the key topics will be for tomorrow's class.
- Post the agenda with key questions labeled sequentially.
- Open the class with four minutes of silence while students journal privately about the discussion that will follow. Even if it weren't for the benefit of those less inclined to speak up, this practice encourages a much more mature, less impulsive level of dialogue.

- Open the class by asking students to turn to a neighbor and quietly discuss what will become the topic of the class-wide conversation after four minutes.

Sometimes—often, in fact—the students who need to rehearse and vocalize an answer before they dare to give it out loud have no opportunity to ever reach a triggering point of readiness. This is because the boisterous, impulsive students' hands go up immediately, even if they only plan to fill the gap between the question and their actual answer with a common stall tactic of "Well, um, Mr. Gottlieb, the answer to your question is basically that—" In such a meandering introduction, nothing has really been said, but internally, the brash child has grabbed the conversational brass ring and stalled long enough to be able to come up with at least a plausible answer. In that same amount of time, the more reticent girl has held her hand at her side and perhaps come up with a better answer, but it's too late now. The impulsive child has garnered the right to speak.

As we have noted earlier, a study was done of classrooms throughout the United States across all age groups. The average length of time between the end of a teacher's question and the moment the first student is called on was found to be 0.9 seconds, and no, that isn't nine seconds. It's nine-tenths of a second. No wonder so many classroom conversations include only the same students over and over and over again. No wonder so many of these discussions never really seem to get to higher levels of thought and reflection.

Take a moment.

Dare to take five or even tens second before you call on anyone.

Say directly, "I'm waiting to see more hands. I want to hear from all of you."

Make it a prodding invitation.

We owe it to everyone to allow time for rehearsal. Even the impulsive boy is likely to come up with a better answer if he now has to wait ten seconds before he answers a thoughtful question.

GIVE A PARTICULARLY SHY CHILD A SILENT CUE

The educational pioneer Richard LaVoie (whose classic videotape *How Difficult Can This Be?* should be seen by teachers in every school in the country) offers the following scenario for dealing with the child who is reluctant to speak up. Whether the child's hesitation is because of slow language processing, risk aversion, or a kind of internal perfectionism in crafting just the right answer, the solution proposed is the same.

Take the shy girl aside one afternoon after class and tell her that you want to hear from her more often even though you understand that she may be a little nervous about speaking up.

Tell her that you would like to help her practice participating comfortably in class. The agreement you make is that you will never call on her unless you have come over to stand directly in front of her seat. You can continue to talk for a moment after you position yourself in the warning spot, but then invite her in, asking her a question you feel certain she can answer. Let her spend the rest of the period when you aren't near her seat really thinking about the lesson, and not reflexively dreading something that most of the time isn't going to happen.

Relieved of such constant anxiety and dread, you may discover that her hand begins to go up voluntarily as she discovers that she can survive the ritual of speaking up in class.

WELCOME A CHILD INTO THE CONVERSATION WITH PARTICULARLY WARM EYE CONTACT

We all likely have a sense of how long a teacher or any public speaker will keep his or her eyes on us as part of their scan of the class or audience. We have just as hair-trigger a sense of when the teacher is singling us out for attention.

A teacher who wishes to have a student speak up can gaze at that student a little longer than the typical scan, share a warm, expectant smile, and through body language welcome them into the discussion.

It's not foolproof, but it's actually surprising how often a student will shortly thereafter, feeling really seen, speak up and become part of the dialogue.

HONOR THEIR PARTICIPATION WITH SIMILARLY WARM EYE CONTACT

When Reticent Rita finally speaks up, it may be embarrassing to her if you offer direct praise. The linger of warm, appreciative eye contact—just a split second longer than the typically fleeting audience scan—can honor a student's participation far more effectively than direct, public praise.

PRAISE THEM ALOUD

At the very least, catch her for a moment as she's heading out the door after class to say, "Whoa, that was a terrific point you made. Thank you for speaking up. I was hoping someone would understand just exactly what you did. That was terrific. It's great to hear from you."

And even in class, a quick "Brilliant!" can perhaps cause a blush, but sometimes a blush is a glow of pleasure.

BE A FRIEND

For some quiet, lonely students (and not all quiet kids are lonely), you may be a kind of best friend. Like it or not, you may be in a position to help a child who arrives at school and spends most of the day by him- or herself with no one really to talk to. As professionals, we can all set limits on our time. (There's no reason to fear that a lonely child hungering for friendship is going to appear, backpack and sleeping bag in hand, on our doorstep.) But many students go through seasons of profound social upheaval. Some experience seasons of transient depression, during which they withdraw. Some are doomed to yearly stretches during which they fail to connect socially with anyone else in the class.

A chat about a book report written, a chance to stay back from recess to help you clean the guinea pig's cedar shavings, or a quiet time changing the bulletin board can really help. It won't always happen, but sometimes in the silent, shared activity arises a kinship for a child estranged from his or her family, from the bustle of the popular kids, from the latent, sleeping dreams within this student.

DON'T ALLOW RIDICULE

There can be no ridicule, no laughter, and no snicker at anyone's expense in your class if you are ever to lure them out of their protective shells. It is vital to the safety of everyone, but it is particularly vital to the shy ones.

The quiet children in our schools are deeply risk-averse, gun-shy, and even fun-shy after a time. If the wisenheimers in the back of the room are ever once allowed to cackle at an error or indiscretion, if the know-it-alls are allowed to cast even a knowing glance at each other, there is little hope for drawing out the quiet, for connecting with the lonely, for relieving their silence.

Make your classroom—from the first day and forever—one in which the only thing that can't be tolerated is intolerance itself, and if there is a case of ridicule, however oblique or subtle, stop the action then and there. Even the most over-lookable instance of ridicule is noticed by many and felt by the victim.

Stand strong and foursquare with anyone thus victimized. The victim has been isolated. Turn the tables on the victimizer and let them feel the power of isolation.

Dead silence.

Serious eye contact.

A step forward.

And don't let the victimizer off the hook.

"Never again. Not in this class."

Dead silence.

LOOK FOR POSSIBLE FRIENDSHIPS

Sometimes, every so often, it is possible to notice a friend for the lonely boy before he can even begin to believe it himself.

I haven't had the chance to do this often, but I will always remember the chances I have had with a satisfaction that equals any of the cognitive gains I might have supported in my teaching. One of those times, Kamaal and Chester were two boys in my third grade class. They were almost too dutiful. Their parents rode them close and hard, and they were in to see me over any bump in the road. Kamaal and Chester had good parents but parents who couldn't yet see that part of real love is letting go. Failure can prompt real growth. Challenge can build real strength. They wanted the road paved and patrolled all the way to adulthood, and all the while, their sons ached alone, afraid to displease, fearing the consequences of displaying anything less than perfection.

It was late in the year, but I was home for the weekend, musing this time not on Tom Foolery and Renegade Jones but on Kamaal and the sadness that so deeply veiled his brightness. Then I thought of Chester, with his little eyeglasses and his handkerchief-in-the-pocket impossible childhood, and I had an idea. All through the long Sunday afternoon, I mused on it. I tried to imagine what they might both really like.

On Monday morning at recess, I asked them to stay in. Looking wobble-eyed and seasick on the calm waters where we stood, they waited for me to pass sentence.

"I've always been interested in submarines," I said, "but I don't really know anything about them."

They blinked in unison.

"And I was wondering if you two would be willing to go home over the course of the next week and work together and learn all that you can about submarines. Maybe build a model. Maybe do a cut-away drawing. Maybe look up submarine disasters. Maybe learn about the history of submarines or the biggest one or anything you want. And come in next Monday and teach me."

They blinked a lot and then turned to each other. Their smiles were almost hugs. That lunchtime, I called each of the boy's mothers and told them what I had perpetrated. I shared with them my suspicion that they might really become good friends over time. I politely encouraged them to set up a few afternoons in the coming week when the boys would be able to get together to work.

Now it may surprise you that I never saw any sort of submarine research from the boys. By the following Monday, they came up to me and said that they weren't ready yet. I smiled and said that was fine. It was extra credit, as they knew. I just thought they might have had fun with it, anyway.

"Oh, we are," Jamaal insisted, his eyes shining.

The submarine project was never mentioned again.

After a couple of weeks had gone by, I asked the boys if they would like me to move their seats closer together. I could see them jumping up and down the hall as they headed off toward art class.

At the end of eighth grade, they were still the closest of friends, and I take no undue credit for this. Even with the vagaries of who proved to be in whose class, and how soon they were classmates again, I suspect they would have found each other eventually.

Nothing—and nothing even after all of these years looking back on my time at that school—brought me more deep, rich, laughing pleasure than the crazy little chance I thought of on a Sunday and put into motion on a Monday that brought to life two boys who deserved so much more attention than what dutiful quiet might have earned them.

REMEMBER THOSE WHO ALMOST SEEK TO BE FORGOTTEN

Our schools are filled with all makes and models of children, but in our meetings, in our discussions that fill up entire afternoons, in our consultations with the counselor or school psychologist, we spend perhaps 90 percent of our time talking about the same 10 percent of the student body. Most of the kids are just okay, used cars in heavy traffic, going their way, driving through childhood, early adolescence, and adolescence in all of its top-down squealing angst and glory. In the right-hand lane, slow as depression and unnoticed by almost all of the cops, convertibles and carefree caravans drive the lonely and quiet and perpetually uncertain children in our midst.

They matter. They are not unreachable. They are not lost. They are there in plain sight.

I know this because I was one of them for more than three years. For three years and beyond, no one noticed.

And then came Jenny Hankins, the young, risky, golden English teacher mentioned earlier in this book (with the metal bust of a woman wrapped in dry-cleaning plastic), and somehow she sensed that in my paralysis there might yet be poetry, in my permafrost there might yet be portent of spring and the potential for someone to find me.

I am certain that I was unappealing, stiff, quiet, and easily startled. When we were told to find a partner for a project or a class trip, I rose and turned to Jerry Tabasco. We were nowhere near friends. We had nothing in common—except for the realization that we could count on each other when no one else would choose us.

And I know that I must have been a hard case for Jenny. She taught English, and I was the classic chess and math and science nerd, a frozen figure on a landscape in motion. Her attention, her good humor, and her patience provided a warmth no one else had ever extended, and over the course of a single year, working in her presence just one class a day, I experienced the gradual, life-transforming thaw of a self-imposed ice age.

They are all about us. They are likely more numerous than the disruptive, difficult students we face each day. It is high time that the silent, undemanding children in our schools get their own fair share of attention and support.

As teachers, we can make just this kind of difference in the lives of all the quiet children in our class, if we seek them out and provide the support needed.

Chapter 48

THIRTY-FIVE STEPS
FOR DEALING WITH A
DIFFICULT CLASS

I t can be a case of outright defiance, serious alienation, and utter disregard. Or it can be vastly more subtle. It's not an awful situation exactly. It just feels as if you're trying to listen to a radio that's not quite on the station. There is too much interference. Too many moments of clarity are followed by raking stretches of static. The connection is intermittent, unreliable, and ultimately unsatisfying. You could live with it, but why should you?

The former case is just awful, but even the latter case, which beginning teachers at Packer came to call "benign chatter," is one that demands attention and action.

What follows is a thirty-five-point checklist of strategies to consider in moving forward with a difficult class. At this point in the book, we aren't so much introducing anything new as much as we are consolidating the best advice from many different discussions throughout the book into one easy checklist. Think of it as a place for you to reference as you venture out into the classroom to try out these techniques. Chances are you are already doing many of the activities that follow, and chances are some of them simply don't make any difference. Regrettably, there is no such thing as a perfect prescription for improving connections in a class or in any human relationship. The social, cultural, and academic issues that underlie any group of students are far too subtle and personal to lend themselves to any guarantees, even if you follow any absolute litany of first-do-this-then-do-that rules.

And yet, we have seen that there are clear, predictable steps you can take to improve classroom control, ensure greater connection with the students, and enhance productivity and satisfaction during the course of a period, not to mention throughout the year itself.

The thirty-five steps comprising this critical checklist represent a comprehensive distillation of the most important points related to the effective control of a classroom. No teacher does all thirty-five—at least not with equal effectiveness—but it has been our experience that addressing even a few neglected or unaddressed components of this "master list" will provide dramatic, incremental improvements in the relationship.

BEFORE CLASS EVEN BEGINS:

1. Lead off your lesson plan with powerful provocations.

Behind every concept, every lesson, every reading you plan to cover, there are a score of cool ideas. Don't settle for a plan that just gets the material covered, that just gets the job done. If you're teaching the subjunctive, ask your students why or how the early civilizations might even have thought of or needed such a form. Fascinate them with language. Bring them into what may have even been at the heart of your own first fledgling interest in the subject.

Have a great story to share with your class. Have a provocative question ready for them. Draw them in. There is magic in all that we teach. So much in history can be so human. So much in science can be so thought-provoking. So much in literature can be so compelling.

Before we even put pen to paper when we craft a lesson plan, we have to get in touch with the subject—or *back* in touch with it—ourselves.

2. Map out a variety of activities.

It is hard work just to listen. It is tiring to stay focused. (If you don't believe that, chances are you haven't attended a day-long conference or taken a challenging college course in a while.) As human beings, our attention spans are limited. Our energy is enlivened by variety.

Beyond that, there are students who, however well-intentioned, simply have hardwired difficulty with auditory or visual processing. They are slow or compromised in what they can take in by just listening or looking. Protracted lectures or long stretches with you at the board going over maps and graphs just don't mean to them what they might mean to others.

Help yourself by helping them stay focused. Crack a period into quarters. Jigsaw the activities and *types* of activities deftly together. Vary the learning channel (not just auditory, auditory, auditory, all the time). Change the social dynamic (not just teacher-led discussions). Let them solve problems together. Let there be urgency within the urgency (not forty tight minutes but four tight ten-minute modules). Keep them alert.

3. Notice your allies and build a coalition.

When it begins to feel that you've lost control of the entire class, recognize that that's *never* the case. Within every section, there are students who want the class to go well, who want to learn, gain mastery, achieve, and feel good about themselves. They may be hard to recognize when it feels as if the snickers are universal and the entire class appears to be rising up in surly rebellion.

But they are there. Map out the class in the evening. Identify potential allies and deputies—those who, beyond all of the yuk-it-up folderol, ultimately *want to learn*—and then, one by one, begin to reconnect (praise is key here) with those who want you to succeed and to isolate those who stand against the class's progress.

4. Use a seating chart.

It's very likely that a seating chart will elicit a slew of groans and convictions that you really are uncool.

Go with the uncoolness.

From the moment students enter your classroom, there will likely be a series of small rituals intended to exert their own power at your expense. Instead, make it clear from the moment they enter your classroom that they immediately have to head to the seat that you chose for them.

This isn't some crass and needy power play. This is simple effectiveness. The wrong kids almost always sit in the wrong places. The quiet ones shift to the shadowy recesses at the corners, where their bodies actually cease to reflect light. The spitballers tend to crowd to the back, where they can practice their ballistics from behind a fortress of eager beavers. And yes, even the eager beavers tend to build their dams in the praise spotlights right at the front of the room.

Mix it up. Alternate genders. Bust up the cliques. Carefully place your prospective allies and deputies with care—where they will be free from ridicule and able to exert their own positive influence. Bring the painfully quiet and the ruthlessly rambunctious to the front, and let the go-getters settle in the rear, where the fiery trajectories of their engagement may come to illuminate all those sitting to the front of them.

Take charge. You make the decisions.

AS THE CLASS OPENS:

5. Be punctual.

When students of any age come into a room without a teacher present, they tend to create their own sense of turf ownership, which they will often concede only gradually and begrudgingly.

When they come into a classroom where the teacher is already present and waiting for them, they are immigrants in a world of *your* creation. Whether one is a teacher in a self-contained classroom welcoming students back from a specialist or one is a departmental teacher rushing from one classroom to another, it is vital to be there as they arrive. Or if that is almost impossible to do, require them to wait outside until you arrive. From the moment they enter then, they are moving into their first grade home, the hallowed halls of

American history, or the digital landscape of mathematics. And all lingering chatter, lunchroom rumors, or locker room one-upmanship should therefore come to an abrupt and absolute halt.

6. Post an agenda.

Reflect your organization and inspire their own. Give them a sense of the main idea of each lesson, because some inevitably really won't get it. Model an outline of what you intend to cover or what they are expected to do. Give them a sense of how many activities there will be and how much time will be spent on each. And if you give homework, have the assignment listed in black and white for all to see.

7. Have something for them to do the moment they arrive.

Some teachers have created—and reinforced—a disciplined routine for their students at the beginning of each class. In my eighth grade algebra class, students were informed on the first day that they were not allowed to talk until they had gotten their texts, calculators, and homework out. And I enforced this, even turning away a student who wanted to speak with me for a moment before class.

Other teachers have a "problem of the day" already on the board (or posted on the portable agenda) as the students arrive. For teachers moving from classroom to classroom, we recommend having such a problem already written on a large piece of paper that can quickly be taped to the board or wall so that you can begin the class facing them, watching them, overseeing them as they arrive.

The goal is to get them focused and even get them immersed in your discipline (using both meanings of the word) from the moment they enter the room.

8. Start on time.

Allow a gradual arrival, and you will get a gradual arrival.

Consider that even two minutes lost to a dilly-dally entry wastes 5 percent of a forty-minute class. Span this over a 180-day school year, and nine full days have been lost unnecessarily to muted muttering and mindless milling about.

Give those who arrive punctually something to do immediately, and give those who may be inclined to saunter toward your classroom a little incentive to quicken their pace. If tardiness has become an issue, flash them an occasional three-question pop quiz that begins the moment the class is scheduled to start. There are no repeated questions. Those who arrive late will soon come to realize that you mean business, that you are the marshal, and that this is your town.

9. Instill a sense of urgency.

Say, "Today we've got a *lot* to do."

Set it up immediately. Those who interrupt the pace of the lesson aren't so much "breaking our rules" as they are "interfering with everyone else's progress," which is a vital distinction to help you stay aligned with the class.

Say this with a smile, warming to your subject, and back it up with your own sense of pace and importance.

AS THE CLASS UNFOLDS:

10. Remember the power of praise.

Yes, there are occasionally direct compliments, but more often than not, in the course of fast-paced dialogues and discussions, the typical teacher only makes extended comments on a student's response when it is *wrong*.

We need to be just as quick to expand on a moment of praise as we are to clarify or correct an incorrect answer. We don't need to spend that much time on long-winded praise. Just giving an enthusiastic "Wow!" or "Brilliant!" or "Did you all hear that?" with lingering eye contact can create a moment of pride and an eagerness for others to join in.

If things have gone downhill for a long time, it may be galling to imagine praising a bunch of kids who have come to seem like doomed and unrepentant hooligans. It may be hard to imagine that there even *is* an intellectual, productive side to them. And this one fact—this failure to praise or even to see anything praiseworthy—is often the principal barrier between life as it is…

and as it could be. We have seen too many classes that are mired in dissension where praise has just gone by the boards. And quietly, inexorably, students begin refusing to respond when there is no hope of being made to feel good about such a response.

Come back to the power of praise. Catch them being good or less bad. Call home. Praise them personally. Co-opt them. Begin to win them back one by one.

11. Move!

Nothing may be more stultifying than a teacher who sits down in a chair, on a desk, or on a lab table throughout the course of a lesson. Even remaining standing at our desk, at the board, or at the front of the room allows the potential energy flow in a classroom to dissipate and grow stagnant. If we have chosen to remain seated—or even to remain standing without real move-ment—and there is a chronic, underlying listlessness in the classroom, we have no one to blame but ourselves.

It is vital for us to commit—not for a time, but until it becomes absolutely second nature to us—to moving about the room. This movement will not only awaken the ionic flow within the room but within ourselves as well. It will help us stay focused and energized. It will reduce our tendency toward hot and cold spots around the room, and it will exert our influence over what can otherwise become sleepy or indifferent backwaters within the class.

12. Make your transitions crisp and swift and just as urgent.

We have seen too many teachers who have crafted wonderful lesson plans, who have led with apparent urgency, and who have developed a rich variety of activities and then let the transitions diffuse the entire momentum of the class. They have to cross the room and refer to their lesson plans. They haven't assembled all of the necessary equipment. They have presented incom-plete instructions so that they have to interrupt the momentum with belated reminders and clarifications. ("Wait a second. Can I have everyone's attention again for a minute?")

Internalize your transition points so that you don't have to lose momentum looking them up. (Here's where a posted agenda can really work to your advantage, helping to cue you for the next activity.) Better yet, *plan the transitions* so that each activity segues naturally into the next. The small amount of time (which will diminish as you get good at it) invested in focusing on these brief but critical transitions will begin to pay off in sharpening focus and momentum from the first day.

13. Remember the power of wait time.

The single most important thing we can provide the nervous, the reticent, *and* the impatient with is *time*.

When we follow the customary inclination to engage in quick-question/quick-answer ping pong, the same players emerge, and the same spectators are left in the background. By expanding wait time—through journaling, partnered dialogue, or simply saying, "I'm not calling on anyone until I see more hands," and actually waiting for those hands—we will draw many former onlookers into the activity. We will not only hear more voices, we will also elicit excitingly different perspectives. We may well discover some sleeping achievers out there, and we will greatly build the opportunity for unification with the entire class in a shared recognition that "we're all in this together."

14. Ensure that they talk and listen to each other.

We are frankly tired of seeing classrooms in which front row students only speak loudly enough for the teacher to hear and then watching the teacher wonder why the rest of the students aren't more engaged. In part, seating arrangements can open up real dialogue, everyone facing each other instead of so many backs. (Horseshoes are wonderful for this.) In part, too, the active teacher works to ensure that students are speaking not only to him or her but to the rest of the class in volume and in eye contact.

And we must be very careful that we don't just scold those who tune out when it is *our* turn to speak. We must be at least as attentive to those who do the same to their fellow classmates. Building a genuine, wide-ranging, increasingly inclusive pattern of class participation is an ideal toward which we should all be working. Requiring each student to speak loudly and clearly enough for everyone in the room to hear is the first major step. Beyond that, it is vital that we pay particular attention to encouraging them, especially as they begin to respond to each other's statements just as they do to ours.

15. Call on the cross-talkers.

Cheryllette is answering the question you've just posed. MoonDoggie is snorkeling over in the corner with his pack of friends. Turn on him warmly and abruptly, and take a strong, controlling step in his direction.

"MoonDoggie, do you agree with Cheryllette?"

Or say, "MoonDoggie, what did Cheryllette just say?"

Let him fumble with an answer. Let him pretend to agree with what he couldn't possibly have heard. Let him somehow even manage to repeat what she had said. No matter what, hold the pause. Let your eyes show that you are disregarding whatever he says, that the answer itself is unimportant, that it is finished. You asked the question not to get an answer but to deliver a message. Let the silence filter in around him like a slightly uncomfortable fog. You don't even have to say anything. You have done what you can to make sure that he understands—that his private partying is busted, finished, kaput.

16. Drawing in the inattentive.

It is a disservice to those who have attention difficulty to let them wander off until they are waist-deep in some "Big Muddy" of their own imagination. It is even a disservice to our own aspirations for the greater unity of the class.

It is also a disservice to embarrass the child with ADD or to take up class time lecturing on the evils of inattention.

To that end, here are two simple tricks to keeping everyone focused while avoiding any embarrassment or wasted time.

Call on them gently, and repeat the question. Allow them the repetition to land back on Earth and to fashion an answer. Being inattentive isn't meant to be willfully disrespectful, unlike throwing knives at your gizzard.

Or simply, as you are speaking, insert his or her name into the middle of a sentence, and move on. Jeffrey may have been playing CandyLand somewhere out along the frozen wastes of Kamchatka, but he'll very likely hear his name even across the silent vacuum of space.

If it is permissible and appropriate in your school culture, sometimes there are students who are so caught up in their little goofball antics or students who are so lost to ground control that a hand placed fleetingly on their shoulder as you pass can reawaken their attention and focus. This sends a quick message: "This is the classroom. This is where you are. You matter. Come back. Join us."

Note that in some circumstances related to the age of the students and in some locales so distorted by the looming vultures of litigation, it will not be deemed appropriate in any circumstances to touch a student. Please determine if this is the case in your school before you use the previous technique.

17. Don't honor those who call out.

Make it a rule from the very first day that you will not—under any circumstances—take answers from those who call out. Even if the best answer in the history of the universe is called out, pretend that you didn't hear it. Don't interrupt the flow. Don't lecture. Ignore it completely. Lift your eyebrows inquiringly and look about for someone who is actually raising his or her hand.

18. Develop—early on, if possible—a simple key for getting everyone quiet.

As clichéd as it may sound, simply counting down from five—and heaven help the child who's still talking at zero—can provide a swift point of focus. We have seen other teachers lightly strike a chime or quietly raise a hand, and each student, upon realizing what is going on, also grows silent and raises a hand.

Simple, individual, and focusingly quiet.

19. When the chatter grows rampant and noisy, talk under it.

There is a great temptation to shout over the noise of a class.

But kneeling and whispering can suddenly deputize many members of the class. Let them hush each other as you blithely continue to whisper the homework assignment or tell them what's going to be on the test this Thursday or recite your grocery list in Pig Latin.

20. Use the power of silence.

If it gets boisterous enough, simply stop. Use the power of silence. Let it emanate.

Breathe. Make strong eye contact with the last of the talkers. Wait for the stillness to echo like silent thunder all about the room. Wait four more seconds. Then start with a crisp bang.

21. Address the issue before you go ballistic.

Ah, the number of times we've watched teachers pretend that nothing was wrong and forge bravely on with the lesson while their complexions reddened and that telltale vein began to bulge in their foreheads. When they lose their temper, they lose it but good—with a wild Donald Duck outburst that must, in some way, secretly delight the students. Perhaps it's as unsurprising as it is sad that having witnessed this loss of control, that same cluster of unsympathetic students gathered in the back corner of the room will be drawn to provoke it again and again.

Keep your reaction cool and quiet and understated. When you feel your pulse begin to ping, sit on the corner of your desk and stare out across the infinity of patience.

You can wait.

22. Express indifference about their progress.

In judo and ju-jitsu, much of the power is derived from using the momentum of the assailant against him- or herself. Instead of standing up to your students relentlessly, let them through.

Look at your watch. Look at the calendar.

Say "Next year, you're going to be going on to algebra/Spanish II/fourth grade. You will be the ones who aren't prepared. You tell me when you're feeling ready to learn."

Or try saying, "You've got homework tonight that isn't going to be easy. I was planning to spend twenty-two minutes previewing it with you. That would have made it a lot easier. We're now down to twelve minutes. My night is going to be easy. You tell me when you're feeling ready to learn."

And then sit and wait until they're *more* than ready to learn.

23. Use the power of our authority.

This is, of course, the big one. It can and should be used at any point: No means no.

Draw the line in the sand. No averted eyes. No unconscious self-effacing smile. No warble in your voice. No stutter-step back toward the protective fortress of your desk.

It is time to accept the fact that it's our challenge, that it's our job, that it's our responsibility to be the authority in the classroom. We need to own that authority.

We may need to practice it before it becomes second nature, but even before we enter the classroom, even before the first student arrives, it is vital that we feel, own, and unleash the power that is ours.

24. Meet him or her for a confidential one-on-one in the hall.

You know the routine. You've got something to say, but you don't want to raise the stakes and escalate a low-level confrontation by saying it publicly.

Wait until he is just about to leave, and then leave at just the same moment alongside him. Send his friends on their way. Close the distance. Ask him a question: "Why do I want to speak with you?"

Let him dodge and feint, but let him feel the proximity of your dissatisfaction along with your awareness that he can do so much better, that his behavior is a betrayal of his true nature. Then send him on his way.

And watch him like a hawk the next day so that you can monitor positive improvement in this area or warn him with sudden, unwavering eye contact that you are a bird of prey.

25. Meet him or her for an announced one-on-one in the hall.

This time the assault on the peace of the classroom or the pace of the lesson is severe enough that the rest of the class has to be notified. You will handle the matter privately, but everyone will know it.

26. Call home.

Enlist the parents. Put them on notice. If you don't, they may later blame you for a failure to try at the very least. Perhaps they will back you, support you, and accept the possibility of a partnership. Remember to say: "I need your help."

27. Kick them out.

Send him or her to the office. Let the class see this demonstration of the consequences of busting the limits. Let the class see how much more smoothly things flow in his or her absence. Let the class see that you mean business, and let the student sweat a bit in the principal's office.

Make sure that you walk down to the same office as soon as class is finished to make sure that the student arrived, that the principal has the *whole* story, and that the disciplinary hierarchy has been activated seriously and effectively.

28. Kick them out with a forewarned supervisor.

This time, the perpetrator has been so consistent in his or her misbehavior that you've told your supervisor to expect the student and to scorch the miscreant's shoes with dragon fire. Add to the child's understanding that not only was he or she way outside the bounds today but that he or she has been outside often enough that even the supervisor knows it.

29. Conduct a solo intervention.

The first day of the year is the time when you should lay down the law, set the tone, and establish routines and expectations of conduct.

But it is never too late to intervene, to say enough is enough, and to declare *this* the first day of the rest of the year. It is never too late to provide revolutionarily explicit expectations—crisp, clear, and crunchy—to map out seriously consequential follow-through and to serve notice that there's a new marshal in town.

30. Ask your supervisor to mediate an intervention.

Sometimes you may need a serious cease-fire, with a resonance of hope built upon a dialogue and guided by a recognition that things have to get better. In such a situation, there may well be some fault on both sides. Now is the time to address it. Now is the time to move forward.

As teachers, we acknowledge that we have some responsibility for the poor tenor of our class, whether or not we really know the reasons. The purpose of this type of intervention is to courageously elicit student feedback (and to own up to our own missteps if possible) and then state categorically that we will heed what we have heard. And now, we too have some things to say.

The students have spoken. Then we stand shoulder-to-shoulder with the supervisor. The law is laid down. The year begins anew.

31. Ask your supervisor in to declare martial law.

Things are out of control. The kids aren't making much progress. You've tried just about everything. You've already declared your own new first day of the year and found that things devolved into a sad replication of the past imperfect. Now, the time has come. Enough is enough. You've done what you can. It's time to make *serious* use of the disciplinary hierarchy.

The supervisor and you are there just as they arrive. Nine minutes later, you are alone with a class now shockwaved to silence and aware that you have friends in high places.

Then, swift as a flash of chain lightning, you unroll a lesson from on high and make it the best class you've led all year. Enough was certainly enough. Let's see what can happen when the monsters have been lion-tamed back into the zoo.

Let's see what they are really capable of.

AND AFTERWARD:

32. See the students in other classes and activities.

Actively explore just who these children are and how they perform in other settings.

Let the hooligan surprise you with his work on the cello. Let the quiet girl amaze you with her leadership on the basketball court. Watch analytically as the Spanish teacher gets Raskolnikov to actually raise his hand, and try to figure out *how* the teacher did it.

One of the greatest obstacles to our growth and development as teachers is that we remain so isolated in our own classrooms. We are all overworked and overscheduled, but a single visit to an extracurricular activity or another teacher's class will—guaranteed—leave us certain that it was time well spent.

33. Seek out a confidante, even a supervisor.

If there really is trouble, your supervisor almost certainly already knows of it, and it's better that you approach the difficulty proactively, seeking guidance and support, than that you hunker down and wait for your supervisor suddenly to summon you into the office.

Whatever your relationship with your supervisor, it can be central to your own sense of optimism and activism to have a knowledgeable confidante, an experienced teacher, who is also a good listener. Share your questions with him or her, talk about your uncertainty, and even reveal the pain you may have experienced.

Isolation is the richest medium for our own self-doubts.

34. Try not to take it personally.

Henry was in fourth grade. Henry played the trombone—sort of. Henry had a recital. He totally lost his place. In front of the crowd, he kept blowing away, increasingly randomly. He felt the first hoof-beats of a panic attack.

And then he began to lift off skyward. From high above the stage where the young boy blew his hapless horn, he looked down on himself as if from far,

far away. It was almost as if it was no longer happening to him but to a child he could observe and sympathize with. Eventually, the brass teacher came out and escorted him gently off the stage, and the audience clapped with enthusiastic empathy.

Everyone has been there. Few of us have likely been able to call on such a precocious defense mechanism. Sometimes, we can look down on ourselves, as Henry did from his angelic perch in the moon clouds high above. Sometimes we can look back at ourselves with the sympathy of age and time. This too shall pass.

There is probably no recommendation in this entire book that will prove harder to fulfill than not to take the pain of breakdown in the classroom too personally. Teaching is intensely personal. This isn't toll-taking or hedge-clipping or wheel-aligning. This is a career about children and their growth. This is a career about our own growth, as well.

This is us out there with them. Alone. With a lot expected of us. Working almost entirely on our own. And when it isn't going well, it doesn't feel good. Most of the time, if we are honest, it isn't because we are so crushed by their lack of progress but because we are so unnerved by our own lack of success at getting through to them.

What is there to do when it's going so badly?

First of all, realize that all that you can do is all that you can do. Beyond that, you can learn, listen, reflect, visit them with other teachers, and observe other teachers with other students. Watch analytically, and pick up a trick or two along the way. Remember to *breathe*.

Teachers are not so unlike parents. We are charged with raising the young, and the young don't always heed us. Sometimes they actually delight in ridiculing our feet of clay. No parent has ever raised a perfect child or raised an imperfect child perfectly.

No one ever said that teaching was easy. And here, toward the end of this book, sharing all that we can, all that we have tried to learn along the way, we will reaffirm that teaching isn't easy. However, nothing worthwhile in life ever is.

As much as you can, keep your challenges in perspective. Keep them in context. And know that we tend to learn the most when we are challenged the hardest. Don't do nothing. Learn along the way.

And know that all that we can do is all that we can do.

35. The best antidote for anxiety is action.

I have experienced more than my fair share of anxiety in life, and I have learned that inaction and isolation are anxiety's two greatest allies.

We conclude this cavalcade of recommended strategies with this one for a reason, partly because this understanding transcends education and our lives in the classroom. In larger measure, when we are facing a challenge in the classroom, the one most important thing we can do, not surprisingly, is to do something about it.

Pain and self-doubt are often immobilizing at a time when the only real springboard to growth isn't a passive wish for relief or rescue but our own willingness to rise, dust ourselves off, adopt some new tactics, and get back into the classroom.

When you are anxious, indecision and inaction are easy and damaging temptations.

Overcome them.

Step forward. Take action.

IN CONCLUSION

There is likely nothing more painful we will ever experience as teachers than the class that is out of control. They challenge our tactics. They undermine our sense of effectiveness. They may even lead us to question our abilities and the chosen course of our lives.

For too many teachers in such circumstances, the result is a kind of passive discouragement, a depressive, inactive response to the pain and the problem. We have accumulated this powerful, thirty-five-step checklist specifically to awaken dormant energies, to underscore the fact that there is a rich range of responses, and to state categorically that, through action and imagination, it *can* get better.

Chapter 49

TWENTY-FOUR STEPS FOR DEALING WITH DIFFICULT OR ANGRY PARENTS

You arrive at school, carefree as a cow in clover. And there, rising from the meadow before you, are Jackal and Hyena Madbull, the most notorious, clover-hating parents of the entire student body. Their look suggests they have been waiting for hours—hours of sleepless antagonism—for you. You are no longer a carefree cow. In their eyes, you seem to be cattle awaiting slaughter.

Not every parent conference is difficult, but when it is, you would do well to prepare thoroughly. Sometimes, you know in advance that it's going to be difficult. Sometimes, it is the Kindly family or Apparently Innocent, who have always smiled at you benignly in the halls, that turns out to be difficult.

Has this happened to you? If not, it may be that you:

1. Haven't set a foot into a classroom yet.
2. Are *way* overdue for a storm of torch-bearing parents, howling death threats outside your window.
3. Are protected by angels from on high.

At some point in our careers, each of us will find ourselves facing an angry parent.

Parents, just like students, are sometimes inclined to test relatively new teachers. On some level, they may want to make sure that their children are in good hands. Sometimes, if we're honest, we did something that might have raised questions.

No matter what the reason or even how valid their complaints are, you have become the villain in their world for the moment. It is up to you to do everything possible to establish and maintain your professionalism.

As someone who has mishandled such meetings in the past, I can affirm that there is very little else in the course of the school year that will weigh more heavily on one's memory and one's feeling of confidence in teaching than the experience of a withering assault from an arch-plaintiff and a mishandled course of action as the respondent. On behalf of each of us who will face such encounters, the following list of time-tested and proven techniques is offered to help you deal with these situations in a professional and effective manner.

1. Ask what the meeting is about.

If you are asked to set up a meeting, dare to ask in advance for one sentence revealing what the meeting is about.

Sure, if Mrs. Cuthbertson fixes her eyes on you and asks pointedly for a meeting with you just shortly after you have sent her beloved Norbert to the detention center for high crimes and misdemeanors, it is natural to assume that is what the meeting will be about. Even so, as someone who has prepared more than once for a meeting and been dead wrong about the parent's agenda, I can speak strongly in favor of asking for a "single sentence" revealing what the meeting is about. Chances are that it *will* be about young Norbert's comeuppance, but if not, you will have time and guidance with which to prepare for the real purpose of the meeting.

We urge you to try to limit the answer to your query to a single sentence. Otherwise, you may get both barrels between the eyes right then when she is most raw with outrage.

2. Schedule the meeting with some tactical awareness.

You don't want to appear to be putting her off, avoiding the confrontation, or dismissing the importance of what she has to tell you, but time, even twenty-four hours, can cool a fevered parent.

If you have any control over the scheduling of the meeting, *don't* schedule it for late in the day or any time on a Friday and certainly never just before vacation. Don't set yourself up to go home for the night or the weekend or all through the gales of the winter break and obsess before your own lonely hearth about the vicissitudes of the profession.

If you feel you have any discretion, then schedule it for early the next day. This sounds like a prompt response, but it allows another night for the family to sleep on their unrest and perhaps even gain some more balanced perspective. It necessarily limits the length of any meeting, and it allows you to get yourself back into the classroom, into the support of colleagues, and into the balanced perspective that can arise by attending to the business of the day.

3. Have an exit strategy.

Know in advance that if the conversation does get out of control, you have a prepared, reflexive safety outlet. Fighter pilots are trained ad nauseam in how to reach the lever for the ejection seat, because in the panic and duress of an impending crash, the mind tends to go blank. We strongly counsel that you heed the same advice as that given by our leading *Top Gun* instructors. If your fuselage is wasted with gunfire and you feel the conversation wheeling out of control, your altimeter clacking steadily downward toward a certain doom, have in mind something completely wise and completely memorized, because you probably won't be very good on your feet at such moments.

Here is a good example: "Ms. Cuthbertson, this is a very important issue to me, and it doesn't seem that we're making much progress. I'd like to include Mr. Delphinium (the department head, principal, etc.) in the conversation. I'd like to adjourn now and find a time when all three of us can sit down and work this out."

This acknowledges that, however dreadful and unwarranted the issue may be to you, you consider a successful resolution important. It states the obvious—that you're not making much progress. It avoids blame, and it posi-tions *you* as the one who will reach out to your supervisor (otherwise, they may immediately storm up to your supervisor's office).

Have these lines or something similar ready to roll out. Say them with what-ever smile you can muster, stand up with a sense of closure, and take charge of ending the meeting. You have stated your desire to make progress. You have affirmed your willingness to meet again. Do so, and get back to them swiftly with a time and a date.

4. Do your homework.

Be prepared. (This is an important correlate of step one—making sure you do the *right* homework.) Ask around about the student and parent, especially among other teachers who have worked with them before.

But be sure to keep your homework notes out of sight. I know a very experi-enced teacher who, anticipating a difficult conversation, went back to teachers who had taught the child in years past. He had assembled a very worthy set of notes with which to gain perspective on the meeting, but he left the notes face up on the desk beside him. The mother read the notes upside-down. When she saw "Mother can be very difficult," she proved *precisely* how accurate that was.

5. Welcome them with a smile.

However much you dread the impending encounter, put on a smile. It may lighten the mood. It may give you confidence—or at least the appearance of confidence. In any case, there's no downside to smiling.

6. Listen thoroughly.

Think of their emotional message as a massive, brutal wave rushing headlong toward the sweet and innocent sand where you wait. Don't plunge out into the tide. Don't interrupt it. Spend some of your silence as you listen trying to understand the feeling as subtext. Is the anger based on some insecurity? It often is. Remember that there are few people more vulnerable in this world than a parent who is concerned for the well-being of his or her child. True, the parent may just be feral, but just as often, the parent may be deeply uneasy about a child who isn't turning out to be the next "lord of the manor" or "lady in waiting." It is hard to be a parent.

7. Make note of incorrect statements.

The only exception to uninterrupted listening is if, in the course of a litany of complaints, the parent raises a point that is clearly in dispute. Them saying, "And then when you went after my Little Bo-Peep with that flanged mace…," may inspire you to bark out an immediate denial. You shouldn't do so, yet it is important to note that a wild overstatement should not simply be absorbed in silence. Neither should it lead to an out-and-out confrontation then and there, for it is only going to escalate if the parent hasn't had his or her full say.

The correct response to any outrageous misstatement along the way is essentially to note the point and to allow the parent to continue. To place such a verbal Post-it note, it is necessary to raise the index finger of your dominant hand and to say calmly, "I want to come back to that point, but please go ahead." You aren't rushing recklessly into the tide, but neither are you accepting the purported facts with a silence that might be mistaken for acquiescence.

8. Breathe.

Breathe deeply. Think Zen breaths. Lower your heart rate.

When confronted, it is biologically imprinted in the species that we tend to develop precisely the short, rapid breaths that prepare us for fight or flight. I have no idea if biology supports what seems obvious, but my experience is that extended short, rapid breathing brings in insufficient oxygen and fails to pump waste gases from the depths of our lungs. This can't help us when we're already feeling a little frantic and febrile.

Work quietly behind the scenes to overcome the millennia of evolution, and breathe deeply for the thoughtful absorption of the words and the confident resolution of the crisis. They won't know, and besides, they can't stop you.

9. Take notes throughout the course of their "presentation."

Take your notes seriously. It may help you to focus on things other than your own defensiveness. It will allow you to flag points that you want to come back to. It can create a "paper trail" in case the situation continues or even escalates. It gives your trembling hands something to do. Most importantly, it conveys the impression that you are taking the complaint seriously.

10. Conceal your notes.

At the end of the meeting, put the pad containing your notes face down. No need for Ms. Cuthbertson to see the voodoo doll you've doodled of her or the word "bonkers" you've etched in rabid red. Keep your notes professional, no matter how unprofessional your inner feelings may be.

11. Time your response.

This point is one of the most critical in the entire list. In step six, we warned you against running headlong into the incoming crash of the wave. Here we are pointing out that the time *to* respond is when that wave of the parent's diatribe has crashed and has become foamy froth upon the beach. That is the time to wade in.

12. Begin by paraphrasing what the parent said.

Capture, if you can, the feeling and the words. Be careful of sounding patronizing ("Oh, Mrs. Somnambulist, I *validate* your feelings!"). Be careful of sounding argumentative ("And then, if anyone can *believe* it, you dared to say that—"). State the issues as neutrally and honestly as you can ("It feels as if you think I haven't been clear enough in my instructions" [or] "I've been holding Angela to different standards than others" [or] "I simply lost my temper with your son.") And then pause for a reaction. Let the parent fix an adjective here or change an emphasis there. Come to an agreement, if you can, on what the issue is.

13. Don't take comments personally.

No matter what they say, *do not* take it personally, even if it was very personal. Act, as much as possible, as if you are listening from above. Or act as if you are remembering this from a safe and distant future, a place and time in which there are no waves, only sweet and sparkling sunlit waters.

14. Begin your response by expressing a positive image of the child.

This is another crucial point and a strategy easy to overlook in the heat of the moment. No matter how concerned you are, begin with something positive about the child. Finding something positive to say even needs to be a crucial part of your homework.

Disarm them. You may disagree about many things—details, strategies, and the difference between right and wrong—but begin with (and keep in mind) a guiding sense of what is in the best interests of the child.

15. Admit any mistakes.

If you do wish that you'd handled a situation differently, say so.

Pat Haggerty was a terrific kid I taught in the eighth grade. He was a strong student and had never really gotten into serious trouble, but he had goofed off one time in a health class enough that he was given a detention, which simply meant serving the lunch period (during which he would otherwise have been allowed to go out to lunch) sitting in the middle school office.

Halfway through the period, I saw the door open and a classmate sneak him a forbidden McDonald's bag. Needless to say, students on detention were not allowed to have curb service provided by wily confederates. It caught me at just the wrong moment and mood. I yanked the bag from his hand and snarled, "You're here because you broke the rules and even now you break another!" I flung the bag unceremoniously in the trash. I had never spoken to Pat that way, and a short while later, I realized that even if I had been *somewhat* right, I had just plain lost my temper.

Mr. and Mrs. Haggerty, who had always been warm and supportive parents, were waiting in my office when I arrived the next morning. I ushered them in and said, "You know I'm glad you came in. I wanted to speak with you and with Pat." I recounted the McDonald's incident, as if they were unaware of it. "And you know, later when I looked back on it, I realized that Pat has always been a good kid. He'd done the wrong thing, to be sure, but I had just plain lost my temper. I make hundreds of decisions each day. That one wasn't one of my better ones, and I plan to find Pat later in the day and tell him so. (pause) What can I help you with?"

Needless to say, they were a little speechless. They were looking back and forth from each other to me with strange, unexpected smiles. "Oh, okay," was the unspoken message. Case closed. Handshakes all around.

Now we're not advocating constant apologies, but sometimes, we do make mistakes. And taking the initiative can spare us a lot of grief in the end. (Sometimes, I've even called home before the end of the day, before the student even got home to report what happened, to tell a mother that I had handled a situation poorly.) It helps to emphasize the fact that we make hundreds of decisions each day. And any of us who insists that every one of our decisions is right on the money is holding up an almost impossible—and very unrealistic— standard of performance.

As a species, it has always felt to me that one of our most unfortunate characteristics was our resistance to saying, quite simply, that we're sorry. In the right situation, how refreshing, how relieving, how open and honest it is to simply acknowledge that none of us in education and none of us in parenting can lay claim to perfection.

16. Make your key points.

Try not to answer each of the parent's points. Tell the story in your own way, with your own perspective. Be specific. Saying "Norbert was shouting in the middle of the assembly in a voice that many others could hear, saying that the principal was a 'buck-toothed she-devil!'" is clearer and less subject to interpretation than saying he was behaving "obnoxiously."

17. Envision a positive outcome.

No matter how difficult it may be to believe, anticipate a positive outcome. Work toward a partnership. Try to find some common ground, even if it is only nestled in a long-shot possibility that the child really might someday become a reasonable facsimile of a functioning adult.

18. Show the potential for growth.

If it applies, focus on a gap between what the boy could be and where he is now.

There are parents who defend and excuse and dismiss all kinds of substandard behavior. One of the simplest ways to deal with this is to be the one in the meeting who expresses the most positive view of the child. For example, you could say, "It has always seemed to me that Genevieve has the potential to be as responsible a student as anyone else in the fifth grade—" (Pause while the parents try to argue with this, as they have with everything else you've said.) "And I just think that her recent habit of burning books and practicing her lupine howl during tests is undercutting what she could be. We all want her to succeed and to be what we all know she really can be."

This offers a way to bring in present negatives (e.g., no homework, chronic biting of other children, spontaneous outcries that the death rays have got her) in the larger context of a more positive, potential image. While it touches on the current troubles, it offers a framework for optimism and a reminder to the parents that this behavior likely *wasn't* what they dreamed of when they first nuzzled her in swaddling clothes.

19. Be open to a genuine response to what you've had to say.

Give the parents an opening to respond to what you've said. It doesn't have to be the following: "Okay, it's your turn to scream at me again." It can be much more pleasant:

- "Does this sound at all familiar?"
- "I can tell this sounds surprising to you. Have you ever seen anything like this at home?"

- "I realize that this wasn't how he reported what had happened. What are your thoughts?"

And then listen thoroughly again.

20. End with a positive statement.

Try to summarize the meeting with a positive statement you both can agree with. "I just want him to be happy/to reach his real potential/to be the kind of sensitive young man we both know he can be." Try to suspend disbelief. Believe in a Norbert that really will someday outgrow this latest penchant for gnawing the legs of his classmates. "I really want to do all I can to make this a good year for him."

21. Work toward concrete action steps and set a timetable.

End the meeting with some solid statements of what will be done next and when, such as the following:

- "I promise to call you any time Archie doesn't have the homework in on time."
- "I intend to change the seating chart by the beginning of next week so that he and Reggie aren't sitting so close to each other."
- "I will email you every Friday with a tally of the number of times he's gone ahead and passed surreptitious notes to Veronica. Maybe you and he can make an updated bar graph of this at home each weekend."

22. Be sure to follow up in a timely fashion.

If you don't follow up in a timely fashion, you're setting yourself up for trouble. Unless you had promised to follow up with an email on Friday, for example (in which case it is vital to flag this on Friday's to-do list), it is important to do something that day. Swift follow-through can go a long way to demonstrate that you were listening and responsive. If you think Ms. Cuthbertson was lethal at this meeting, just wait until she comes back in to complain about your lack of follow-through, perhaps this time to see your supervisor. Regardless of the unreasonableness of her original complaint, she can now state unequivocally that you promised something and didn't deliver.

23. If the meeting ended unpleasantly, notify your supervisor promptly.

If the very idea of this gives you the willies, imagine your supervisor's response if you *don't* get to frame the situation first. Get in there pronto. Be the one to characterize the situation. Afterward, the parent may be able to get his or her story across, but it will be editing *your* perspective. Don't leave your supervisor to be blindsided by a furious parent who is reporting an incident that, regardless of anything else, the supervisor feels you should have shared.

24. Finally, read *Difficult Conversations*.

Difficult Conversations (Stone, et al., Penguin, 2000) is *the* great book on how to handle such situations. I often pluck my own copy from the bookshelf and immerse myself in it whenever I'm on the way into what I know may become a tense and difficult conversation.

IN CONCLUSION

As teachers interacting with children of all outlooks and backgrounds, we are constantly exposed to view. As educators who must not only lead the educational journey but also call students to account and report on their progress, we are almost equally exposed to the far less contextualized view of their parents.

Sometimes we can anticipate an impending conflict. Sometimes we are blindsided. Whatever the genesis of the difficulty, having to meet with an angry parent can be one of the most memorable, painfully difficult experiences in any school year. Having a strong, almost reflexive sense of how to be prepared is no guarantee that the encounter won't be uncomfortable, but that preparation, that planning and perspective can go a long way to ensuring that you remain professional and responsive throughout. Beyond that, such preparation can vastly improve the chances for a positive possibility of partnership.

PART 7

Appendices or Worth Noting

A WHISPER ABOUT CLASSROOM ETIQUETTE

This section applies to those teachers—most often middle and upper school teachers—who must share a classroom with colleagues. Surprising levels of irritation can arise between any sort of roommates. Working in close quarters with others, coupled with differences in attention and style can needlessly create tensions between colleagues. Being open with those colleagues about preferences from the beginning of the year can create a sense of shared enterprise and mutual ownership of the space. Let's look at some effective ways to do this.

BEFORE THE YEAR BEGINS:

Bulletin boards

Some teachers take to bulletin boards, as if they were repressed interior decorators. Others simply wonder why they didn't leave the cinderblock alone. But lest some eager designer arrive in late August and festoon every square centimeter of bulletin board space with photographs from their summer vacation, it is probably best to find out which colleagues are sharing the classroom and have an open discussion about the division of presentation space.

Seating structure

This one is more urgent, because it is far more difficult to begin and end each period with the tedious, noisome realignment of desks. As noted in a preceding chapter, there are styles and structures for setting up student seating that can go a long way toward achieving more effective focus and attention. If, however, you feel outvoted or simply inclined to compromise, it is vital that you retain the right to move the desks into a position that accommodates your teaching style for that particular day. Obviously, at the end of the period, return them to the agreed-upon alignment. Just as obviously, enlist the students in this process, or else you will still be pivoting while they are waiting and end up chronically late for your next class.

The teacher's desk

It's worth a simple discussion at the beginning of the year, including perhaps a decision as to who gets which drawer. Even more, teachers often accept the orientation of a classroom's furniture exactly as they find it in the late days of August. This initial conversation may represent an easily overlooked opportunity to optimize the arrangement in the room.

AT THE END OF CLASS:

Erase the board.

It's that simple. If you must retain a corner of it for posterity, with a "Please Save" note attached, that's probably fine—if you've cleared it with your classroom-mates. However, don't let the next teacher come bustling in to find the slopped spaghetti of your equation-solving spilled all over the board, over the chalk tray, and onto the floor.

Get out of there on time.

If you must have a lingering conversation with a student, take it out into the hall. Let the next teacher have his or her own space on time. Life in the hinterlands of the Faculty Lounge will be far more agreeable.

Don't work in the back of the classroom during the next period.

Period. It's the next teacher's space. You may not be in the way. You may be creating a seminal lab on the exorcism of devil's food cake. Let them have their own space, all the way to the back wall of the room.

Keep the room supplied.

Don't accidentally leave a classroom with only dry dry-erase markers or stubs of chalk the size of a newborn's pinky toe. Don't hijack the preceding teacher's prized red pen. If the chalk has been getting shorter and shorter (as chalk will usually do), it will win you points in the Emily "The Educator" Post Hall of Etiquette Fame if suddenly there are some gleaming new, Dover-white cylinders in the chalk tray, as a gift from you to those who share your space.

Special events and activities

If you are planning on holding a Atonal Hootenanny or having students bring in their life-size replicas of the Great Pyramid of Giza on a rainy Thursday morning, talk to your colleagues about this well in advance. It may be that the tone of the relationship will be calmer than it would have been, had they not been forewarned.

WHAT ADULTS REMEMBER: CHARACTERISTICS OF AN EFFECTIVE TEACHER

A s we mentioned early in this book, one of the very first activities we do as part of our three-day workshops is to focus every single one of the educators in attendance on the most effective teacher they ever had. We break participants into small groups for discussion. For a time, they engage in simple, affectionate memory. Then we turn them loose to distinguish the specific characteristics that made their memorable teachers so effective. We conclude the exercise by soliciting the full list of characteristics named.

The following list is presented, as theirs are, in no particular order. The items are not grammatically parallel.

We offer it not because any of us can or should aspire to the godhead envisioned by the full combination of all of these characteristics. We present it partly to underscore the behaviors *not* on the list that may be tempting to us, particularly as young teachers—to be cool, overly friendly, oblivious of boundaries, uncomfortable with our authority. Wisely, those never show up.

The larger reason for presenting these characteristics of an effective teacher is to allow us to reflect on each of these characteristics. In good measure, most of us will (if we are immodestly honest) possess most of these characteristics, but there may be some that (with equal honesty) we might admit we can always work on.

While we have perhaps leveled a rain forest or two with charts from these gatherings, the fact remains that the characteristics identified are almost identical from group to group and year to year.

For your pleasure and reflection, we present the following characteristics of effective teachers:

- Caring
- Generous
- Validates who we are
- Creates a safe environment
- Establishes a warm rapport—with boundaries
- Punctual
- Challenging
- Fast-paced
- Hardworking
- Inspires a sense of wonder
- Funny
- Emotionally connected—with the subject and students
- Dynamic
- Entertaining
- Instills confidence
- Available and approachable
- Lively
- Structured
- Organized
- Embraces "tough love"
- Strict
- Holds high expectations
- Knowledgeable about the subject
- Enthusiastic
- Creative

- Calm
- Accepting and embracing of differences
- Articulates clear expectations
- Establishes predictable routines
- Patient
- Warm
- Positive
- Encouraging
- Consistent
- Provides clear examples
- Explicit
- Fosters independence
- Creates a spirit of mutual respect
- Has a deep love for children
- Makes students feel competent
- Provides individual attention
- Passionate about the subject
- Kind
- Empathetic
- Articulates clear objectives
- Well-prepared
- Connects well with *all* students
- Original
- Embraces a variety of methods
- Inspires curiosity

WHAT STUDENTS WANT: ADVICE FROM THE KIDS

Our students are astute teacher-watchers and have very clear opinions about how teachers should teach and how they should behave in the classroom. The work Christine and I do to support students when they face an academic challenge often leads to conversations about what works and what doesn't work in their relationships with teachers. We have interviewed students about what helps them and what doesn't help them to become successful, engaged learners.

Following are some of their comments about what "good" and "bad" teachers look like.

Good teachers care about their students, whether or not those students are successful in our particular subject. Students are painfully aware of the fact that certain teachers seem to care far more about the students who are "good" in their subject. Upon these students, a teacher may unconsciously lavish smiles, encouragement, and praise. The students who don't feel as able or successful in that subject—and who could no doubt use the encouragement more than anyone—are sometimes left to fight an uphill battle against a difficult subject in an environment that seems less than fully supportive. Some of us have a naturally positive sense of inclusion that enables us to have (and extend) positive expectations to everyone in our classes. For those of us who may quietly admit that there are weaker students whom it is harder to like or harder to hope for, it is vital that we be consciously mindful of how hard it is to learn something that doesn't come easily. We even recommend taking the time to get to know students in other ways so that we can experience them as successful people in other arenas— perhaps in a different subject area, extracurricular clubs, the arts, or sports. Seeing them in other, more successful circumstances can help us to create and maintain an environment of optimism in our classroom that is essential for the hard work it takes to learn.

When we are giving extra help, we shouldn't just repeat what was said in class. Students need teachers to use different words and different examples and also be willing to go over it more than once. If what we had said in class was sufficient, the student wouldn't be there for extra help!

It's almost laughable, but it's true. Almost more than anything else, students don't want us to be boring. This isn't just a question of charisma or energy. It has to do with a commitment, from the first moment our pen touches paper in a lesson plan to the use of a variety of approaches and activities. We need to perform the following duties:

- Learn how our students learn best.
- Adapt to the different needs of the students in our class.
- Be mindful of the different modes of information processing.
- Keep students on their toes. Active involvement in the class helps sustain the attention necessary for learning.
- Break the class time into chunks and apply different modes to provide variety.
- Stimulate visual, verbal, aural, social, and kinesthetic pathways to keep our students maximally engaged.

Ask the class for feedback. At the end of a unit or marking period, it is very easy to distribute index cards and ask three simple questions. What worked for you? What didn't work? What do I need to know about you as a learner in order to teach you better? We should report back to the class what we have learned and what we're going to do about it.

Respect goes both ways. It is vital that we model and apply the same behaviors we expect from our students. Our tone of voice and our interactions with students set the standard in the classroom. Students are sensitive to—perhaps more than anything else—inconsistency and what they may see as hypocrisy. ("He gets to joke around all period long, but if I make a wisecrack, I get yelled at.")

"I like it when teachers use real life examples and relate the information to something I know and understand." This is a basic tenet of the psychology of learning—that we build new learning onto a scaffold of previous knowledge and experience. The more we can stimulate previous knowledge or use analogy and metaphor to explain a new concept, the more likely our students will be able to build new understandings.

Beyond these key points, students are clear about what bad teaching looks like:

Bad teachers let their pride and ego get in the way. They say mean things and get personal in their criticism. It can be a challenge at times to maintain that cool and clear-headed distance when confronted by an angry or anxious student, but it is never okay to stoop to a hot-headed level of interaction with a student. It diminishes our credibility as the adult and can irreparably damage our relationship with that student and with any student who witnesses the interaction.

Bad teachers forget who the grown-up is in the relationship. Although it can be tempting to be "one of the kids," one of the most fundamental requirements of teaching is that we remain the adult. From the moment we sign a contract, from the moment we accept the responsibility and the paycheck, we are being hired to lead, not to hang out. Students need and appreciate trustworthy role models for being an adult. Our media is filled with so many examples of how *not* to grow up, that is becomes ever more imperative to provide our students with an example of positive possibility.

Bad teachers use sarcasm to hurt kids. It is important to remember that sarcasm is *not* the same as humor. Sarcasm always has a target, and that target is meant to be hurt by the comment. Beyond that, sarcasm parades as a compliment with a nasty scorpion sting hidden in its tail. Don't ever use it.

Bad teachers allow their unconscious feelings to hold sway. It is imperative to know ourselves well, to commit, to self-examine, and to learn about who we are as a person, as a teacher, and as a learner. What makes us anxious, upset, or angry? Which kind of kid is likely to kindle a negative response? What triggers our own sense of insecurity? The more we become aware of our own foibles—everything from our preferences to our pet peeves—the less likely we will let them loose on unsuspecting students. There is an art and craft to teaching. There is a profound, infinite skill base in educating the young. We will never be fully proficient. All that we can do is commit to the self-reflective practice that can foster ongoing learning, discovery, and growth.

A NOTE ON MONTESSORI EDUCATION

Rich had spent all of his professional career working in relatively traditional—if sometimes progressive—school environments. In the course of those years, he had seen any number of educational trends come and go: Open Classroom, Back to Basics, No Child Left Behind, just to name a few.

In the spring of 2005, he realized that there was one serious educational philosophy that hadn't exhibited the foreshortened half-life of most educational fads. It was approaching its hundredth anniversary, and it was quietly continuing to gather support.

Montessori education is the breakthrough approach developed among the impoverished children of Italy at the beginning of the twentieth century by Maria Montessori. Out of a curiosity to further his own professional development, Rich signed on for the first cycle of Montessori leadership training in the summer of 2005. It was a revelatory experience for him. Maria Montessori had created a setting in which each child was able and encouraged to explore the world at his or her own pace, following his or her own style. Within several years, Rich had made the move to a small Montessori school west of Boston, where the children work independently, guided by wisely trained teachers and the inspirational design of materials that invite individual exploration and learning.

By the nature of human beings and children in particular, the great majority of this book will apply to students in any school, but by the very nature of the Montessori philosophy, the role of the teacher in a Montessori environment is decidedly different from one in a classroom with rows of desks, chairs, and lab tables. In their more individualized guidance of the young and in the largely decentralized model of classroom education, Montessori teachers seem to have somewhat less need for some of the disciplinary models outlined in this book.

Nevertheless, the need for mutual respect, positive tone, and sensitive discipline is vital to classrooms everywhere. Regardless of the school they attend, students will test their teachers in almost any setting. As we have stated earlier in the book, they do so not to overthrow us or humiliate us or drive us into another career but to be reassured that someone is confidently in charge. Just as younger children seek the comfort of their parents and just as adolescents are strengthened by the corresponding strength in their parents, students everywhere are encouraged in their own growth by warm, strong, consistent adults. While there will certainly be differences in the application of the teachings in this book, education everywhere is fundamentally about the children who seek to be seen as who they are and to be imagined as who they might yet become, as their learning liberates them to pursue their own growth.

FINAL WISHES

We honor you for your decision to serve as an educator. Perhaps even more significantly, we honor you for your decision to remain in education, challenged and growing throughout your career.

We conclude this book as we do each of our workshops—with our own set of final wishes.

> We wish you…
> A growing sense of confidence…
>> and a life-long spirit of humility…
>>> There's lot to learn along the way,
>>> and the learning never ends.
>
> A process for effective planning…and meaningful action…
>
> A good teaching friend/veteran/mentor/confidante…
>
> An ongoing readiness to learn…

An ongoing readiness to listen…

An absolute readiness to establish limits…
>They are testing you to force you to establish those limits.
>>Limits are fundamentally reassuring.

A readiness to explore…and to go on exploring…

Some useful tactics…
>and an ever-expanding skill base….

An ability to take care of yourself…
>Your own best energy is the most important thing you can to share with the kids.

And finally…
>a sense of humor
>and a gentle patience with yourself
>>as you learn along the way.

THE AUTHORS

Richard H. Eyster entered the field of education at age sixteen as an assistant in an inner-city Head Start Program. At nineteen, he started a summer day camp for young children. By twenty-one, he was working as a third grade teacher in New York City. In the years since, he has taught every grade but tenth, leading self-contained, lower school classrooms and teaching English, computers, and mathematics. Eyster has served as a department chair, board member, and middle school principal. A graduate of the University of Michigan, he received his masters in education from Teachers College, Columbia University. Mr. Eyster is currently head of school at The Summit Montessori School in Framingham, MA.

Christine Martin also began her educational career early on, teaching mathematics and working as a middle school dean of students before moving on to lead a groundbreaking department of learning specialists serving students in grades five through twelve at the Packer Collegiate Institute in Brooklyn, NY. Martin graduated from Boston University, and she is engaged in ongoing graduate work in educational psychology at Fordham University. Martin is currently the chair of the learning skills department at Packer, where she also directs the New Faculty Mentoring Program, coaching both veteran teacher-mentors and new faculty.

INDEX

A

ADD. *See* Learning differences

ADHD. *See* Learning differences

Administrative assistants, 279–280

Agendas, 170, 323

Assessment

  alternative forms of, 213–214

  bonus problems, 222

  comments, 222–223, 225–226, 242–246

  emerging opportunities for, 208

  extra credit, 222

  grades, 219–221

  of group projects, 224–225

  and ongoing dialogue, 222–223

  and parent conferences, 247–252

  potential for, 216–217

  red pen, 221

  self-correction, 221

  tests, 212–217

Authority, 330

B

Birge, Walter, 261

Birthdays, 55

Bullying, 58–62, 187–189, 314

Business office, 281

C

Challenges, from students, 12–13, 79

  See also Discipline; Testing, of teacher

Classroom
knowing students outside of, 51–56
life outside of, 255–258
promoting values outside of, 27–28
sharing, 351–353
Cooperative learning model,
191–198, 224–225
Counselor, 54, 280
Covey, Stephen, 275
Custodian, 280

D

Difficult Conversations, 347
Directions, 193
Discipline
contacting parents, 111–116, 331
hierarchy, 105–107, 136
intervention, joint, 123–130,
131–137, 332
intervention, solo, 118–122,
331–332
isolation of student, 99–101,
103–104, 330–331
martial law, 131–137, 332
mediation, 123–130, 332
and popularity, temptation of,
81–84
and power, 75, 80, 88–90
preventative, 93–97
principal's office, 331
saying no, 86–88

seating, 93–97
silence, 91–92, 329
and supervisors, 105–106,
107–108, 331
support from students, 76–80
and tardiness, 172
See also Students, difficult
Discussion, classroom
best practices for, 177–190
components of leadership of,
175–177
inclusion in, 180–182
intervention in negative interactions in, 187–189
participation in, 181–190, 327
Dyslexia. *See* Learning differences

E

Effectiveness, 5–6, 355–357
Email, problems with, 113
Empathy, 294
Energy, 162–164, 176, 178
Etiquette, classroom, 351–353
Expectations
for discussions, 180–182
expectations sheet, 151–156
for homework, 228–230
setting, 39–43, 149
Extracurricular events, 55

F

Family situations, need to know, 53
Favoritism, 45–46
Feedback
  from students, 47–48
  to students (*See* Assessment;
    Grades; Homework)
Files, 52–53
First day, 148–150
Flirtation, 81–83, 84

G

Getting-to-know-you games, 54
Gossip, 296
Grades, 18, 219–221, 222–223
  See also Assessment
Group work, 191–198, 224–225
Guidance counselor, 54

H

Health information, students',
  53–54, 283–286
Homework
  assigning, 202
  collecting, 233–236
  correcting, 234–235, 237–240
  debate over, 227–228
  expectations for, 228–230
  late, 231
  long-term projects, 230–231

I

Instructions, 193
Isolation
  of act, 13
  of student, 99–101, 103–104,
    330–331
  of teacher, 10, 11, 43, 80 (*See also*
    Unity)

J

Journal writing, 54

L

Lateness, 172, 324
LaVoie, Richard, 311
Learning differences, 301–306
Learning specialist, 280–281
Lesson plans
  energy in, 162–164
  for final three minutes, 199–204
  leading off, 320
  questions to address in, 158–159
  variety in, 165–168
  See also Planning
Letters, handwritten, 29–30
Letters from home, 52

M

Maintenance supervisor, 280

Matsui, Shiro, 215
Medical records, 53–54, 283–286
Montessori, 363–364
Movement, 178–179, 325

N
No, saying, 86–88
Notes, handwritten, 29–30
Nurse, 281

O
Office, principal's, 107–109, 331
Outcasts, 58–62
 See also Students, quiet/shy
Overplanning, 150

P
Parent conferences, 247–252
Parents
 and comments, 242–246
 conferences with, 247–252
 contacting, 28–30, 111–116, 331
 difficult/angry, 337–347
 praising students to, 28–30
 providing fair warning to, 245–246
Participation, 181–190, 308,
 309–313, 327
 See also Discussion, classroom
Passion, 162–163

The Peter Principle, 271, 273
Phone calls, 28–29
 See also Parents, contacting
Planning
 agendas, 170
 for beginning of class, 169–173
 daily (*See* Lesson plans)
 expectations sheet, 151–156
 for final three minutes, 199–204
 for lost days, 142–145
 for opening days, 147–150
 overplanning, 150
 power of, 159
 and preventing misbehavior,
  177 (*See also* Discipline,
  preventative)
 questions to address in, 158–159
 for small group work, 191–198
 for year, 142–145
Popularity, temptation of, 81–84
Power
 and discipline, 75, 80
 feeling, 88–90
Powlen, Cob, 167
Praise
 believable, 34
 of difficult students, 20–21, 299
 of entire class, 22–27
 of good students, 18–19
 methods of, 34–37
 power of, 16–17, 324–325
 reinforcement of values by, 24–25

sending home, 28–30
specificity of, 30
unifying effect of, 26–27
utility of, 20–21
value of, 17–20
Principal, 107–109, 331
See also Supervisors
Projects, group, 191–198, 224–225
Psychologist, 280
Punctuality, 322–323
See also Tardiness

R

Reputation, 295
Resources, outside, 283–286
Ridicule, addressing, 187–189
See also Bullying
Routine, 323

S

Sarcasm, 27
Seating, 60–61, 93–97, 309–310,
321–322, 326
Self-description, 52
Shyness, 180–182, 307–317
Silence, 91–92, 329
Standards, 45–46
See also Expectations
Students
advice from, 359–362

difficult, 20–21, 289–300, 319–335
(*See also* Discipline)
knowing, 51–56
quiet/shy, 180–182, 307–317
Supervisors
and conferences, 251
and contacting parents, 112–113
and discipline, 105–106, 107–108,
123–130, 131–137, 331
and intervention, 123–130, 131–137
relationships with, 262–278, 333
Syllabus. *See* Lesson plans; Planning

T

Tardiness, 172, 324
Testing, of teacher, 12–13, 79
Tests, 212–217
See also Assessment
Time, outside classroom, 255–258
Tone, positive, 63–64
Trust, 45–49

U

Unity, 26–27, 80, 321

V

Values
promoting outside classroom, 27–28
reinforcement of by praise, 24–25

Variety, 165–168, 321
Victimizing. *See* Bullying
Visualization, 6

Z

Zilboorg, Peg, 149